Experiential Landscape

An approach to people, place and space

Landscape

Kevin Thwaites
Ian Simkins

Routledge
Taylor & Francis Group

LONDON AND NEW YORK

This is for Angela, Ann and Amy, Kathryn, Elinor, Rebekah and Nicholas

First published 2007
by Routledge
2 Park Square, Milton Park, Abingdon, Oxon OX14 4RN

Simultaneously published in the USA and Canada
by Routledge
270 Madison Ave, New York, NY 10016

Routledge is an imprint of the Taylor & Francis Group, an informa business

© Kevin Thwaites and Ian Simkins

Typeset in Melior by Alex Lazarou, Surbiton, Surrey
Printed and bound in Great Britain by The Alden Press, Witney

British Library Cataloguing in Publication Data
A catalogue record for this book is available from the British Library

Library of Congress Cataloging in Publication Data
A catalog record has been requested for this book

ISBN10: 0-415-34000-4 (pbk)
ISBN13: 978-0-415-34000-7 (pbk)

Contents

Acknowledgements

This book represents the latest port of call in an ongoing journey of thinking, teaching, research and practice, begun nearly a decade ago, to explore people–space relations and reflect on the implications for theory and practice in landscape architecture and its related disciplines. Since both of us, at different times and in different ways, had our formative schooling in landscape architecture at an establishment with a sustaining reputation for social and community awareness, it is perhaps not surprising that wanting to know how people tick remains central to our ethos of landscape architecture. A first debt of gratitude must go therefore to those with whom I (KT) shared many years, first as student and later as colleague, in the Landscape Architecture Department at Leeds Metropolitan University. In particular, John Kirkman and Cliff Hansford, both strong early influences but sadly no longer alive, and also Chris Royffe, Alistair Taylor and Colin Treen, the original architects of their Department's Landscape Design and Community programme, a special and unique learning experience, exposure to which has taught hundreds of landscape architecture graduates that people matter first when making good outdoor places. Much later, Colin, as my PhD Director of Studies, bore witness to the crude beginning of some of the ideas that eventually grew into experiential landscape. I owe Colin a lot: without his clarity of thinking and steady

intellectual nerve few of them would have got off the starting blocks. We also want to say thanks to Alan Simson at Leeds who engineered the first meeting between Ian and myself and in consequence unwittingly laid the foundations for us to begin to get to grips with the business of realising that, for many people, the "landscapes" that affect them most are those that weave together the routine of daily life, at the doorstep, in the alley, the street and the street corner. I am also indebted to Ian Heywood, also at Leeds Metropolitan University, for first drawing my attention to the ideas of Expressivism.

More recently our work on experiential landscape has benefited immeasurably from the support of colleagues in the Department of Landscape at the University of Sheffield and our thanks and appreciation go to all there for helping to create and sustain an environment in which ideas can develop and flourish. Working in an academic environment provides the special privilege of being able to work out developing thoughts with students. Through our teaching and research activities we hope to have benefited the educational and professional development of the many students we have worked with, both here and abroad. But we have found, and believe, that the best teaching is always a two way occupation and it is hard to overestimate the contribution that students we have worked with have had in helping us clarify foggy thinking, test methods and bring perspectives we would never have thought about. Inevitably there are too many to mention, but special thanks and appreciation go to Tom Johnson, Chris Davenport, Ruth Reay, Martha Alka, John Clayton, Gareth Proctor, Kelda Platt, Antonia Paul, Tim Spain and Robert Kelly, ex-Leeds Metropolitan University Landscape Architecture students who enthusiastically offered themselves as early experiential landscape "guinea pigs" helping to develop and pilot some of the initial mapping methodology and contributing to a paper about it. More recently we are especially indebted to University of Sheffield, Post Graduate Landscape Architecture students, Fran Curtis, Peter Koch, Neil Northrop, David Wesselingh, Lu Zhong, Veronica Meacham and Steve Watts for their contribution to chapter eleven. We are also very grateful to Alice Mathers, Ellie Lloyd and Laurel Truscott for their valuable involvement at Kirby Hill.

As work on experiential landscape has developed it has become increasingly a collaborative venture and we are extremely grateful to have the sustaining support of colleagues, Claire Dobson, Beth Helleur, Alice Mathers and Sarah Worthington who together constitute www.elprdu.com, bridging the gap between academia and practice and broadening the scope of experiential landscape. As part of the international UStED Alliance (Urban Sustainability through Environmental Design) www.elprdu.com benefits from overseas collaboration in teaching, practice and research and we are pleased to enjoy the continuing support and encouragement of UStED colleagues, Sergio Porta (Milan), Ombretta Romice (Glasgow), Barbara Golicnik (Slovenia), Marcus Zepf (Switzerland), John Renne (New Orleans).

Finally, we would like to thank the inhabitants of Kirby Hill, particularly Jean and Gareth, for their contribution to chapter nine. Also thanks to the many children and staff who have been involved in Ian's work with schools throughout the Yorkshire region and North East, especially Mike and Vicki, for their support and encouragement during the fieldwork.

All photographs are those of the authors save for those in Figures 1, 4.4, 5.11, 5.12, 5.31, 7.4 and 7.7. Thanks and appreciation to Beth Helleur for these.

Base Mapping: Reproduced by permission of Ordnance Survey on behalf of HMSO © Crown copyright 2006. All rights reserved. Ordnance Survey Licence number 100045659.

A way of seeing

"The tree was easily identified. It stood a short distance from the main entrance to the ministry, a large acacia tree with a single wide canopy that provided a wide circle of shade on the dusty ground below. Immediately beside the trunk were several strategically-placed stones – comfortable seats for anyone who might wish to sit under the tree and watch the daily business of Gaborone unfold before him. Now, at five minutes to one, the stones were unoccupied."

The man approached the tree cautiously. Staring at Mma Ramotswe, it seemed as if he wanted to say something but could not quite bring himself to speak.

Mma Ramotswe smiled at him. "Good afternoon, Mr Sipoleli," she said. "It is hot today, is it not? That is why I am under this tree. It is clearly a good place to sit in the heat." The man nodded. "Yes", he said. "I normally sit here." Mma Ramotswe affected surprise. "Oh? I hope that I am not sitting on your rock, Mr Sipoleli. I found it here and there was nobody sitting on it." He made an impatient gesture with his hands. "My rock? Yes it is, as a matter of fact. That is my rock. But this is a public place and anybody can sit on it, I suppose."

Mma Ramotswe rose to her feet, "But Mr Sipoleli, you must have this rock. I shall sit on that one over on that side." "No, Mma," he said

hurriedly, his tone changing. "I do not want to inconvenience you. I can sit on that rock." "No you sit on this rock here. It is your rock. I would not have sat on it had I thought that it was another person's rock. I can sit on this rock, which is a good rock too. You sit on that rock."[1]

This passage comes from Alexander McCall Smith's book, *Morality for Beautiful Girls* (2001, pp.120–121), about Botswana's most famous lady detective, Mma Ramotswe. Setting aside the fact that this encounter is fictitious for a moment, what exactly is going on here? What makes two people so apparently animated about a stone? Thinking about this helps highlight some of the central themes of this book.

The exchange between Mma Ramotswe and Mr Sipoleli is an example of the phenomenon of place attachment. The rock is important to Mr Sipoleli because he sits on it frequently and it has become embedded into his routine to such an extent that he has established what environmental psychologists might call a temporary territorial claim. Both he and Mma Ramotswe are perfectly well aware that this is a public place. The rock technically belongs to no-one, is available to all who wish to sit, and yet at the same time it is

---

1 The name of Mr Sipoleli has been substituted here for the term 'Rra', which appears in the author's original text.

intensely private. You can sense Mr Sipoleli's indignation as he sees Mma Ramotswe sitting there and he is confused and does not know quite how to respond. Rationally he knows he cannot complain. He knows it is not really his rock; it is not as if there are not any others to sit on after all. But nonetheless, he feels a strong sense of personal attachment to the rock, an emotional bond of sorts that has a tangible impact on what he feels and how he behaves when someone else is there, on his rock. It is not just the rock, of course, that generates this feeling. The rock is one of several beneath a tree and together they define a space and provide a sense of location. The shadow cast and the enclosure enveloped by the tree canopy strengthen this and the shadow edges mark a threshold differentiating an internal realm from the wider public environment beyond. All these components no doubt add to the attraction for Mr Sipoleli and might explain why he chose to sit there in the first place. The arrangement of objects makes a space to belong, albeit temporarily.

But Mr Sipoleli's rock is actually much more than part of an arrangement of objects, space and patterns of sun and shade; it is also a place of experience. Mr Sipoleli enjoys feelings of shelter from the hot sun, of comfort and rest, surveillance, solitude and meditation, and probably from time to time socialisation with occupiers of the other rocks. These experiences, accumulated and consolidated with the passage of time, combine with the physical elements in a more complex whole which defines part of the life of Mr Sipoleli. The occupation of the rock is a part of what brings a form of order to Mr Sipoleli's life. It is part of a pattern, a routine woven together from the relationship that Mr Sipoleli has built up with his everyday surroundings. It is a form of order that is hard to see and that Mr Sipoleli himself is probably barely conscious of until, that is, someone interferes with it. When it is not available it induces an emotional response, a sense of loss, an impact on the quality of Mr Sipoleli's life even though, like here, it may be a relatively small and short-lived one. It is almost as though this place is an extension of Mr Sipoleli himself and just as much a part of his identity as his finger-print.

Mr Sipoleli's place is a totality of spatial and experiential dimensions and, as such, a part of what we will call his experiential landscape. An experiential landscape is, then, as much a product of mind as of the material world. If it is meaningful to say that individuals, and possibly whole communities, have such experiential landscapes that they carry with them and that affect their daily lives and habits, the question we are concerned with here is, how can we see these and understand their properties and characteristics? This, along with the implications for those who make new outdoor places, is explored in the following pages.

The concept of experiential landscape
Revealing hidden dimensions of experience

Before we begin with the main body of the book, we want first to sketch out what we mean by experiential landscape by trying to give an introduction to the main characteristics. We hope that as we move on we will be able to add depth and detail to explain more fully why we think it is important to look at the human-environment relationship in this way, setting out its philosophical and theoretical context and then describing some of the methodological components that help us to make experiential landscapes visible. It is important that experiential landscape is understood within this wider framework because we are trying to present a way of looking at the world as much as describing a set of tools and methods for understanding and making new outdoor places. But before this we felt it would be useful if readers had an overall impression of the central concept in the hope that it will help to make what follows more meaningful. Because we work in the discipline of landscape architecture, in academia and practice, our thoughts and ideas are rooted in this context. They are meant to be especially relevant to those involved in the study and practice of landscape architecture and urban planning and design because these are the professional groups mainly concerned with how the outdoor environment where most people live, work and play is shaped and designed. But not exclusively so, and we hope that anyone with an interest in the rela-tionship between people and their outdoor world will find something of value.

Experiential landscape is the term we will use to conceptualise a holistic relationship of outdoor open space and a range of human experience. Our intention is to provide a means by which experiential aspects of people–space relations can become more prominent: how, as scholars and practitioners, we can understand and make outdoor places. The concept of experiential landscape is structured in such a way as to provide those involved in analysis and design of the outdoors with a vocabulary and methods that can help them read the experiential potential and character of existing outdoor settings, inform how they are changed and how new ones are made. We see the experiential landscape as a spatial and experiential whole constituted from outdoor places that people use during ordinary daily life. It is the realm usually encountered sub-consciously, the ordinary setting of daily routine and the incidental spaces and features people encounter which through regular use come to mean something, rather than special places that people would make a conscious or planned decision to visit, for days out and holi-days for example. This might be generalised as the built environment made from the collective of building edges and doorways, streets, yards and alcoves, alleys and squares, etc. The experiential landscape is the mundane rather than the special

1

The ordinary setting of daily routine

because most people's routine experience, that which impacts on the quality of daily life most, happens here (Figure 1).

It is important to be clear that the experiential landscape is not conceived as a collection of set-piece locations linked together, but as a totality of varying spatial volumes experienced sequentially. Gordon Cullen captured the essence of this when he talked of passing through a town as "a journey through pressures and vacuums, a sequence of exposures and enclosures, of constraints and relief" (Cullen, 1971, p.10). Into this journey a complex range of subjective meaning and association is injected as a consequence of what people feel and do as they move about. As people pass through their spatial surroundings its form and configuration both engenders and becomes imbued with experience. It is as though an experiential dimension of the bodily self reaches out beyond the skin to draw aspects of the surrounding spatial world into what it is to be fully human. This holistic conception of human-environment relations is similar to that advocated by, for example, philosopher Arnold Berleant who, in an investigation of environmental aesthetics, suggests that we must try to reconceptualise our world to take into account that we do not exist in isolation from our environment but rather as part of a continuity that includes it. It is a view that heightens the ethical responsibility for how we design and make changes in this realm because as Berleant points out, "what we do in environment we do to ourselves" (Berleant, 1997, p.121).

We imagine the experiential landscape to be constituted from more localised experiential landscape places. What we mean here is that although we see the experiential landscape as unbroken continuity it is not a uniform continuity. It varies in character locally as people move about their surroundings and experience them in different ways. In the concept of experiential landscape we focus on a range of fundamental experiences. These include, for example, that people develop a sense of orientation, that they come to identify and attach significance to particular locations, and that they can become aware of an overall sense of containment or coordination by which they might identify their neighbourhood or distinguish different city quarters and districts in the wider public realm. We will try to show in chapter four that these three general categories of human experience are fundamental to human life quality, but it doesn't stretch the imagination far to accept that if people cannot easily orientate or understand their place in the world then quality of life is likely to become compromised. Kevin Lynch was well aware of this in the development of his ideas about city imageability. "Let the mishap of disorientation once occur, and the sense of anxiety and even terror that accompanies it reveals to us how closely it is linked to our sense of balance and well-being. The very word 'lost' in our language means much more than simple geographical uncertainty; it carries overtones of utter disaster" (Lynch, 1960, p.4).

We will show later that these experiences can be conceptualised in spatial terms collectively as centre, direction, transition and area. Centre relates to the experience of location, direction to the awareness of continuity and extent, transition to where we feel a sense of change occurring, and area to the wider sense of environmental coordination that can give a sense of being somewhere as opposed to somewhere else. We will group these terms together in the acronym CDTA, partly for convenience of expression in the text, but more importantly to represent that these spatial–experiential components must be understood as distinguishable sensations within an indivisible whole. CDTA provides the basis of a vocabulary to tie experiential and spatial dimensions of place perception together. Experiential landscape places are holistic relationships of CDTA distinguishable within, yet inseparable from, the wider experiential landscape (Figure 2).

We will later develop the concept of experiential landscape by highlighting a range of environmental properties and characteristics associated with stimulating sensations of centre, direction, transition and area. Some of these define generic forms of the four components and others specific types of them. So, if we take the concept of centre by way of example, we can say that the term centre represents the spatial experience of location or proximity: the experience of centre is what gives us an awareness of "here". This sensation tends to occur when certain environmental properties are present and these include where we feel contained or enclosed, from which there are views beyond and where points of entry and exit can be perceived. Our research and field observations have also shown that the sense of centre seems more intensively felt in places constituted from smaller-scale centres and these tend to occur where there is convergence of opportunity to pause and rest, where people may gather, and because of this where the predominant sensation is that of occupation rather than of movement. These environmental properties are what we refer to as the generic properties of centre. In other words, that whatever else might work to encourage a sense of location, some or all of these properties are usually evident. There is, however, a finer level of detail that appears to distinguish different ways in which people experience the sense of centre. So, in addition to the generic properties we have outlined, if, for example, there are facilities like shops or places that hold some kind of social meaning, for work, play or ceremony, for example, or where there may be pronounced physical features like monuments, trees etc., then the sense

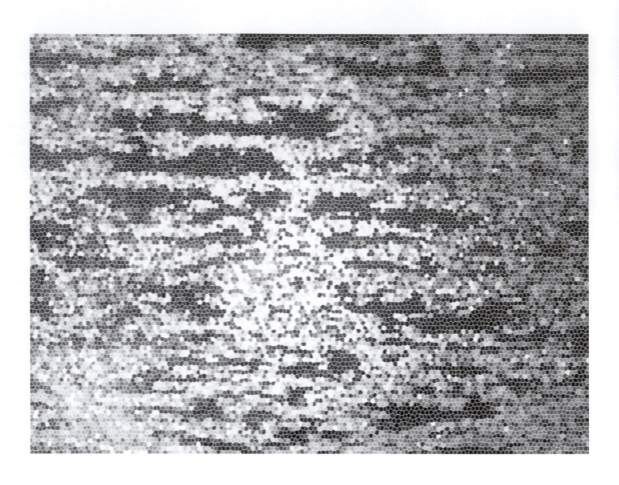

of centre might build up because a location has a pronounced imageability. We can say then that centres that exhibit this range of properties are so because they are socially imageable. Although differences are fuzzy rather than clear cut, nevertheless this makes them distinguished from other types of centre that become significant due to social encounters or because of their respite or restorative benefit to people. So what this means is that it is possible to distinguish three types of centre: social imageability, social interaction, and restorative benefit. Similar levels of detail apply to direction and transition whereas area has a slightly different characteristic that we will talk about later.

It may be useful to say a little more about space and place here, in particular that we draw a clear distinction between space as abstract and value-free containment, and place as something imbued with significance arising from human psychological and behavioural activity. Eminent geographer

Yi Fu Tuan has discussed this distinction in relation to the way that architects may sometimes talk about the locational qualities of space (Tuan, 1977). Endowing space with locational qualities is the same as saying that the space is a particular kind of place: one that delivers locational sensations to occupiers. Tuan also points out that architects might equally well speak of the spatial qualities of places. Here places are assumed to have certain properties, that of spatial dimension. Tuan's purpose here is to draw attention to the fact that, whereas space and place cannot be used interchangeably, they mean different things but require each other for full definition. Experiential landscape places can be understood this way too. For Tuan though, there is another distinction between space and place and this is that space is assumed to be something that allows movement, whereas place is associated with pause, "...each pause in movement makes it possible for location to be transformed into place" Tuan, 1977, p.6). The

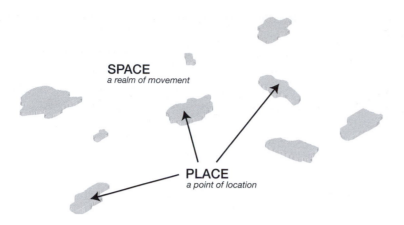

SPACE
a realm of movement

PLACE
a point of location

3

Place as a pronounced point of location against a general background

pauses that Tuan refers to here may be long, such as the purposeful occupation of somewhere for a period of time, or it can be so fleeting as to be hardly noticed, such as the way that the eye might momentarily rest on a particular building or feature within a broad panorama. What this implies is that space can be understood as the area defined by a network of places. Consequently it tends to suggest that places are intrinsically locational in nature and that they are separated by a background of space which, itself, is not place (Figure 3).

An alternative conception we have tried to develop in this book is that place perception is intrinsically a phenomenon of continuity. One does not step into place and then out again. Instead some form of place experience is always present; it is just that its characteristics change as people move about. Some places do have an emphatic locational character. They are perceived as pauses, rests or stops, as Tuan suggests. But in reality people move between these pauses and the question that we ask here is, during this travel, does the sense of place simply switch off until one arrives at the next pause? It makes no sense to us to answer yes to this and so we propose instead that the character of place experience simply changes, indeed is in a constant state of flux, as we move around. CDTA gives us a way of describing the nature of these character changes for intervals along the journey. For example, at a place with a strong sensation of location, the experience of centre will be heightened, but will probably be accompanied by a relatively less emphatic awareness of direction and transition. All this within an awareness of general background coordination, or area, also sensed to a

lesser or greater extent according to the prevailing circumstances. As one moves away, it is possible that the sense of centre will gradually diminish in favour of a stronger sense of transition that may be fleeting or sustained, and as one moves further, the sense of direction for a while may predominate, or we may feel again a strong sense of centre but this time at a different location. CDTA provides us with a conceptual means to read the changing rhythm of place experience during our journeying about (Plate 1).

CDTA are, then, abstract representations of different facets of our experience of place in the world defined in both spatial and experiential terms. As we move about they are carried with us and they vary in our awareness of them according to the circumstances at hand. They are, in some sense conceived as the fundamental building blocks of place experience, but it is important to remember that they are not separate, discrete entities assembled together to form experiential landscape places, but instead represent distinguishable variations in the continuity of place experience detectable at specific locations. The concretion of these experiential landscape places is what constitutes the experiential landscape, and because of the human subjectivity involved, one person's experiential landscape will not be the same as another's. A person's experiential landscape is uniquely their own.

The seamless and holistic nature of this conception of experiential landscape can perhaps be usefully elaborated through analogy with musical experience. A starting point for this can be found in Walter's attempt to encapsulate the holistic nature of place experience by asserting that place has a topistic reality just as a person has a subjective reality and an artefact an objective reality (Walter, 1988). The essential nature of a place's topistic reality is given by people's feelings and emotional expressions so they have a real and tangible emotional content that comes from human participation and expressive action. In Walter's conception, places are nothing other than the location of experience and in this sense he is suggesting that our physical surroundings are really emotions in material form. Assigning such an explicit emotional dimension to place highlights the dynamic nature of place experience.

Such places can never be static fixed and determined, instead they change, develop and evolve in continuous flux, through time, according to what happens there and according to the meanings and associations that people project there. When new structures, buildings or landscapes, for example, are built this is but the first step in a continuous and dynamic process of building, demolition and rebuilding, during which meaning, significance and values evolve. This unfolding life is the way the topistic reality of place rises and falls, ebbs and flows through time and location in a rhythmical and symbiotic dance of situated human action and emotional expression. Such a conception of place seems to us to describe something that is less and less like an assemblage of defined and distinguishable settings, no matter how well integrated, and more and more like the fluidity of musical experience.

Yi Fu Tuan has drawn attention to the way in which sound and space can be related by highlighting that spatial impressions can be evoked by different sounds. "The reverberations of thunder are voluminous; the squeaking of chalk on slate is 'pinched' and thin. Low musical tones are voluminous whereas those of high pitch seem thin and penetrating. Musicologists speak of 'musical space.' Spatial illusions are created in music quite apart from the phenomenon of volume and the fact that movement logically involves space. Music is often said to have form. Musical form may generate a reassuring sense of orientation. To the musicologist Roberto Gerhard, form in music means knowing at every moment exactly where one is. Consciousness of form is really a sense of orientation" (Tuan, 1977, p.15). What this shows is that the phenomenon of music is not only intrinsically holistic, in that the whole is greater than the sum of its notes, chords and constituent phrases, but that it is seamlessly sequential and can also be considered as a type of form capable of delivering a sense of orientation. These characteristics are common to the concept of experiential landscape we envisage. Before developing on this, however, we should highlight one important difference between musical experience and place experience. This is that most people experience music as being finite with definite beginnings and ends. This is not the same for place. As long as we

remain alive, place is always there, an inseparable part of what in fact it is to be alive. It cannot be stepped out of or switched off as music can. It is instead an omnipresent dimension of human existence the characteristics of which are in a continual state of flux, changing always as we pass through time and through our physical surroundings. But with this proviso music and experiential landscape are analogous in useful respects and this helps to provide a picture of the conception of place that is its fundamental foundation.

First of all, consider some of the characteristics of musical experience. To begin with music is a sequential phenomenon: we do not get it all in one chunk, it comes to us in a sequence, its character changing in complex ways as it develops and unfolds. Also music is not just heard, it is felt. Most people would recognise that music induces often profound emotional reactions. We can feel the swelling and diminishing, the tension and relief, the mystery, the anticipation, the wonderment, the climax, as though our bodily sensations were being carried along in harmony with the unfolding variations in the musical sequence. Music can also be experienced as a whole in the sense that we can recognise an entire symphony as a whole phenomenon with a character and qualities distinguishable from those of other symphonies. Simultaneously, though, music is also experienced as an accumulation of its component parts, each of which may be short or long distinguishable passages: recognisably contained entities within the whole symphony, but strung together seamlessly and harmoniously so that the final effect of the whole is always greater than the sum of the component parts.

Interestingly, it is possible to give a visual expression to the changing characteristics of the musical sequence through the fluctuating light emissions often seen on hi-fi graphic equalisers and other types of musical mixing equipment. These display the balance of volume in different frequencies or instruments in a musical passage at intervals throughout its length. The dance of the bars on the display screen allows certain details of the characteristics of the music to be read as it unfolds without interruption and without break. This, we believe, is similar to the way our place experience appears to us: as a harmonious interplay of parts and whole in a seamless continuity of changing character and scale (Plate 2).

We can illustrate this by taking a look at a journey through a small sequence of courtyards in the old town of Sitges, near Barcelona in Spain in a way reminiscent of the way Gordon Cullen demonstrated his concept of serial vision in *Townscape* (Cullen, 1971, p.17). Cullen shows a plan of what appears to be a small walled town and then imagines taking a walk through it, illustrating his journey with eight sketches to show how the scene changes as he goes. The purpose is to illustrate how the unfolding sequence of revelations created by changes in spatial volume, landmark features, gaps, corridors and gateways, induces a seamless awareness of fluctuating sensations catching our attention and drawing us on in a dynamic spatial rhythm of here, there and change.

Like Cullen, we are concerned with how the sensation of direction is stimulated: drawing a person through a journey by means of a series of visual revelations. But we are also concerned with the wider experience of place character throughout the journey and with how we might understand the nesting or enfolded impact of scale. Returning to the musical analogy for a moment, we can tell the story of the Sitges sequence as a journey through a town with reference to the fluid way that music gradually unfolds and develops. In doing so we want to highlight the inter-relationship of three things: first, the seamless fluidity of change in character, or personality, throughout the piece; second, the way in which nuances of changing character can be captured and revealed at intervals; finally, the way in which variations in scale become apparent as woven into the whole experience (Figure 4).

Perhaps the first thing immediately apparent from the six photographs representing our passage through this journey is that, taken as a whole, there is a sense of overall coordination. The vernacular style of the architecture with its white stucco surfaces, stone details and repetition in the use of arches, the grey cobbled floorscape, all contribute to an identifiable whole. In musical terms this represents that the whole ensemble has a recognisable identity that sets it apart from others. It is equally clear though that this whole has a series of distinguishable components.

1. The first photograph reveals an open spacious character, but one that holds future possibility in the doorways, windows, arches and ornamental detail in the distance.

2. Moving on the sense of future possibility develops and begins to intensify revealing the direction that the sequence will take, hinting at some of the qualities yet to come and how they themselves may introduce still later qualities.

3. Entering the tunnel generates a more abrupt change of tempo, introducing notes of strong containment and control. There is a sense of compression and possibly a tension induced by diminishing light levels and the close proximity of doors leading to realms unknown. Attention is simultaneously drawn to the visual rewards of ornament around doorways and arches at close proximity, and to the still distant escape into the light and space beyond.

4. Gradual emergence from the tunnel brings a sense of release as the spatial compression relaxes making way for the light and the open once more. Additional features – the tree, the colonnade, the steps – gradually increase their sense of presence introducing new notes and nuances to the journey.

5. The spatial rhythm changes again, from the right side open space at the start of the sequence to the left side now. A note of high drama occurs with the abrupt arrival of the heavy ornamental doorway, emphasising the rhythmical shift from right to left by attracting the eye to its prominent setting above the stone entrance steps. It has a stately baronial air of authority.

6. Finally, approaching the door yields a final climax of detail, holding the attention and suggesting a continuity of experience, possibly of a dramatically different kind, beyond its threshold.

The experience of change in this sequence does not, of course, happen in a series of self contained jerks, as the static photographs imply,

4

A journey through Sitges old town

but as a seamless continuity. Just as a musical symphony contains, and is made up from, distinguishable passages each of which has its own particular characteristics and nuances that are recognisable in their own right and at the same time contribute uniquely to the whole, so too does the journey through this townscape sequence.

The seamless and unfolding change in character through a musical symphony can be made visible in the pattern of light emissions on a graphic equaliser display. This gives us a model that can make patterns in place character visible in experiential landscape too by using the CDTA language. The graphic equaliser bands display variations in qualities of the components present in a musical sequence as it unfolds. It does this in an unbroken flow preserving the sense of continuity yet allowing frequency characteristics to be read at any interval throughout the sequence. To this extent the bands of light emission constitute a form of language allowing an aspect of the unique characteristics of a musical passage to be understood at any point. CDTA provide similar opportunities for reading experiential landscape. Like the balance of frequency in music they can never be separated from one another, because place character is defined, not in terms of either one or the other, but as the balance evident between them. Sometimes, as in photograph three of the Sitges sequence, a sensation of transition may speak more loudly than other components, for example. Yet these components do not disappear, they are either more quiet or temporarily dormant, and they will reappear with varying degrees of emphasis later in the passage. Neither do they stop and start in abrupt chunks. Like musical frequency, changes in CDTA balance happen seamlessly with movement through space and time. In the Sitges sequence, what one experiences is not six discrete locations at all but a continuity of spatial experience within which the six locations exist, depicted as frozen moments in the photographs, in a fluid continuity. Recording the relative intensity of CDTA anywhere along the sequence is, then, a record of the experiential landscape character at that instance, just as the graphic equaliser light patterns display aspects of the character of the musical passage at that instant (Figure 5).

As well as changes in character throughout the sequence, revealed as frequency variation in music and balance of CDTA intensity in experiential landscape, there are also scale implications. One of the characteristics of music is that it works, again seamlessly, on different levels of scale, holistically as if the parts and the whole work in harmony together. At the finest grain of scale, individual instruments work as if they are extensions of the musicians themselves, bringing intonation and expression that makes the same score simultaneously recognisable but also different, unique in style and expression to particular players, bands or orchestras. This acts to bring personality to the notes which are the basic building blocks of musical expression. Notes group together sequentially and holistically, independently or together as chords, to create melody and these in turn group to form distinct passages or suites which also have a life of their own within the overall symphonic whole. Change any of these parts and the manifestation of the whole can be subtly or dramatically altered. Change the overall symphonic arrangement, perhaps to create a softer or more edgy performance and this one decision will influence the way that the subordinate parts have to behave to express this intention. The whole and the parts work together as if in symbiotic totality.

The same is true of experiential landscapes. CDTA are simply expressions of spatial experience that are scale independent. As well as being present in different intensity to form the experiential character of a place at an instant on a journey, they are also detectable at different levels of scale. So if we look again at the Sitges sequence, focusing for

5

Recording the relative intensity of CDTA at intervals along a journey

	Social Imageability	Social Interaction	Restorative Benefit	View	Movement	Threshold	Segment	Corridor	Ephemeral	Thematic Continuity
Strong										
Moderate										
Weak										
	Centre			Direction		Transition				Area

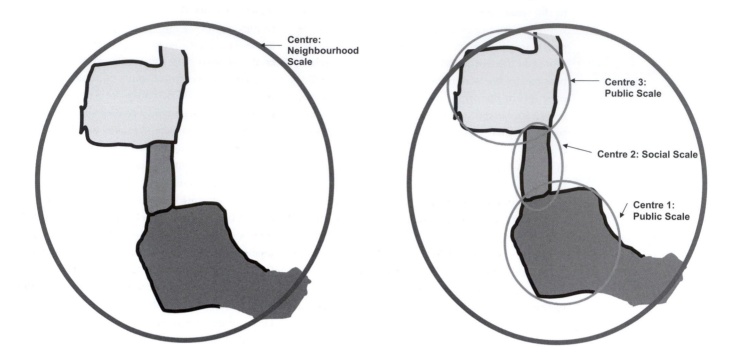

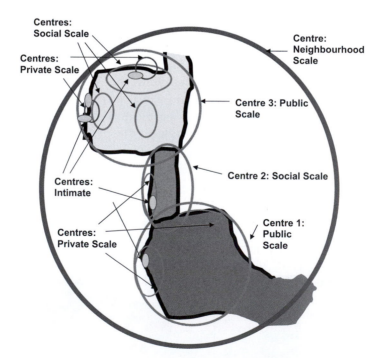

Clockwise from top left

6

Sitges old town: a centre at the neighbourhood scale

7

Three smaller centres nested in Sitges old town

8

A multiplicity of nested centres at different levels of scale in Sitges old town

simplicity of example only on centres as the general sensation of location, we can see that the overall sense of coordination might constitute a sense of centre when viewed at the scale of the wider town. It in fact determines a sense of location as a distinguishable neighbourhood, one of many that coalesce to make up the whole town. This neighbourhood seems itself to be made from a collective of centres at smaller levels of scale. So, for example, there seem to be three distinct centres: two constituting the main squares and a third in the corridor between. The two squares exist at a public level of scale whereas the corridor, although still a public place, seems to have properties that emphasise a smaller more social level of scale. This is because the compressed space encourages close social contact, encouraging social interactions, particularly in the doorways (Figures 6, 7, 8).

This could also be said of the colonnade in the second square, and the steps, all of which encourage and support social activity. Personal scale centres are evident at the location of doorways. Yet more intimate scale centres are detectable as one zooms in to become aware of ornamental detail or features, such as the decorative quality of the door joinery and knocker, where appreciation of them requires close quarter contact.

The multi-layered musical anatomy arises from the complex interplay and blending of sound expressions at different scales working together to preserve an overall structure but within which are nuances and variations that add personality. So too does the experiential anatomy of a town seem to work. Intimate and personal scale gives fine grain variation and personality whilst at the same time aggregating to form social and then public scales, which themselves provide the structural consistency for creating coherent neighbourhoods and then wider towns and cities. This is what we have called the experiemic scale and we will talk more of that later (Plate 3).

Preface

"There is a quality even meaner than outright ugliness or disorder, and this meaner quality is the dishonest mask of pretended order, achieved by ignoring or suppressing the real order that is struggling to exist and to be served" (Jacobs, 1961, p.15).

Experiential landscape is a conceptualisation of people and outdoor settings that attempts to begin to overcome this suppression. It takes as its starting point the outdoor environment as a primarily experiential entity and that realising the real order to which Jane Jacobs alludes depends on realising that human functioning and the spatial and material surroundings cannot be meaningfully decoupled. Human experience must be given greater prominence in how we understand outdoor places and how we make new ones. There is no shortage of information to help of course but, as Steven and Rachel Kaplan observed, relevant research, particularly within their own field of environmental psychology is not always easy to operationalise in the design disciplines (Kaplan, Kaplan and Ryan, 1998).

The approach taken in the development of experiential landscape is that this is partly to do with the way we conceptualise space, a fundamental medium to people concerned with the design of the outdoor environment. Experiential landscape is a concept of the outdoor environ-ment that draws together spatial and experiential dimensions as a unified whole. Normally it is only the spatial dimension that is visible to us and this, along with the material elements that define it, is what designers of outdoor places primarily pay attention to. It seems though that what Jacobs and the Kaplans, and many others besides, really mean is for the environmental design professions to be more aware of the expe-riential consequences of what they do and this involves recognising more forcefully that the picture of order revealed by the spatial realm is only a partial one. Projected into it and inextrica-bly bound together with it is human experience. Without this extra dimension space remains a vessel, a container for human experience, and for many scholars and researchers concerned with the human-environment relationship this has seemed incomplete and unsatisfactory.

American psychologist, Mayer Spivak, writing in *Architectural Forum* in 1973 made a significant distinction between space and place when he said "it is what people do in space that makes that space into a place" (Spivak, 1973, p.44). Spivak's assertion was that there is a finite number of environmental experiences that contribute the repertoire for fulfilled human life which he called archetypal places. Setting aside the inherent determinism, the significance of Spivak's ideas lay in defining archetypal places as a kind of fusion of human behavioural and psychological functioning and the special circumstances in which it happened. It was something that not only makes a clear distinction between the notions of space and place, but also gives the definition of place an explicitly human experiential dimension. That place has an intrinsic human dimension is echoed by others and has become a cornerstone of what has subsequently developed as place theory. This has meant that the idea of a sense of place, a concept very close to the heart of landscape architecture, was not necessarily to do with properties that a particular physical setting had, but just as much to do with what people did and felt. This presents the environmental design professions with a significant challenge. It is hard to imagine that anybody working in this area would wish to do anything other than make new places that deliver experiential opportunity and social relevance. But if we are to accept that outdoor places are not just receptacles for human experience but are actually defined partly in terms of them, how do we respond to this in our analysis and design work? The approach taken in experiential landscape is to try to conceptualise experience spatially. Because space is the fundamental medium of landscape design and spatial manipulation is how we go about making new places, then if we can understand something about the spatial dimensions of human experience, if indeed such a thing is conceivable at all, then we might be able to see how to imbue this fundamental medium of outdoor design with greater experiential resonance. Experiential landscape is a way to make hidden experiential dimensions in outdoor places explicit and by this means help people make better outdoor places.

Section one of the book begins by sketching out a philosophical context for the development of the experiential landscape concept with an exploration of ideas about the human-environment relationship. We first take an overview of the prevailing world view and its influence on the development of environmental design disciplines, highlighting problems that seem to continue to stand in the way of genuine people-friendly approaches. In response we explore ideas that contribute an alternative world view supporting a more holistic view of human-environment relations which ties together more closely human behavioural and psychological functioning with the settings in which it occurs. Key elements of this are traced to counter-enlightenment movements associated with aspects of Romanticism which although all but over as an influential cultural movement by the late nineteenth century continue to resonate in recent times within the growth of some eco-centric aspects of the modern environmental movement. This helps to underpin a more ecological, holistic view of human-environment relations, elements of which have been explored in the context of landscape architectural theory but have not really taken root. The general characteristics lean towards a more phenomenological philosophy emphasising experiential dimensions and this provides foundations for human psychological functioning to be at the heart of the way the concept of place is understood.

This philosophical overview is then taken forward to a consideration of the theoretical implications for landscape design and begins by discussing how the professional development of contemporary landscape design has taken place over a relatively short time against a background of Modernism. We argue that the gradual professionalisation of landscape architecture has emphasised the requirements of practice possibly at the expense of philosophical exploration and theoretical maturity. This may have contributed to approaches that stress aesthetic, economic and technical proficiency over human experiential considerations and may at least in part be responsible for why important developments in environmental psychology, specifically the development of place theory, have remained largely overlooked by the mainstream. We follow this with a brief account of some aspects of place theory to establish elements relevant to the outdoor environment before moving on to discuss principles underpinning the development of the experiential landscape concept in section two.

Section two begins by building from these theoretical foundations to first establish the background to the experiential dimensions at the core of experiential landscape. This draws fundamental aspects of human experience into three categories related to orientation, place attachment and neighbourhood awareness and we show how these can be related to spatial concepts. This forms the theoretical cornerstone of experiential landscape and establishes how experiential landscape places, the components of experiential landscape, are conceived as integrations of spatial sensations called centre, direction, transition and area (CDTA). The properties and characteristics of each of these components and the way they connect in a vocabulary of experiential landscape are outlined in detail. CDTA provides the means by which experiential landscapes can be made visible and we show how this is achieved by means of a range of field observation and participative techniques that can generate maps representing graphically the distribution of CDTA. These maps have potential as an analytical tool augmenting conventional survey and analysis techniques with explicit experiential information. It also has potential in design decision-making and geometrical implications relevant to this are also discussed in this section.

A final section shows how the experiential landscape approach has been applied in a range of contexts beginning with examples to show how the experiential potential of residential settings can be read from the spatial configuration. This, however, is a limited application of experiential landscape because it does not take inhabitants' patterns of routine life into account. As such, findings from this application of experiential landscape remain provisional, but they are never-theless a potentially important addition to conventional site survey and analysis work because they highlight the relationship of spatial factors to user experience and can help focus subsequent public consultation. This is followed by an account of the way experiential landscape mapping techniques were used to reveal aspects of the identity of the north Yorkshire village of Kirby Hill. In this case the emphasis was on methods for resident participation to gather information with which to generate experiential landscape maps for individual participants. We show how individual maps are layered using computers to reveal the cumulative pattern of place experience for the Kirby Hill participants and what this enabled us to conclude about the nature of village identity and community life. Another example of experiential landscape application concerns work done with schools. In this case we describe how experiential landscape participative techniques are adapted for use with school staff and young children to draw out the school's collective personality, a particular form of the concept of area that defines what is unique about a particular school community. Examples are described that show how experiential landscape concepts can be used to steer environmental improvement work towards more experientially rich outcomes. We conclude this section by looking at how experiential landscape can underpin the study of a waterfront site in Leeds, generating insights about the nature of city centre neighbourhood in urban regeneration and design.

Section One

Human-environment relations

Introduction

"Nature is not out there, a place apart from us. We have, instead, a continuity of humans and natural world. What we need now is to reconceptualise our world in a way that comes to terms with this, for what we do in environment we do to ourselves" (Berleant, 1997, p.121).

If Arnold Berleant's philosophical position that what we do in environment we also do to ourselves is accepted, then how can this be understood and operationalised in approaches we adopt to shape our outdoor environment? The concept of experiential landscape is essentially an exploration in search of some answers to this question. Experiential landscape is not however solely concerned with the development of new tools and methods for practice: it is also concerned with trying to understand the reasons why we seem to have found difficulty accommodating experiential matters into open space design practice and with making some suggestions about how things might be improved. To do this we need to begin with exploring ideas about the human-environment relationship and particularly to highlight how these ideas have influenced the development of modern landscape architecture specifically. Our assertion in doing so is threefold. First, that

human-environment relations should form the principal philosophical foundation for landscape architecture and urban design but that hitherto this is underdeveloped in their intellectual fabric. Second, is that this has brought about a largely subconscious acceptance of a particular concept of human-environment relations, increasingly challenged today, that may be partially responsible for a subjugation of experiential concerns in outdoor place making. Third, is that this can be overcome. We will talk about some of the philosophical, theoretical and methodological implications to support our argument for a humanistic and socially inclusive approach to open space design in which human emotional expression and psychological functioning have primacy.

Central to this aim is that techno-scientific rationality and dualistic human-environment relations characterise a world view increasingly thought within environmental design disciplines to be a constraining influence, especially in relation to understanding place experience and particularly the complexity of meanings and associations people have with places they routinely use. Evidence for this can be found in the often lively critical debate that has emerged in the landscape architectural academic and professional press since at least the early 1980s. This highlights growing concern about perceived limitations in landscape architecture's intellectual development thought to be affecting its capability to develop landscapes conducive to the achievement of human fulfilment. If there is limitation and deficiency here then this should be a significant concern in a society which is increasingly asking environmental design professions to be more conscious of quality of place and what this means in terms of human life quality and approaches to design. These concerns have been variously expressed but generally appear to focus on perceptions of excessive bias toward utility and style at the expense of social and experiential concerns in the design of landscape. Koh (1982), for example, blamed a technological bias. "What mattered most was the technical know-how of putting site and structure together...Designs frequently became professionally excellent but socially irrelevant, unresponsive to the ecosystem, and alienating user groups" (ibid., p.77). Later, Howett (1998) focused on aesthetics. "In practice, however, primacy is most often given to aesthetic values in judging the success or failure of a given project" (ibid., p.80), a sentiment echoed by Ken Worpole the same year in a commentary in the *The Guardian* newspaper about the lack of human life in the photographic coverage of the award winning Royal Albert Dock piazza "...human needs are sacrificed on the altar of design and aestheticism in many British towns...People tend to go missing in the pristine imagery of architecture and design where life's untidiness is regarded as an aesthetic intrusion" (Worpole, 1998). Blamed in particular are aspects of landscape architecture's philosophical foundations and theoretical development which have been considered immature, narrow in scope and largely derived from related discipline areas.

Opinions as to why landscape architecture has developed this way are various but there is evidence for a convergence of view pointing to the dominant influence of the doctrines of Positivism and its Enlightenment origins. This is thought to have fuelled a preoccupation with methods which aspire to the analytical solidity of science, a bias towards quantitative considerations, and a subjugation of experiential and emotional dimensions of place experience. There is also thought to be a strong reductionist undercurrent in landscape architecture which, although rarely explicit in practice, is regarded as a considerable influence on the mind-set adopted by landscape architects serving to reinforce a prevailing view that complex problems can be more easily understood, and then resolved, through analysis of the components from which they are perceived to be made. This appears to be regarded as the fundamental root of a bias in landscape architecture's intellectual development that has come to privilege objective, analytical methods in design and a conception of human-environment relations characterised by separation and division. It is argued that this led to over-emphasis on rationalising modes of thinking applied to manufacture and manipulation of the physical components of the environment, impeding the achievement of meaningful landscapes and human experience of them.

This background has influenced the intellectual underpinning and practice of landscape architecture, but it is based on a particular world view which has arisen relatively recently in history and, although dominant in Western society, is increasingly challenged. The question raised here is, are there other philosophical systems that are more helpful and, if so, what implications might they hold for our approaches to outdoor place making? This section first sketches out the prevailing world view, highlighting features of it that sustain human-environment dualism, arguing that its consequences are problematic as a philosophical foundation for environmental design disciplines trying to understand people-place relations. We follow by showing how this philosophical inheritance has shaped many of the values underpinning contemporary professional landscape architecture. After this we move on to explore an alternative world view, characterised by a more integrated conception of human-environment relations which has a more phenomenological character and emphasises experiential dimensions. It takes forward to the next section an integrated conception of the human-environment relationship so that the theoretical and methodological implications for the concept of experiential landscape can be considered.

Chapter 1

A prevailing world view

Enlightenment human-environment relations and the separation of humans from environmental experience

The concept of human-environment relations associated with modern landscape architecture originates predominantly in the Scientific Revolution which gradually unfolded over two centuries from 1500–1700. Before 1500 nature was experienced in terms of organic relationships, symbolised by *the great chain of being* (Lovejoy, 1974) in which existed an interdependence of spiritual and material phenomena concerned with understanding the meaning of things rather than with prediction and control. The beliefs upon which much of this world view was founded began to be undermined by Copernicus's hypothesis in 1543 that the earth did not occupy a privileged position at the centre of the Universe. This was given additional support by the astronomical studies of Kepler, who said of his work, "My aim in this is to show that the celestial machine is to be likened not to a divine organism but rather to a clockwork" (Horton, 1956), but became established as a valid scientific theory following Galileo's work in 1632. Galileo was the first to combine scientific experimentation with mathematical language to formulate and communicate

his findings. These are central tenets of the scientific method developed and vigorously advocated by Francis Bacon in England and they remain cornerstones of scientific theory and practice today. This empirical approach and the development of a mathematical description of nature began to raise the significance of measurable and quantifiable properties like movement and shape and to diminish the significance of subjective properties like colour, taste and smell for example.

Since Bacon, the goal of science has been to acquire knowledge by drawing general conclusions from experimental procedures which were then to be tested and verified by further experiments. In addition to being attributed with the development of the modern scientific method, Bacon's significance extends, for some, to the domineering and aggressive metaphors used in his writings. Merchant's (1980) interpretation of Bacon is highlighted by Capra (1982) to assert that the advance of science was accompanied in Bacon by a view of nature as an entity to be subjugated and enslaved and from which secrets were to be tortured by scientists using mechanical devices. This stands in stark contrast with the ancient organic, nurturing concept of nature and fuels the development of a mechanistic world view in which human self confidence, in its ability to transform and control nature, would eventually replace earlier thinking altogether.

The new confidence which was to arise from scientific progress is perhaps most evident in the work of Rene Descartes. Descartes' philosophy is a significant influence on the conception of human-environment relations predominant in today's Western cultures. The belief imbued in Bacon's scientific method, that the only reliable truth came from scientific inquiry, was elevated by Descartes to the status of a scientific philosophy. Its aim was to distinguish truth from error in all fields of learning: the measure of truth lay only in its capacity to withstand scientific scrutiny. In this quest Descartes developed a new method of reasoning based on the mathematical language he believed was the key to a complete understanding of natural phenomena. Central to this is Descartes' belief that the essence of human nature lies in thought. The evident power of the mind allowed access to certain knowledge through processes of intuition and deduction: an analytical method of reasoning which involved breaking down complex problems and thoughts into smaller fragments and placing them in logical order. Descartes' method made mind more certain for him than matter and drew him to the conclusion that the two were separate: a rational, thinking self inhabiting a material body which was in itself no more or less significant than the animal, plant or mineral matter from which the world was made (Taylor, 1989). Descartes' method of reasoning, and the general world view it contributed to, have remained a dominant influence on Western scientific thought and wider cultural development for more than three centuries. Its success as an approach to intellectual problems has been immensely valuable, especially to the realisation of increasingly complex technological projects since the industrial revolution. During his lifetime, Descartes' vision of nature as a complex machine, governed by mathematical laws, would remain a conceptual framework only. It would be Isaac Newton's mathematical achievements during the seventeenth century which, through providing a consistent theory for all objects in motion, appeared to confirm Descartes' concept of nature as a mechanical system (Capra, 1982).

During the eighteenth century, the Newtonian mechanistic theory of the universe and the belief in the rational approach to human problems would underpin the Age of Enlightenment. These intellectual achievements were to finally eclipse medieval notions of spiritual and material unity and a nurturing organic world, and become the prime influence on the current Western culture. Particular features of this growth in emphasis on the power of reason include:

– higher status for mental over manual activity;
– the primacy of analytical procedures leading to fragmentation in thinking;
– a reductionist attitude from a belief that complexity can be understood through analysis of its parts alone;
– quantitative criteria raised above qualitative criteria as the measure of truths and reality;
– natural phenomena are absolute and complete and can ultimately be determined as such by the application of rational procedures (Lincoln and Guba, 1985).

In particular, these developments have shaped the dominant contemporary conception of human-environment relations. Central to this are changes in the way the notion of self and nature are understood (Taylor, 1975). The definition of a pre-Enlightenment self rested on the assumption of an external, divinely created hidden order. The Enlightenment stood in reaction to this, attempting to establish that there was no hidden order beyond what might exist in some natural laws or mechanisms. If this kind of hidden order did exist it was not part of a system of meaning or aims, meaning lay only in the thought and action of the human subject. Against this background the modern enlightened subject becomes self-defining, reliant on his/her own powers of reason and requiring no external influences. This unshakeable faith in human reason, along with access to the secrets of nature via rational experimental practices, led to a surge of cultural optimism and a belief that humanity would make great progress once irrationality, ignorance and superstition were eradicated. Civilisation had become synonymous with the acquisition of reason and knowledge within a conceptual framework characterised by:

dualistic separation of mind from body, human from environment, individual from society, thought from deed; and a view of nature as a machine, determined by mathematical law and open to rational investigation (Capra, 1982).

A belief that mind and matter were fundamentally different and separate, coupled with a shift in the image of nature as organism to nature as machine has profound consequences. Life resided in the mind, separate from and contained within a material body. The body became part of a wider material environment made of matter, an assemblage of essentially lifeless mechanical entities without any intrinsic purpose or spirituality of its own. Stripped of life and soul, nature was no longer respected as an organism. As Caroline Merchant colourfully elucidates, there was no longer a cultural constraint on its treatment. "The image of the earth as a living organism and nurturing mother served as a cultural constraint restricting the actions of human beings. One does not readily slay a mother, dig into her entrails for gold, or mutilate her body...As long as the earth was considered to be alive and sensitive, it could be considered a breach of human ethical behaviour to carry out destructive acts against it" (Merchant, 1980, p.3). The ethical implications of our treatment of environment can be extended further with the introduction of ideas advocating the interconnected nature of the human-environment relationship. Here the environment is regarded not simply as an independent entity we ought to respect but as an extension of what it is to be fully human. In this case if we do wrong we harm, not just a nurturing other, but our own selves. The implications of this will form part of our discussion in chapter two.

Enlightenment thinking brought about a world view in which the acquisition and study of knowledge became increasingly displaced from the world as lived. Developing particularly from the work of Descartes, human life was distanced from nature as scrutiny of the physical world through mathematical precision and empirical clarity replaced faith in experience. This paved the way for the fragmentation of the pre-Enlightenment cosmology into separate bodies of self-contained knowledge, each developing to become increasingly self-referential, specialised

and isolated. In architecture, the scientific revolution brought about the establishment of the Ecole Polytechnique in the late eighteenth century in which architecture was taught as science based on rationality and logic (Perez-Gomez, 1983). A theory of architecture derived from pure methodology and technique developed, rejecting the intuition and metaphor of earlier masonic apprenticeship traditions. By the mid nineteenth century this development, according to James Corner's interpretation (1990), saw theory reduced to a form of technical knowledge: a methodology for production and repetition in which architecture and gardening became purely technical operations with a formal purpose. The post-Enlightenment concept of theory as a set of operational rules provided the background against which contemporary landscape architecture was to develop. This theoretical foundation has, according to Corner (1990), brought about an excessively technological school in landscape architecture, based on Positivistic problem solving, resulting in a separation of human experience from the environment which he believes weakens landscape architecture's potential "as the great mediator between nature and culture" (ibid., p.77).

Positivism arose from the Enlightenment as a family of philosophies which owes much to the Newtonian mechanistic world view in which the universe is considered to consist of fundamental parts assembled into larger complexes governed by laws of nature. Positivism involves the explicit description and explanation of factual phenomena. It requires assertions about reality to be capable of test by scientific method and to withstand detailed and objective scrutiny. Although its major influence was in providing a new rationale for doing science, it became associated with a general philosophical doctrine embracing social as well as natural phenomena with the work of French philosopher Auguste Comte in the nineteenth century. The historical development of Positivism is generally regarded to have been slow and complicated, leading to different views about what it implied. Lincoln and Guba (1985) draw from a range of representative authors on the subject to highlight that the way Positivism is defined in its detail depends to some extent on the position and purpose of the definer. Whilst acknowledging a substantial underlying consistency, they conclude that certain idiosyncrasies are evident which raise questions about its philosophical solidarity. Nevertheless its basic tenets survive today as the dominant methodological paradigm in both social and natural sciences and as the foundations of the prevailing culture of Western society.

Theory development in landscape architecture has taken place within this context and a number of commentators associate it with limitations in the approaches it adopts. Corner (1990) asserts that Positivist principles underpin a contemporary concern in landscape architecture with the acquisition of tangible and objective knowledge before any action is taken and the scientific description and explanation of design processes. These concerns combine as a methodological theory strengthening a belief that humans can explain, control and manipulate their surroundings. The growth of complex analytical procedures in design like those developed by Alexander (1964) and McHarg (1971) is thought to be rooted here, leading ultimately to a belief that outputs are accounted for and legitimised by the procedures involved. This point is echoed in Lyle's (1985) distinction between *real* processes, which include imaginative vision and speculative free will and the veneer of *formal* processes overlaid for professional expedience. Other aspects of landscape architecture to which Positivist influence is attributed include a principal concern that good environments can be rationally prescribed through design, independent of users' personal, social or cultural variations and that human well-being can be beneficially modified by the results. This approach is considered by Koh (1982) to arise from a view of the environment as an objective entity, reducible to basic elements for scientific evaluation. Positivist principles are considered by these commentators to be a significant influence on the logical level at which landscape architecture takes place: mainly as an activity focused on the solution of site design problems. The landscapes that result from Positivist attitudes are variously considered to be in some sense incomplete: "deserts of quantitative reasoning" (Corner, 1991, p.118); "mathematically

efficient and economically profitable while the poetries of place have been blindly erased." (ibid.); "professionally excellent but socially irrelevant" (Koh, 1982, p.77). What these comments appear to imply is a lack of, or at least a narrow consideration of, human experience in the production of landscapes through this approach. This, coupled with a deterministic view that human well-being could be modified by change to the physical environment, led to design practices whereby users of the finished landscape were effectively excluded for reasons of ignorance or lack of taste.

Despite the pervasiveness of Positivism within Western culture its tenets are becoming increasingly challenged by experimental and theoretical findings. Lincoln and Guba (1985) draw together challenges and critiques of Positivism; highlighting five assumptions upon which Positivism rests that are, they assert, increasingly difficult to maintain. They are:

– "an ontological assumption of a single, tangible reality 'out there' that can be broken apart into pieces capable of being studied independently; the whole is simply the sum of the parts;
– an epistemological assumption about the possibility of separation of the observer from the observed – the knower from the known;
– an assumption of the temporal and contextual independence of observations, so that what is true at one time and place may, under appropriate circumstances (such as sampling) also be true at another time and place;
– an assumption of linear causality; there are no effects without causes and no causes without effects;
– an axiological assumption of value freedom, that is, the methodology guarantees that the results of an inquiry are essentially free from the influence of any value system (bias)" (Lincoln and Guba, 1985, p.28).

The challenge to Positivism is a significant factor because if, as commentators suggest, it has had a strong influence on the development of theory and practice in landscape architecture, the credibility of the intellectual foundations of landscape architecture are called into question. Not only is Positivism associated with weakness in landscape architecture, but its very credibility is open to challenge.

A less explicit, but nonetheless significant component of landscape architecture's cultural background is the process of instrumental rationalisation, a widespread characteristic of contemporary society. Rooted firmly in the Positivist mind-set, it is regarded to be a characteristic of the culture of Modernity and according to Taylor (1991), one of the features of it that many people experience as a decline or loss, even within a so called developing civilisation. Main features of the instrumentalist viewpoint include: the separation of humans from the environment as well as other aspects of Enlightenment dualism; a view of the environment as consisting of raw materials for human use; an emphasis on economic efficiency over other criteria in the measurement of social progress. The impact of instrumental reason is widely apparent across all aspects of society but has particular relevance here for its influence on environmental and social attitudes. In many ways a liberating influence, it is nevertheless associated with an excessive tendency to search out the most economical application of means to an end, or cost-benefit analysis. The emphasis on economic growth at the expense of other considerations has led to: insensitivity to the needs of the environment; social planning based on financial assessments of human life; and the dominance of technological solutions to environmental and social problems (Taylor, 1991; Capra, 1982). In addition to its general influence on the economic and technological orientation of modern society, the primacy of instrumental reason contributes to a polarisation in society. Those who favour technological solutions to human and environmental problems are countered by those for whom an accelerating technological civilisation represents a form of social decline, with increasing loss of contact with nature and loss of social cohesion as a result of an imperative of domination over the natural world. These sentiments are clearly resonant in critics of landscape architecture's current approach. Counter-positions are often characterised by an appreciation for pre-industrial societies and craft traditions etc., which are perceived to involve a closer, more empathic relationship with the natural world. These challenges to the dominance of instrumental rationality have persisted in various ways since the Romantic period and survive today in the modern ecological-environmental movement (Taylor, 1991). At extremes, this appears as a wholesale rejection of the anthropocentrism of instrumental rationality in the deep ecology movement developed particularly by Arne Naess in the 1980s (Naess and Rothenberg, 1989).

The professionalisation of landscape design

Against this general background, the intellectual character behind the development of approaches to landscape design can be traced more specifically. Before 1800 English landscape design was related to the theory of painting, in particular the Neoplatonic theory of Ideas. Artists strove to represent as closely as possible supposed universal Ideals of which everyday objects were thought to be imperfect copies. To imitate nature through art meant to produce images of Ideal nature and not the nature which appeared to the senses. This provided pre nineteenth century artists and landscape designers with a clear theoretical framework for their work. But towards the end of the eighteenth century interpretations of nature began to change. Nature as Ideal became replaced with a nature of empirical reality, a consequence of the Enlightenment and rise of scientific rationalism. Faced with a new interpretation of nature derived from what was accessible through the senses alone, the objective of landscape design as an art through which to imitate nature made less sense to practitioners. Without the Ideal of nature to aspire to, it seemed all that was left was to imitate wild nature, a conclusion which undermined the theoretical stability which had been enjoyed by landscape design's association with the arts, and led to fragmentation and eclecticism in style.

Turner (1996) draws attention to the arrival of empiricism as one of three stakes driven into the heart of landscape theory during the nineteenth century, the other two being the choice of the term landscape architecture as the professional title, and the growth of scientific functionalism during the twentieth century. Just as the word "nature" had earlier acquired a different interpretation, during the twentieth century the word "landscape" had become associated with any topographical product: the kind of landscape meant by geologists and geographers. Turner's point here is that if this definition of landscape is the one to predominate in landscape architecture, it equates the production of a landscape with the production of a building by an architect. Such a landscape is reduced to a kind of artificial product or commodity which results from professional intervention instead of an expression of a higher ideal. James Corner (1991) takes a similar view in his implication that landscape architecture is synonymous with aesthetic land-engineering, outputs from which are driven by technical imperatives and are frequently spiritually empty. The third of Turner's stakes, the advance of scientific functionalism during the twentieth century, has been widely cited as a principal influence on the development of design as a problem-solving activity (Koh, 1982; Lyle, 1985; Moore, 1993). This is a factor which holds considerable significance for the growth and characteristics of professional landscape architecture and repeatedly attracts criticism as a factor which contributes to the production of soulless, invariant places, devoid of human meaning or value. Corner (1990) is especially explicit about the influence of modern scientific thinking on contemporary landscape architecture, tracing its impact from eighteenth century landscape aesthetics, through nineteenth century eclecticism, the purist aesthetics of Modernism and the excessive Positivism of the post war era: "...the theoretical foundations of our contemporary profession have evolved directly from the fallacies of modern scientific thinking. They are simply extrapolated from a narrowly focused, one-sided and contradictory doctrine with which we still live" (ibid., p.75).

Coherent and cohesive theory in landscape design, strong as a result of its association with the fine arts, failed to survive the post-Enlightenment period, having been weakened by changing views about nature and excessively influenced by accelerating techno-scientific

rationality. In this context what has come to be understood as theory in landscape design has become increasingly associated with the establishment of operational rules and procedures aimed at repetition and reproduction. These factors appear to have contributed to the detachment of professional landscape architecture from important aspects of its cultural and intellectual roots, leaving its development open to influences which are explicitly modern in character. Instead of theoretical cohesion grounded specifically in the new profession, a multiplicity of working theories has persisted: a situation which is widely cited for its contribution to the maintenance of confusion within the discipline and weakness in the output of the profession (Rosenberg, 1986; McAvin, 1991). Rosenberg (1986), in particular, foresees considerable difficulty in overcoming this whilst landscape architecture remains in the grip of a mind-set driven by a dualistic conception of human-environment relations.

Modern landscape architecture has roots in urban planning as well as the arts and historic landscape and garden design from which much of its formative theoretical underpinning is generally assumed to derive. The North American City Beautiful Movement was initially a specialisation within landscape architecture before developing into a separate, more scientific profession and discipline. In the United Kingdom, the Scottish scientist, sociologist and geographer Patrick Geddes described himself as a landscape architect in 1903 and through close friendships with Lewis Mumford and Ebenezer Howard became an influential urban theorist and practitioner helping to develop Garden City ideas and other town planning practices. Geddes is generally credited with promoting the humanitarian belief that planning and design practices should be based on a thorough understanding of the prevailing social, cultural and geographical circumstances. His solution eventually evolved into the survey-analysis-design (SAD) approach that still characterises landscape architectural training and practice. The essentially linear, objective procedures that today characterise survey-analysis-design have attracted criticism because of their apparent derivation from techno-scientific functionalism and its supposed de-humanising consequence (Turner,

1996). The weaknesses often attributed to SAD based approaches, however, do not appear to lie with its visionary origins but with its subsequent unimaginative interpretation. Geddes' (1915) requirement for a synoptic appreciation of *Place, Work and Folk* seems to have become increasingly reduced to mere cataloguing of information: "ritual behaviour" according to Turner (1996, p.39) which is detached from the creative act of design. Although Geddes' motives were to remedy overemphasis on the arbitrary aesthetic or technical decision-making prevailing in city planning at the time, in doing so he appears to have taken a developing landscape architecture a further step away from its roots in the arts and firmly established the foundations from which it became possible to characterise design as a methodology for solving site-based problems through the application of sets of rules and procedures.

The rise and crisis of design methodology

Developing as a professional activity in the early part of the twentieth century, closely associated with urban planning, bereft of clear theoretical foundations and detached from earlier intellectual roots, contributed to a reinforcement of modernist influences on landscape architecture's growth. This is particularly evident in how the need for professional recognition and credibility was addressed, leading to a strengthening of SAD based, or more generally, analysis/synthesis problem solving models as a defining characteristic of the profession. Two principal factors are significant here: one, development of the primacy of abstract spatial awareness in which the concept of space is understood purely in terms of sets of Cartesian coordinates; another, the developing concept of design as a problem solving activity.

Abstract spatial awareness has its origins in the shift from a traditional, mimetic representation of nature in art to the non-figurative work of Modern artists. In abstract art the ground of meaning is in perception of the artefact itself. To hold meaning it was no longer necessary for art to express or signify any external idea, tradition or intention of the artist. Meaning was personal and left to the individual to decide, based on the prop-

erties of the image itself. These ideas found their way into architecture through Bauhaus inquiries into the nature of pure form and geometrical space as part of a quest to identify the elements of a universal language of form. The concept of space arising from these ideas embodied no values other than those derived from mathematical and geometric properties. These principles were explored in architecture at the time most notably through the work of Mies Van Der Rohe and later in landscapes by Eckbo, Burle-Marx and Barragan for example. Space understood in this way contributed to the reduction of landscape to a set of abstract properties and widened divisions between the making of landscapes and the human lived experience. This is a consequence which prompts thinly veiled exasperation from Corner. "Imagine the audacity or simple suspension of belief, necessary to reduce the complexity of living landscape to the sheer placelessness of pure form" (Corner, 1990, p.74). In these circumstances, perhaps more than ever before, what was tasteful and beautiful was determined by specialist experts.

A defining characteristic of contemporary landscape architecture is its focus on site-based problem solving activity. The concept of design as a problem solving activity also has its roots in the Bauhaus, especially in the axiom *form follows function*. A rational two-stage model of design developed in which an objectively gathered database of functional requirements preceded the development of form to solve the requirements. Design decisions were encouraged to be made according to quantifiable and objective information. By doing so designers felt their creativity would assume the sought after solidity, authority and legitimacy of scientific rigor. These claims held particular appeal for the relatively new profession of landscape architecture, anxious to establish recognition and credibility. The development of ideas about design as a problem-solving activity became reinforced with the growth of interest in design methodology. The idea of design as a legitimate subject to be studied in its own right is relatively recent: the first literature about design methodology began to appear in the late 1950s and early 1960s (Jones, 1980). The relevance of this development is twofold: first, it is the context within which SAD-based approaches to design in landscape architecture were refined and raised to the status of a dominant methodology; second, two of the principal proponents of design methodology have since questioned the legitimacy of design as an appropriate subject for independent study: a view based largely on the realisation of interdependency between problem and solution (Alexander, 1964; Jones, 1980).

That design can be conceived as an activity, capable of independent and objective study at all, dates back to the demise of craft evolution and its replacement with the *design by drawing* tradition. Earlier craft evolution was characterised by an interdependent relationship between thinking and the application of technical skills in the making of things. Jones (1980) refers to an account of the traditional wagon maker's craft to exemplify the point. Craftsmen did not draw their ideas and cannot generally give rational reasons for the decisions they make. Form was continuously modified so that the shape of objects evolved through trial and error over long periods. Information about the object existed only in the product itself, the knowledge of the craftsmen and the patterns and jigs used in fabrication. Because there were no drawings or other symbolic forms to record information, study of the process of its creation could not be conceived of outside the creative act itself. The separation of the trial and error of craft evolution from the process of production by using scale drawings paved the way for an approach much better suited to the demands of a growing technological society. Making drawn representation of things separate from and in advance of their fabrication makes it possible to: split up production work into separate components which can be carried out by different people; plan and coordinate many different craftsmen to a common end; and speed up the process of production. This separation also makes it possible to scrutinise design as an activity in its own right, independent of its context.

One of the most influential forerunners of the academic study of design methodology was the mathematician, architect and town planner, Christopher Alexander. His *Notes on the Synthesis of Form* (1964) is an attempt to compare design problems with arithmetic. Mainly through

study of primitive peoples Alexander came to believe that form could be considered to be the physical manifestation of underlying forces. These forces could be natural, social or forces of association, for example, linked with the lives and habits of people. The essence of this point of view would remain intact and become developed in his later work, but at this time, in the context of general dissatisfaction with the limitations of traditional design methods to solve complex problems, Alexander looked to his mathematical background for a way to get to the underlying structure of form. His reason was based on the knowledge that arithmetic convention allows complex numerical problems, impossible to handle mentally, to be solved quickly and easily. Alexander thought that an equivalent design convention (or method) ought to enable designers to come to solutions for increasingly complex problems. This appeal to the logic of arithmetic would also provide designers with a means of validating solutions in a manner analogous with science and would reduce over-reliance on formal rules derived from history. Human intuition, whilst recognised as valuable, would be made accountable by testing it against a method, thereby avoiding excesses of wild artistic individuality and the shrouding of incompetence.

Alexander's *Notes on the Synthesis of Form* is considered to have fuelled a subsequent development of interest in the academic study of design and problem solving methodology. Design and psychology converged in a blossoming of new methods which included procedures like brainstorming, synectics, value analysis, systems engineering etc. (Jones, 1980; Parnes, 1992). Their influence in architecture, engineering and landscape architecture was not to replace design by drawing but to make it increasingly rationalistic, more analytical, systematic and open. Although varied in their components and procedures and in their field of application, all new methods were attempts to externalise the design process, to expose the hitherto private thinking of the designer.

The appeal of design methodology in landscape architecture appears to have been motivated by a sense of professional insecurity. John Kelsey's article *A Design Method* (1970) not only draws design methodology into landscape architecture, but also reveals something about the condition and aspirations of the profession at that time. Kelsey clearly sees one of the major problems facing landscape architecture to be the acquisition of interdisciplinary recognition and respect. That it does not enjoy this is attributed to the nature of its objective: the abstract utopian ideal of "optimum external environment" (ibid., p.425). The tone of instrumental rationality implied in this aspiration seems reinforced by his wish to remove the "romantic nonsense that often goes for rational thought" (ibid.). Another problematic aspect of practice emphasised is the dominance of the operational and management aspects of projects which supposedly reduce the amount of design time available to between 5–10% of the project time. Kelsey sees the solution to these problems in adopting a rational design method to make more efficient and productive use of limited design time and to expose the workings of landscape architects to scrutiny, encouraging interdisciplinary cooperation and mutual professional respect. Kelsey sets out a nine-step method out of which, at step nine, "The landscape based plans should arrive as no surprise to anyone" (ibid., p.428).

The method he suggests has the flavour of the industrial production line: human intuition is present but controlled by procedures for divergent and then convergent thinking drawn directly from the new design methodologies and confined within early stages of the procedure. Thereafter new creative insight is discouraged to the extent that it is almost as if it were thought to be damaging, or in some way compromising to the legitimacy and validity of the resulting product. Creative thought is replaced by logical deduction as the procedure progresses toward the production of plans which seem regarded to be an end in themselves: fixed and static representations of the prior testing and refining of an ideal. Intrinsic to this methodological approach is that the collection and analysis of data by rational procedures appears to be given greater status as part of the process than is the creative insight of the designer. The desire of Alexander (1964) and others for an approach to design in which human intuition is made accountable has led to its subjugation in these methods.

The general climate of Modernism, coupled with a perception of the increasing complexity of problems and doubts about the capability of traditional design methods to cope; fears about how design outputs can be legitimised within a growing techno-scientific society; and insecurities within an immature profession, have all contributed to the adoption and development of excessively rational design methods within landscape architecture. As Lyle (1985) points out, these often appear to have more to do with meeting the demands of productivity and efficiency in professional practice than making high quality landscapes. Although highly varied in detail, procedure and degree of formality, design processes in contemporary landscape architectural practice and education appear to have their roots here and lead to a number of assumptions. These include a sustaining belief that a good method produces a good output, implicit in which is that the quality of the output can be judged against the quality of the method used to produce it rather than against external criteria: user experience for example (Alexander, 1964; Kelsey, 1970; Jones, 1980). Also there is a belief that intrinsic modern design problems exist to be solved in society and that the best way to solve them is by application of rationalistic procedures which at best control intuitive impulse and creative expression and at worst diminish them to the level of token entertainment (Kelsey, 1970). In some instances the complex abstract procedures which emerge as a result of this assumption are given the status of theory in landscape architecture (Steinitz, 1990).

Soon after the beginning of a growth in design and problem-solving methodology, two of its principal exponents began to raise questions, both about the use of method and about the legitimacy of design methodology as an academic discipline. Seven years after the publication of his *Notes on the Synthesis of Form*, Alexander rejected the whole idea of design methods as a subject of study, partly because he thought it was absurd to separate the study of designing from the practice of design. Similarly, Jones, in his introduction to the 1980 edition of *Design Methods* and four years later in *Essays in Design* (1984), also highlighted the interdependence of problem and solution in criticisms of design methodology. Designing as problem solving alone is "a dead metaphor for a living process" (Jones, 1980, p.xxiii). Jones extends his criticisms with the following reasons.

- A tendency to involve a split between intuitive and rational thinking. Jones' belief is that both are required working together in design.
- Methods are to do with a search for certainty in design. Design is about uncertainty.
- The application of design method seemed more to do with a process of control than a process of creation.
- They were often complicated and therefore tended to hinder clear communication and participation: a clear failure to achieve one of their principal goals.
- Designers often became swamped with information and locked into rigidity of procedure which obstructed common sense and intuition and obscured clear sight of the design situation.
- They were often regarded as a complete substitute for thinking for oneself.

The crisis of design methodology seems founded on a failure of nerve based on what, as a subject, it has become, rather than on a fundamental objection to the idea of design taking place within organisational frameworks of any kind. This seems rooted in two main issues: first, scepticism about the legitimacy of the subject of design methodology at all and second, concern about the consequences of over reliance on methods. The first issue, stressed by both Alexander (1964) and Jones (1980), is based on the view that the study of designing is context dependent: it is only meaningful within the specific design situation. This means that the method used in any given situation should arise from that situation and is not necessarily transferable to other situations, and designers' intuition is not just involved, but is unavoidable. The second concern, emphasised initially in Jones but increasingly apparent in Alexander, centres on methods which: divide intuition and rationality; strive for certainty and control; and result in disincentives for designers to think because of rigid and formal procedures.

Once again, it is possible to overturn these concerns and envisage the characteristics of methods which may be more acceptable to these critics. For example, methods which unite rather than separate intuitive and rational thinking, accept uncertainty as part of a process of creation, and engage the imagination and individuality of designers within flexible processes grounded in the design situation. The essence of this was clearly apparent to Christopher Alexander and has contributed to the development of his early ideas into a more qualitative pattern oriented approach underpinning his publications *A Pattern Language* (1977) and later *A New Theory of Urban Design* (1987).

Summary

Against the dominance of this cultural background, theory in landscape design developed from the clarity and stability enjoyed through its association with the fine arts to a position in which theory became successively less cohesive and was weakened and fragmented by the time it began to develop as a profession in the early part of the twentieth century. Loss of continuity with previous theoretical traditions, along with influences from urban planning, appears to have weakened its intellectual foundations resulting in a loss of humanistic roots. The rise of rationalistic problem solving methods became a defining characteristic within a new profession developed in response to these circumstances. Growth of interest in design methodology in the early 1960s contributed towards a reinforcement of these characteristics in landscape architecture as a means of providing a relatively new and insecure profession with interdisciplinary respect. The value of human experience, intuition and imagination diminished in the face of criticisms of subjectivity, idiosyncrasy and romantic individualism. Criticisms of landscape architecture in the 1980s and 90s stand principally in reaction to this tradition. Fuelled partly by a loss of confidence in the concept of design methodology as well as observation that the landscapes which result from approaches built from this inheritance are considered to be unsatisfying, a desire for change in direction is becoming increasingly evident. Calls for new approaches, processes, methods and paradigms appear to emphasise the resuscitation of the primacy of human experience as the basis for making new landscapes. The importance of the design situation is emphasised as having intrinsic value and uniqueness and there is an acceptance of uncertainty and variety as qualities to be celebrated and encouraged instead of sterilised or hidden.

The desire for intellectual development and new approaches in landscape architecture appears to focus on a more complex conception of the environment and the role which individuals and groups play in the definition of its qualities and meaning. Social and cultural aspects are emphasised, in addition to the physical fabric, in an equal partnership of dynamic, interconnected and interrelated influences. This holistic view is quite different from the one which has underpinned the development of landscape architecture as a professional activity and is now behind a growing interest in steering towards a new direc-

tion in its future development. John Dixon Hunt (1992), one of the most outspoken critics of landscape architecture's intellectual inadequacies, sees these views forming part of resurrected theory. He suggests that landscape architects should discover what people want from public and private landscapes, that a new agenda of meanings should be established, and that locality should be exploited. This view highlights that addressing problems in landscape architecture's output that are perceived to be related to overly rationalistic approaches involves the three related considerations of human interrelatedness with the environment, a recovery of meaning, and response to context. These essentially human-oriented, qualitative and experiential principles do not correspond with the positivistic and techno-scientific roots from which the mainstream of modern landscape architecture is derived. If this is the case then what alternatives are available for us to consider? This will be the topic of the next chapter.

Chapter 2

An alternative world view

Introduction

We now follow on with an exploration of ideas relevant to a more integrated concept of human-environment relations. This presents a world view different to that characterised by Enlightenment thinking and supports a more holistic view of the human-environment relationship that ties together more closely human behavioural and psychological functioning with the settings in which it occurs. Key elements of this can be traced to counter-enlightenment movements and found in the tenets of more recent philosophical and cultural ideas. The Romantic movement in particular emerged as a revolt against material changes in society which accompanied the growth of cities and industrial expansion during the eighteenth century. As a discernible cultural movement, the Romantic challenge to the Enlightenment was relatively short-lived, lasting until the mid-nineteenth century. But vestiges of Romantic thought remain today particularly within the growth of the modern environmental movement, and this has helped fuel challenges to the Enlightenment concept of civilisation that have gathered pace over the past two decades (Lincoln and Guba, 1985). In part this is related to increasing awareness of environmental and ecological threats, argued by some (Schumacher, 1973; Capra, 1982)

to be a direct consequence of the Enlightenment's techno-scientific legacy, and by cultural and scientific developments in the twentieth century which challenge fundamentally the stability of its deterministic and dualistic foundations. This has underpinned interest in a more ecological, holistic view of human-environment relations, elements of which have been explored in the context of landscape architectural theory but have not really taken root. The general characteristics lean towards a more phenomenological philosophy which provides foundations for human experience to be at the heart of the way the concept of place is understood. The implications of this for the design of outdoor places will be explored later, but first we want to focus on some of the broader philosophical influences on human-environment holism.

The Romantic movement and Expressivism

The European Romantic movement began in Germany in the second third of the eighteenth century, between 1760 and 1780 according to Berlin (1999), and in many ways represented the antithesis of Enlightenment thinking. Romantic thinkers in Europe constituted an artistic and intellectual movement which found expression in literature, music, painting and drama, and which can be seen as a reaction to material changes taking place in society at the time. Emphasis on organic metaphors and human lived experience countered the mechanistic world view and primacy of human reason. A holistic concept of nature as an undivided whole countered Enlightenment reductionism and reintroduced a world view in which humans and environment were unified in a single seamless expression of a supposed absolute world spirit of nature. Romanticism emphasised the value of feelings, emotions, imagination and experience as being equally valid means of access to knowledge. All aspects of nature, culture and society were analogous with organisms involved in continuous, dynamic and evolutionary change (Taylor, 1989). In contrast to the determinism and closure of the Enlightenment, Romantic thinkers believed that it was not possible to know with certainty what the world was like in itself, because human knowing was conditioned by contextual and subjective influences.

Romantic philosophers raised to prominence the value of the whole of human experience, rather than reason alone, as a route to truth. One of the significant effects of Romanticism was the freedom with which the individual could now interpret life in his/her own way. Individualistic expression became a requirement of a good life. Affirming the rights of individuals and the primacy of feelings paved the way for a particular branch of Romantic thought related specifically to the way that human life comes to a sense of self-awareness and fulfilment. Charles Taylor (1975, 1989) has called this Expressivism, a theory of the human-environment relationship rooted in Isaiah Berlin's interpretation of the German philosopher Herder. It arises from Herder's reaction against the dualistic anthropology of the Enlightenment and his preoccupation with the uniqueness of groups and societies, especially the inextricable relationship between the human personality and the life it leads in environmental and social contexts. Herder was a thoroughly holistic thinker and, in Expressivism, connectedness and integration among all things are emphasised over dualistic separation.

Expressivism asserts that full realisation of human fulfilment lies in interdependent relation-

ship with acts of expression. It involves an aesthetic appreciation which stresses the quality of experience evoked over the intrinsic properties of objects. This provides for a fuller definition of an individual as someone defined by acts of expression. The crucial issue here is that human expressions are not seen simply as a means by which objective and independent material or artistic products are produced: paintings, poetry, music, furniture or buildings, for example. Instead, people are assumed to be realising something about themselves through their expressive actions and achieve fulfilment by doing so. This is an explicitly phenomenological perspective, elaborated in detail by Merleau-Ponty and others more recently, in which people are defined, not in terms of their material bodily presence, but in terms of what they do and where. A key feature of Herder's belief discussed by Berlin (1965, p.95) is the mutually dependent human-environment relationship in which groups and societies both shape and are shaped by their environment.

Expressivism arises from Romantic affirmations of the primacy of human experience over reason, and the removal of the Enlightenment mind-body and human-nature duality. Its central tenets affirm that human fulfilment is inextricably linked to a kind of human experience in which creative activity is seen as an expression of the personality. Human fulfilment depends on opportunities for this kind of expressive activity being available routinely. It is important to stress that, unlike its Romantic origins, Expressivism does not imply a return to a pre-modern view of nature as an ordered entity already imbued with meaning which humans need to recognise and respect. The human subject is central to the realisation and articulation of meaning through expressive activity. Expressions are related to contexts: they are communicative and therefore depend on language and other expressive beings for their significance and value; they are also constrained by nature because humans are an inextricable part of nature. Contexts are not fixed and absolute but dynamic and changing and conditions applying in one context cannot necessarily be transferred to others. Contexts are understood as integrated and interdependent relationships of the individual and the individual's expressive activity as well as the physical, social, cultural and historical circumstances which prevail (Berlin, 1965). In many ways this outlook resonates with the later development of place theories to which we will turn in chapter three.

As well as affirming individual rights, Expressivism can also be shown to carry collective responsibilities, derived from the need to act in ways which avoid compromise to one's own individual expressive potential, and that of others. These reconciliatory features are implied in Expressivism's social emphasis, requirement for communication, and the integrated conception of human-environment relations. According to the tenets of Expressivism, achieving fulfilment implies not only use, or even enjoyable use, of landscape, but a level of engagement with it through which some element of personal expression can be given form, whether in the material sense of *made form*, or as *found form* in the sense of psychological satisfaction gained from identifying, and then attributing value to, preferred locations. This is a holistic conception which raises the significance of the environment as an entity which is fundamental to human fulfilment, not simply in terms of a repository of goods, such as clean air and water, attractive scenery, food and recreational opportunities etc.; nor even as a nurturing organism, the survival of which is required for the maintenance of human life; but as an entity which is integral to human being, from which we cannot be meaningfully separated.

The historical development of the human-environment relationship can thus be traced through these changing conceptions of the human self. Pre-Enlightenment conceptions defined in relation to a larger divine order were replaced, with the development of scientific rationality, with the modern concept of a self-defining human subject, separated from an external environment. Enlightenment thinkers, through promoting the primacy of the human power of reason in self-definition, brought about a dualism separating the rational self from an external and objectified material nature with no intrinsic significance. Individuality prospered as intellectual activity began to be given more status than manual activity. Romanticism, developed in reaction to Enlightenment dualism and its excessive empha-

sis on human reason, established that the modern concept of a self-defining self need not be derived from reason but from an understanding of human subjects as integral to an inner Nature. The source of unity and wholeness which Augustine had found only in God could now be discovered in the self (Taylor, 1989). Romanticism is close to the development of landscape architecture because of its influence on the modern environmental movement, and sometimes Romantic values are coupled with ecological attitudes and presented as an antidote to perceptions of excessive techno-scientific thinking (Pepper, 1984). But, for some in landscape architecture, Romanticism holds connotations of regression and sentimentality which are thought unacceptable as a philosophical basis for approaches in landscape architecture. It is dismissed as irrelevant to modern society, and something that a modern landscape architecture should not be associated with (Kelsey, 1970; Stiles, 1992). Expressivism extends beyond its Romantic roots by recognising that human expressive activity does not simply communicate aspects of a larger pre-existing natural order but actually defines what the human self truly is and has the potential to become. Expressivism is important to our discussion here because, among other things, the rights of individuals include a collective responsibility to maintain environmental conditions which do not restrict the rights of other expressive individuals. This makes it an intrinsically sustainable philosophy, environmentally and socially, and one that requires the focus of attention to be placed on the relationships among people and their settings, and not on either, as if they were separate entities.

A human-environment dialectic

Romantic Expressivism presents us with a conception of human existence that cannot be separated from its environment. Instead it appears to establish humans and environment as two distinguishable components of the same whole, rather like the two sides of a coin. It also shows that the nature of the relationship between human and environment is not one of passivity but is active, characterised as a continuous exchange, a subconscious dialogue through which people develop their full potential through acts of intuitive expression. Here, the environment is not an external container in which people exist, but a means of expression, a voice through which people define themselves and communicate that to others. If such a dialectical human-environment relationship is significant to the achievement of fulfilment, then there must be an appropriate interpretative framework within which understanding can take place. One possibility can be found in Hans George Gadamar's development of philosophical hermeneutics in which he establishes that understanding is necessarily dependent on context (Gadamar, 1975).

Hermeneutics has its origin in nineteenth century attempts to develop a theory of interpretation initially concerned primarily with the Bible (Warnke, 1987). This was gradually expanded to include how meaning in any texts or utterances could be comprehended, and attempts were made to develop methods by which this could be achieved objectively. Gadamar extended hermeneutics from its roots as essentially a method of linguistic analysis to establish a philosophical basis which stresses understanding over explanation. In referring to his analysis as philosophical hermeneutics, Gadamar is concerned with a practice which involves the expression of affinity between people and what or whom they seek to understand, instead of an objectified reflection reached by science and methodology (reason): an experience rather than a knowing (Palmer, 1969). Attributing meaning involves a shared language: a common view of a subject matter. In this sense, meaning cannot be attributed to the parts of a situation, an observer and the observed, say, but lies in a relationship between them.

To illustrate Gadamar discusses the structure of game playing (Warnke, 1987). He argues that, although a game has rules which dominate the actions of players, the game cannot be fully understood as a set of rules only: it has to be played. So although the game dominates the players, their playing is essential to its full appreciation and meaning. "A game both determines the actions of its players and is nothing other than these actions themselves" (ibid., p.50). Also, because the same

game can be played differently each time, its meaning cannot be determinate but will change according to the circumstances prevailing at the time it is played. So although the game remains, in some sense, recognisably the same game, it can also be entirely different each time. This introduces the apparently paradoxical concept of entities which are self-identical whilst constantly changing. "Indeed, at issue, according to Gadamar are entities that are 'only in being different'" (ibid., p.51). In this phenomenological analysis, Gadamar is searching for a model with which to present an alternative picture of reality to the Cartesian model in which subjective attitudes (or a rational self), are separated and distinguished from what is objective (Bernstein, 1978). It is used as a prelude to establish how works of art are related to people. They are not, as in the Cartesian sense, merely objects to be viewed by detached spectators, but rather part of a type of participation in which understanding or appreciation is reached through a dynamic interaction between the work of art and the spectator. In this sense, the work of art remains, in some sense, incomplete until it has an interpreter who participates or shares in it. Although Gadamar's principle focus of attention here is with developing a framework of understanding for works of art, this form of interdependency resonates in phenomenological conceptions of place theory to the extent that a place only fully comes into being as a consequence of human action or expression projected at a particular location.

Expressivism and philosophical hermeneutics call for a concept of the human-environment relationship as a fluid and dynamic continuum understood in terms of a relationship of events rather than as an assemblage of elements. In landscape architecture this implies that it is insufficient for landscape to be regarded only as either an aesthetic (merely seen) or a technical (merely used) product of landscape architecture, or an objective entity which is meaningful independent of human interaction. Expressivism affirms landscape as the emergent product of acts of making which have both physical and communicative dimensions. As acts of communication, landscapes, like any other linguistic act, depend on active relationships, or dialectic, between both the senders and the receivers of communications. Hermeneutics is important in this process because it enables the meaning of landscapes as communicative acts to be derived from ordinary acts of interpretation, arising from the particularities of context. In this concept the meaning of landscape does not require highly specialised methodologies of interpretation applied from outside the context. This emphasises a more phenomenological approach in landscape architecture extending beyond narrow aesthetic treatment of physical space to embrace wider considerations in which human expressions are fundamental to the way landscape is understood and meaning attributed.

Environmentalism and human-environment relations

Since the advent of Cartesian dualism it has become possible to conceive of the "idea" of environmentalism: a product of human reason detached from the material and emotional world capable of rationalising values about how the environment should be treated. The environmental ideology most closely associated with landscape architecture is the ethic of stewardship which many regard as the main philosophical preoccupation of landscape architecture in present times. The stewardship ethic has its origins in a combination of ideas rooted in eighteenth century Romanticism and the American Transcendentalists, such as Muir, Thoreau and Emerson, and is characterised by: a bioethic philosophy (the idea that nature has its own intrinsic worth); a belief that human contact with nature is spiritually uplifting (that it holds human values which transcend material well-being); and that nature is holistic (there is more to it than the sum of its parts) (Pepper, 1984). Underlying this is an implication of interconnectedness in which people are seen to be in a sharing relationship with other species (Kellert and Wilson, 1993). There is also a sense of interdependence in the idea that nature and some of its constituent components are necessary to human existence, whilst there are others which hold no obvious or direct human benefit towards which we ought to

exercise responsibility (Allsop, 1972). This blend of pragmatism and altruism underpins what has become the modern ecocentric belief that man is steward of nature: that there is a duty of care which extends to all of nature and not just the parts which are obviously beneficial to people.

Although the ethic of stewardship draws humans and environment together with implications of interdependence and interconnectedness, it does so to a crucially limited extent which maintains humans as separate from and superior, by virtue of the authority required to act as steward, to the rest of the natural and cultural world. Stewardship implies an external world as the recipient of benign acts. Because we are stewards, we are supposed to act in environmentally benevolent ways, but we do so out of moral obligation. This maintains humans in a position of superiority over a separate environment. Attempts to respond to this can be found at the extremes of ecocentric environmentalism. Ecological philosopher, Arnee Naess (1989), for example, holds that if humanity can be conceptualised as so completely inseparable from nature that human-environment duality is replaced by total unification then it is no longer possible to injure nature wantonly because this would mean injuring an integral part of ourselves. Naess' philosophy requires the concept of a "greater Self" (ibid., p.9) which includes other people and nature. If such a level of extreme holism can be achieved then the altruism and moral obligation implicit in stewardship is not necessary. "If one really expands oneself to include other people and species and nature itself, altruism becomes unnecessary. The larger world becomes part of our own interests. It is seen as a world of *potentials* to increase our own self-realisation, as we are part of the increase of others" (ibid., p.9). This implies a change in the concept of stewardship from a response to an external moral law to an internal drive for self-realisation. In many ways an appealing idea as a response to Enlightenment dualism, in reality it is difficult to imagine how this expanded self could ever be experienced, except perhaps in a mystical and highly personal sense. To accept that the interests of the whole will simply be reflected in the interests of its parts seems to require a supreme act of faith.

In anthropological research the concept of environmental stewardship equates with what Palsson (1996) defines as a *paternalist* kind of human-environment relation: a position of balanced reciprocity in which nature is perceived as the recipient of human benevolence and protection. Paternalism is one of three paradigms postulated by Palsson (1996) to draw out distinctions in different conceptions of human-environment relations. The first two, called *orientalism* and *paternalism*, are quite different in their characteristics but both rest upon a dualism between humans and environment. Orientalism is associated with human mastery over the natural world and with its exploitation by humans primarily for material goods whilst paternalism has a more benevolent intent in which both humans and environment benefit. Both not only preserve duality and human superiority but also tend to privilege specialist experts over lay-persons. Both exploiter and steward of the environment are obliged to be adequately equipped for their task irrespective of malevolent or benevolent intent. Although some people could be said to have an intuitive grasp of environmentally benevolent activity, the contribution of specialist experts may become increasingly emphasised as environmental problems become more complex. At extremes, this may have counterproductive consequences by encouraging the view that looking after the environment is someone else's (the experts) responsibility by virtue of their particular specialist skills. The stewardship ethic, ecocentric attitudes and the benevolence and mutual reciprocity of Palsson's paternalism do not extend far enough here because: they imply obligations for humans; tend to emphasise the voice of the specialist few and not of the many; and because of its objectification, actively obstruct a view of environment as integral to human self-realisation. Palsson's third concept, of communalism, seeks to reject the last hidden vestiges of human-environment duality entirely.

Communalism emphasises a human-environment relationship without explicit reference to the existence of either human society or the natural world as independent frames of reference, whether interconnected or otherwise. It attempts to overcome any potentially mystical implications inherent in interpretations of human-environment holism and remnants of human privilege over a recipient environment through appeal to action and activity alone. It seeks to develop an *ecological* theory that emphasises *practice* as its key principle, rather than the application of ideas. It stresses the benefits of generalised reciprocity and the importance of ongoing dialogue between human participants and the wider community of action to which they belong. "The proper unit of analysis is no longer the autonomous individual separated from the social world by the surface of the body, but rather the whole person in action, acting within the contexts of that activity" (Palsson, 1996, p.73). Thus, the concept of self appears to be extended to include activity involving participation and engagement, rather than in terms of an objective entity like *body*, or even *body and mind*. In communalism, then, is the basis for a reconceptualised *self* as contextualised active participation. What is done and felt, and where this happens is what defines a human self here.

Palsson's idea of communalism is derived in part from the early conviction of Karl Marx that society and nature could not be meaningfully separated and is exemplified by reference to hunting and gathering societies. According to Palsson, ethnographic studies have often shown how such societies frequently extend communal relations among humans to the wider realm of environmental relations; often speaking of a communion with nature or, as with Nayaka of South India, personifying supportive aspects of the environment in saying "forest is as parent" (ibid., p.74). Other examples include the rural Colombian *economy of livelihood* described by Rivera (1990) and Gudeman (1992) in which the forces of the human body are extended to include the land also. This wider conception of human life means that rural Colombian people do not see the land simply as an economic resource, but as an extension of life itself. Communalism also holds implications for knowledge acquisition, stressing the importance of knowledge gained through authentic practice within a given context over the textual knowledge acquired by experts which is often then imposed regardless of contextual awareness on the assumption of normative authority. Citing research carried out with the Icelandic fishing fleets, Palsson indicates that this type of knowledge is effectively the collective product of apprenticeship, derived from progressive dialectic within a specific context.

In using these examples, Palsson is clearly conscious that communalism is being associated with a range of pre-modern traditions and is consequently vulnerable to criticism. Recourse to the relative self-sufficiency of, so called, primitive societies; master-apprentice relations; and the implication of craft oriented practices within community settings are all common themes used by those who see challenges to Enlightenment tenets as regression rather than progress. Palsson insists however, that the principles of communalism do not represent a return to naive romanticism. Instead, primarily because they centre on a "dialogic perspective" (Palsson, 1996, p.78), they embrace a more realistic position about the human-environment relationship than that presented by the Enlightenment. The objectifying techno-scientific scrutiny of nature, its component parts and other cultures is, according to Palsson, both unrealistic and irresponsible given the wider ecological and historical context within which human life operates. It is important to note, however, that this does not require acceptance of such an expansion of the human self to the extent that it embraces all of other people, species and nature, as Naess (1989) advocates, into an entirely unified totality. Human self is realised by expressions in environment and environment is realised through human expressions, but self and environment are not literally "one". Taking the idea of communalism as a basis for further exploration of human-environment relationships, a number of key themes emerge with which to structure subsequent discussion. These include:

- the breakdown of the boundaries which define a unitary and isolated human self and its redefinition to include the social and physical context;
- a redefinition of self which stresses dynamic and participatory action;
- an emphasis on general reciprocity through dialectic;
- the primacy of context as a key location of knowledge acquisition and self-identity.

New science perspectives on human-environment relations

The above material has contributed to the development of a holistic conception of the human-environment relationship which emphasises the active role of human expressions to the achievement of self-realisation, and the importance of social and physical contexts. The following further develops this concept by introducing an understanding of the nature of order in holistic frameworks. This is important to landscape architecture because it establishes that order can be understood as an entity related to active relationships of elements within holistic frameworks and is not merely that which results from the assembly of discrete elements, as in a classical Cartesian sense. More specifically, it establishes that, in some perceptions of reality arising from interpretations of scientific findings, there is a dynamic and creative aspect to the way holistic frameworks are understood that derives from a tension between the self-assertion of elements to maintain uniqueness and individuality and their tendency towards integration to maintain the supporting whole. This understanding is relevant to the geometrical considerations we will discuss in chapter seven.

It is important to stress that including this material here is not an attempt to provide the concept of experiential landscape with scientific verification. When we talk about the experiential landscape we mean a conceptualisation, or model, through which we can highlight aspects of the relationship between human experience and its spatial expression. Our purpose here is to highlight that there are some apparent similarities of world view in different intellectual realms and that they have potential to contribute to the development of new concepts which are relevant in landscape architecture. Furthermore, aspects of the so-called new science have been considered in landscape architecture (Rosenberg, 1986; Motloch, 1991; Alvarez and El-Mogazi, 1998) and in the associated disciplines of architecture (Jencks, 1995; Alexander, 2002) and urban planning (Batty and Longley, 1994), which raise questions for the interpretation of new science concepts in these areas. Much of the following draws from the work of physicist Fritjof Capra who has, through two influential books, attempted to highlight the wider philosophical and cultural significance of new science developments. The second of these, *The Turning Point* (1982), is an explicit attempt to draw out the social significance in which he stresses the importance of ecological and holistic perspectives.

The two principal cornerstones of Newtonian science at question here are: that the universe is determinate and reducible to fundamental laws and physical building blocks; and that these can be discovered by people (given sufficient knowledge, technical apparatus etc.) who can then study them as independently existing, objective entities. Theoretical and experimental developments, particularly in high-energy particle physics in the twentieth century present an alternative conception of reality in which, at a fundamental level, the universe appears to consist of a dynamic network of interwoven and interconnected events from which human consciousness cannot be meaningfully detached (Capra, 1975; Zukav, 1979; Bohm, 1980). With this, the solidity of the Newtonian-Cartesian paradigm in science is undermined and alternative holistic and ecological world views are given, for some, scientific credibility (Capra, 1982). Moreover, and more controversially, human consciousness is believed to be an active force in the way some aspects of physical reality become realised in determinate form (Bohm, 1980). In his most recent books about the nature of order, Christopher Alexander acknowledges a series of meetings with David Bohm in the late 1980s and how his concept of wholeness corresponds essentially with Bohm's articulation of an implicate order, a structural characteristic he believes explains scientific observations of sub-atomic systems (Alexander, 2001, p.108). The following material outlines principal landmarks in the development of this paradigm shift in science. It highlights some of the main philosophical claims made and focuses on how they contribute to developing ideas about the nature of order and particularly on the role humans are thought to play.

A wide range of scientific developments spanning most of the twentieth century have, since the mid-1970s, been collectively popu-larised as new science to distinguish it from the mechanistic determinism of the old science associated with Newton. In this context interest has focused primarily on the implications for our world view founded on a realisation that modern physics has a strongly holistic flavour and less on technical and experimental detail. Some have sought to make comparisons between the way scientific findings are described and Eastern philosophical and religious traditions (Capra, 1975; Zukav, 1979) giving elements of the new science explicitly mystical overtones, which some think unhelpful to its intellectual credibility, but which nevertheless are acknowledged to capture the essence of the holistic concepts now widely accepted as central to an understanding of reality revealed by some scientific findings (Davies, 1983).

The beginning of modern physics is generally attributed to Einstein's relativity theories and subsequent development of quantum theory, a theory of sub-atomic phenomena in which the hitherto accepted belief that matter consists of assemblages of discrete material particles independent of human observation was to prove unsound. This discovery has its foundations in two principal facets of experimental investigation. The first is related to the apparently paradoxical properties of sub-atomic particles which allow them to behave as either waves (entities spread out in space) or particles (entities confined to small volumes) depending on the way they are investigated. Capra (1982) highlights that the paradox here is not intrinsic to the sub-atomic phenomenon but arises from attempts to explain it within the theoretical frameworks of classical science. The second facet is the establishment of a precise mathematical form, expanding the conventions of classical science, with which to express this phenomenon: the uncertainty principle of Werner Heisenberg. Fundamentally, the uncertainty principle replaces the determinism previously thought to be a defining characteristic of physical reality with a requirement for indeterminism. Initially formulated in the 1920s it has brought about a significant shift in the way science thinks about and investigates the nature of reality. With Heisenberg's uncertainty principle has come the realisation that physical reality is indeterministic at its basic level. Scientists working in this area no longer talk of matter existing with certainty at particular points in space and at particular times, but of matter which shows tendencies to exist which are expressed in the language of probability. Furthermore, the way in which matter appears in observable form seems to be inextricably linked to the circumstances of observation. What one chooses to observe has a direct bearing on what is observed. This has led some scientists to conclude not only that uncertainty and indeterminism are intrinsic properties of the material world, but that human observation of it, in some sense, influences the way in which the material world appears to us.

These discoveries have brought profound changes to the way in which the fundamental building blocks of the material world are perceived in science. The classical concept of sub-atomic particles as minute solid objects which combine in different ways ultimately to create the macro-world does not correspond with experimental investigation at sub-atomic levels. Sub-atomic particles have no meaning as isolated objects but can only be understood in terms of interconnections between various processes of measurement and observation; processes which appear to include human observers and their experimental apparatus. Nature appears to be "a complicated tissue of events, in which connections of different kinds alternate or overlap or combine and thereby determine the texture of the whole" (Heisenberg, 1963, p.139). A picture of reality thus emerges as a unified whole, within which there are distinguishable components in the form of molecules and atoms etc., but in which, at finer levels of definition, the concept of separate parts does not hold. At the sub-atomic level, particles are not things but interrelationships. This is how modern physics has revealed that the nature of reality is not one of objects, but relationships and networks of patterns. This new world view has been given some experimental verification by John Bell (1987) who was ultimately to develop a theorem (Bell's Theorem) which demonstrated not only that sub-atomic events are intrinsically probabilistic and interconnected, but that interconnectedness is sustained over theoretically infinite regions of space. The

Cartesian conception of independently existing isolated elements subject only to the effects of local causation does not apply to quantum phenomena, leading some scientists to the conclusion that either the universe is fundamentally lawless or fundamentally inseparable (Stapp, 1971).

Central to these, and other, twentieth century scientific discoveries are three key points which are relevant here. First is a holistic concept of reality as an inseparable whole rather than an assemblage of discrete entities. Second is a predominant concern with relationships over parts: indeed distinguishable parts, especially at the sub-atomic level, appear to be idealisations which only become manifest because of interconnections between events. Third is the role of human consciousness, not as a passive observer in an independent objective world, but as an active participant in the way the world becomes objectively manifest. The philosophical speculations of scientists working in this area fall broadly into three distinguishable categories, all of which have in common an integrated conception of the human-nature relationship and particularly a breaking down of the Cartesian mind-matter duality.

Teleology and hidden order

According to Paul Davies' (1987) assessment of twentieth century science, the impression of design in the universe is overwhelming. It is generally assumed that if there is a hidden order underlying the evolution of the universe, as opposed to it being a pointless and random happening, it will have a mathematical nature. Many scientists throughout history have observed the patterns in nature as evidence of hidden order and have tried to extrapolate from them (Penrose, 1989; Poundstone, 1985). For some, quantum theory and the more recent chaos and complexity theories have strengthened the teleological orientation of modern science. Roger Penrose in particular, considers that certain mathematical constructs, for example those relating to complex numbers and especially their manifestation in the Mandelbrot set associated with fractal geometry, have objective existence independent of their creators mind (Penrose, 1989). This is often referred to as mathematical Platonism, reflecting a view in science that an ethereal and eternal Ideal order exists, and that it is of a mathematical kind. Others explicitly include a central role for human consciousness in the development of an understanding of the nature of reality. One of the strongest proponents of unification in material (quantum) and thought processes is David Bohm (1980). His work develops on the earlier statement made by James Jeans in response to the picture of the world that appeared to be revealed by quantum research: "Today there is a wide measure of agreement...that the stream of thought is heading towards a non-mechanical reality; the universe begins to look more like a great thought than like a great machine" (Jeans, 1930). Bohm's primary emphasis is on undivided wholeness, a concept of creative, evolutionary unity so extreme that even the idea of holism as a descriptive principle is rejected as too restrictive and fixed (Bohm, 1980). Bohm's wholeness is conceived as a network of relations called the implicate order which exists folded up in nature, gradually unfolding as the universe evolves to become manifest as the organised explicate order perceived by the senses. The solid objects of our everyday experience are temporary states of stability in an otherwise continuous movement. Bohm includes consciousness as an essential feature, believing that mind and matter are correlated within the implicate order and are projections of some higher order which is neither. As we mentioned earlier, Bohm's ideas about the nature of order at these fundamental levels of scale corresponds closely to those of architect Christopher Alexander to whom we will return later.

The anthropic principle

This stems from the argument about whether it is meaningful in any sense to talk about a universe which contains no intelligent life. At its heart lies the realisation, derived originally from Heisenberg's uncertainty principle, that human consciousness is a necessary condition for bringing nature into being. Human consciousness is then both a product of nature and a fundamental part of nature's process of realisation. The existence of consciousness and the particular

structural characteristics of the universe are thus woven together in mutual reciprocity. This is how the anthropic principle is used to explain why the laws of nature are as they are: they are inevitably found to be in a form conducive to the development of consciousness because consciousness is necessary for nature to be realised. Nature organises itself in such a way as to make the universe ultimately self-aware (Davies, 1987). Expanding this anthropological perspective, Detlev Nothnagel (1996) argues that the nature described by high-energy particle physics is actually a creation of the culture and techno-scientific specialism of the physics community. It is a reproduced nature, defined only in terms of the technical parameters relating to the context of investigation. The idea of progress in physics is, according to Nothnagel, problematic because nature, its referent, is hard to define independently. In this respect we have a view from the physical sciences that seems to resonate with that of Gadamar's philosophical hermeneutics. That the world we perceive and understand is entirely context dependent.

The bootstrap approach

The bootstrap approach is associated with a development in physics called the S-Matrix theory, specifically developed in 1968 by Geoffrey Chew in an attempt to develop a comprehensive theory for strongly interacting sub-atomic particles. Since then it has been expanded into a more general philosophy of nature in which the hierarchical implications inherent in ideas about the existence of fundamental entities, whether material building blocks or mathematical equations, laws etc., are abandoned. Like other interpretations of quantum theory, the structure of the universe is thought of as a web of events, interrelated and in a state of continuous motion and change. S-Matrix theory has it that none of the properties of any part of the web is any more fundamental than any other. Furthermore, all properties observed arise only from the self-consistency of the system as a whole: all properties follow from the properties of other parts. This type of self-consistency is called bootstrapping and is strongly reminiscent of Bohm's concept of enfolded order (Capra, 1982). There are no normative influences, whether externally or internally generated; no entities which can be meaningfully isolated; and no sense of anything more or less fundamental. Again, the idea of bootstrapping, that complex entities develop from the properties of entities that already exist correlates strongly with Alexander's views about the nature of order at the macro-scale. This principle is implicit in his assertions that what he regards as good forms, natural or man-made, arise from processes he calls structure-preserving transformations. We will return to this again in chapter seven.

What emerges from these holistic interpretations of scientific inquiry is that order in the natural world can be conceptualised as an entity in its own right, rather than in the more classical sense as something arising from combinations of related but otherwise discrete component parts. Order itself can then become the unit of study and, although there are differences in detail, something of its intrinsic properties can be discerned. For example:

— it is conceived in terms of networks or relationships of events in which mind and matter are correlated in some way, rather than only as assemblages of material components;
— it is conceived as a state of temporary stability in an otherwise dynamic and continuous process of movement and change, instead of as something static and enduring;
— its structure is analogous to enfoldment rather than assembly;
— there is diversity and uniqueness among distinguishable parts, but only within a unifying whole.

The holistic conception of the human-environment relationship implied here is, however, an extreme one leaning heavily, explicitly so in Bohm (1980), towards an entirely unbroken unification of all phenomena including human consciousness. From this perspective, the structures of the material world are determined, ultimately, by the way the world is observed. Capra succinctly summarises this as implying that "...the observed patterns of matter are reflections of patterns of mind" (Capra, 1982, p.85). This perhaps reflects Capra's tendency toward

mysticism in his interpretations, but it serves to highlight that the holism, or Wholeness (Bohm, 1980), implicit in some twentieth century scientific theory can, if appropriated into the macro-scale, effectively deny the existence of any kind of objective nature. At the extremes of this position, reality is an idea: there are no objective facts about nature which can be separated from human interpretations of them (Pepper, 1996). The obviously problematic consequences of this have encouraged attempts to reconcile the excessive subjectivity implicit with the notion of partial objectivity. This basically means that aspects of the material world, including the human self, are thought to come to realisation in determinate form (are objectified) as a consequence of human expressive action. Here human expressive action can be conceptualised as a kind of force that works to arrest a determinate state within an otherwise indeterminate, fluid continuum resulting in entities (e.g. a painting, a chair, a poem, a human self, a place) which have discernible and measurable objective properties but which can only be understood as partially defined by them. In this sense the nature of reality is neither entirely idea nor entirely material, but something arising out of an integration of the two. The notion of partial objectivity follows Alfred North Whitehead's organicism proposed as an alternative to the mechanistic world view promoted by classical science (Whitehead, 1926). He recognised that objectively discernible entities were part of the fabric of reality, but considered it completely unbelievable to regard them as existing independently of their context. He saw context as a dynamic continuum in which objective properties appeared as only partial qualities of the larger whole. A flowing river is often used to illustrate this concept within which vortices appear as discernible objects in an otherwise continuous flow. This view of material things as states of temporary stability in flux is echoed later by Bohm and since then has been brought into the architectural and design arena through Alexander's view of the nature of order.

Self-generation and the systems view of life

This holistic model of the human-environment relationship makes it possible to conceive of entities which possess objective properties but which can be defined only partially by those properties. One of the most comprehensive attempts to draw wider social implications from this philosophical position as it is supported by science specifically is probably that of Fritjof Capra in his book *The Turning Point* (1982). His schematic new world view rests mainly on an elaboration of the holism he sees implied by the new science and the assumption that it holds for macro-systems like human society, and that it necessarily results in cooperative tendencies rather than simply a relativistic tolerance of multiplicity. These are bold assertions, and whilst they have established Capra's influence on eco-centric environmentalism, are not universally accepted by any means. The principal point of focus here, though, is the contribution Capra's schematic makes to a developing understanding of the structure of holistic conceptions when they are applied to large-scale phenomena like communities.

Capra (1982) emphasises the concept of systems, drawing particularly from biological and ecological models in his analysis. Organic metaphors are used to illustrate the central point that living organisms, ecosystems, communities and societies are all types of system which share common properties. Broadly, he asserts that these are characterised by distinguishable parts (molecules, cells, organs, people, families, communities, societies, nations etc.) which collectively are integrated in the form of a stratified order. Each of the parts can be regarded as wholes in the sense that they are, in various ways, integrated systems, but at the same time are also parts of larger wholes of increasing complexity. This analogy is used to illustrate his central point that the whole is reflected in each of the parts. It is a holistic conception in which order is maintained through the dynamic interplay of self-assertion and integration: two complementary, but opposite, tendencies assumed to be possessed by both part and whole. Entities which are conceived as both part and whole together in this sense are given the name holons, after Koestler (1978). Each component of a system in Capra's terms, whether biological or social, is assumed to consist of entities which have integrative tendencies to function as part of a larger whole, as well as self-assertive tendencies to preserve their individuality. It is a holistic conception which is self-creative, self-organising, and self-sustaining, relying on the nature and activity of the entities which already exist within it for its future form and progress. The precise character and form in which order will become manifest is indeterminate and emerges from the integrative activity of the whole.

In self-generating systems emergent properties are ascribed to nature in which increasing levels of complexity emerge over time as an inevitable consequence of continuous processes of reconciliation between self-assertion and integration (Prigogine, 1980). Changes in macro and micro-structures evolve together as a whole rather than through the interaction of separate parts, and processes are cooperative rather than competitive (Briggs and Peat, 1985). This is a view which gives primacy to that which already exists within the whole as a mediating influence on the individualistic behaviour of parts within the whole, instead of external laws or other pre-given forces. According to Russell (1991), self-realisation is the key with which people become naturally in tune with the group in mutual support. Pepper however is very cautious about the potential consequences if this point of view is taken to metaphysical extremes, emphatically pointing out that a significant weakness rests in the possibility that it will degenerate into "orgies of introspection" (Pepper, 1996, p.300), interpreted by those who seek to raise their levels of self-awareness through faddish therapies and fashionable new pseudo-religions which tend to proliferate at the fringes of New Ageism.

Summary

The above material establishes the nature of some aspects of the challenge to the concept of human-environment dualism to arise from twentieth century scientific inquiry and contributes further to an understanding of holistic conceptions of the human-environment relationship as an alternative. In particular it begins to contribute an understanding about how order and form can be conceptualised in holistic systems, as an entity in its own right, rather than in the more classical sense as something arising from combinations of related but otherwise discrete component parts. Furthermore, activity among elements within holistic systems is stressed as significant to the generation of order which reflects a tension of self-assertion, maintaining individuality in distinguishable elements, and integrative tendency, acting also in the interests of maintaining the supporting whole. We have argued here that this conception of order arises when the human-environment relationship is considered to be holistic rather than dualistic, and that order is what emerges as a consequence of the continuous and active dialogue between the expressive activity of people and its social and environmental context.

The important point here is that this concept requires a fundamental shift in mind-set away from looking specifically at things to looking at relationships among things. It is a mutually reciprocal relationship of people, their activity, and the physical, social and cultural circumstances within which human and environmental attributes achieve realisation through their interaction. As a consequence of this, what it means to be fully human must include environmental attributes, and equally environment must include the human action, psychological and physical, associated with it as integral to a full understanding. There is a dialectic nature to this relationship and, from a human perspective, this means the environment comes to be seen as a dimension of human existence. It functions as an expressive medium through which people gradually and progressively define and redefine themselves and through which they communicate with others. Expressions may involve making physical changes or they may involve the assignment of meaning. Through these expressions the environment is transformed, either physically or in terms of its emotional significance, and as a consequence becomes the embodiment of these human attributes: the objective material properties of the environment constitute only a partial understanding. This holistic, mutually defining human-environment relationship is thus one of

continuous, dynamic and evolutionary change, driven by the activity of people expressed through where it happens. It is derived from conditions existing within the context of the relationship rather than from external influences and its full nature can only be understood, therefore, in relation to that context.

Such a relationship constitutes a form of order in which aesthetic appreciation stresses the quality of the experience rather than the intrinsic properties of objects. It is a form of order that arises specifically from activity within the relationship, understood as a dynamic interplay of self-assertion and integration among parts, and can be visualised as networks of enfolded events rather than assemblages of discrete component parts. From a design perspective, this implies considerable challenges for conventional geometric ordering mechanisms, which are from Euclidean origins and are more concerned about line, surface and form, rather than with the representation of relationship. It suggests the need for a more evolutionary approach to the generation of form. One in which the focus is placed on arranging the organisational conditions necessary to allow form to actualise, instead of prescribing or imposing form through the external prescription of arbitrary style (Figure 2.1).

— The human-environment relationship here is conceptualised as a form of order, a kind of nucleus, generated by the dialectical and

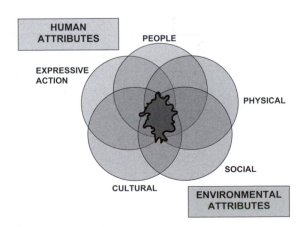

2.1

A holistic human-environment relationship

mutually reciprocal nature of interactions between human and environmental attributes.

- Through these interactions human attributes and environmental attributes are in a state of continuous evolutionary change. This makes the human-environment relationship, as a form of order, indeterminate and progressive towards increasing complexity.
- The character of this conception of the human-environment relationship is that of a form of temporary stability generated from an internal tension to continuously reconcile self-assertion and integration.
- Internal tension becomes manifest in the human-environment relationship as human acts of expression defined by and communicated through the medium of environment. By this means the environment is progressively transformed materially and in terms of the meanings and associations it holds, and people project a sense of self in terms of the environmental attributes that enable this to be developed and communicated.
- Order in this conception of the human-environment relationship is therefore entirely context dependent: it is generated from the circumstances within the relationship system and not from external influences. It is also a form of evolutionary order that is in continuous change and cannot be understood as a static and deterministic entity. The overall character of order here is as networks of experiential events that gradually unfold from inside the system rather than the assembly of independent component parts.

Chapter 3

Landscape as place

So far we have sketched out a broad philosophical framework based on a holistic conception of human-environment relations. We have begun to identify some of its distinguishing features and structural implications, particularly in relation to how order is understood. We have suggested that this may help provide more appropriate intellectual foundations for an approach to making outdoor places in ways more responsive to human experience than the prevailing conception grounded in Enlightenment dualism. Now we want to turn to look at some of the theoretical implications of this philosophical position close to the central purpose of landscape architecture: how to make better outdoor places. A starting point lies with the concept of place.

There is an important distinction to be made between different theoretical conceptions of the human-environment relationship as it underpins and provides a context for theories of place to develop. Altman and Rogoff (1987) have outlined four principal world views to characterise human-environment relations in psychological research. They make explicit distinction between interaction, interdependence and integration. Interaction between humans and the environment is characteristic of what they call *trait* and *interactional* approaches. In both, human psychological functioning and environmental settings

are independently defined and operating entities in which the former varies in response to its interactions with the latter. The principal difference between them is one of equality: the trait approach conceptualises nature as a subordinate influence on psychological occurrences; the interactional approach recognises both as equals. A more holistic conception underpins the *organismic* approach in which integrated systems of independently definable elements form the unit of study. Here, the separation or division between elements is broken down by the assumption of networks or dynamic patterns of relationships. Full understanding of definable elements is reached only through comprehension of the holistic set of relationships between them. This is essentially an ecological analysis (Rohde and Kendle, 1994) in which component parts of a system are assumed not only to interact, but to be in mutual interdependence. The *organismic* approach also embraces the notion of hidden order which acts to guide systems toward a predetermined ideal state.

A further dimension of integration between humans and environment is assumed within *transactional* models. Here the concept of entities consisting of separately definable elements influenced by teleological principles is abandoned. This is essentially a phenomenological concept which, in the human-environment relationship, is focused on experiential or meaningful aspects as they evolve over time. Here humans and the environment are considered to be fully integrated rather than simply interdependent. Transactional models in the human-environment relationship adopt a distinctly humanistic orientation in which the definition and meaning of the environment is seen to be inextricably linked with the activities of people who use it (Tuan, 1979). They in turn are defined by their landscape in a continuous process of mutual realisation: "The natural world forms us and is also formed by us" (Rohde and Kendle, 1994, p.21). The transactional perspective in environmental psychology is especially relevant here because it constitutes the overall paradigm within which psycho-social constructs in environmental psychology continue to be developed. This is a growing area of this field of study in which psychological research is increasingly linked with research in phenomenological approaches in geography, and architecture and planning (Bonnes and Secchiaroli, 1995). It is also the academic framework within which concepts familiar to landscape architecture: e.g. *sense of place, genius-loci*, etc., are located and defined, and where developments in human-environment understanding is developed in terms of *settings* and *place*.

From the early 1970s, the need to adopt a theoretical perspective in environmental psychology defined as transactional has been affirmed by various authors (Ittelson, 1973; Stokols and Altman, 1987). The term transactional is also associated with ecological, socio-systematic and transactional-contextual. These terms have specific definitions and nuances within psychology, but serve to highlight a number of the key characteristics of the human-environment relationship assumed in this approach. One of its aims is to free psychological investigations from the subjectivist-objectivist duality in which the human-environment relationship is seen either in terms of individualistic psychological functioning, or in terms of objective properties of the environment. The transactional perspective aims at reconciliation of this opposition by suggesting a dynamic relationship in which human and environment are integrated aspects of the same unit of

study.[1] Simultaneous reciprocity of influences between the two aspects are assumed in an active, rather than purely reactive, relationship; aspects of change rather than stability are emphasised, as is the systemic and holistic character of the approach (Ittelson, 1973). The human-environment relationship is thus defined in terms of integrated psychological, contextual and temporal facets (Altman and Rogoff, 1987). Context here is defined as people's everyday environmental setting (Stokols, 1987).

In a detailed review of the literature on this subject, Bonnes and Secchiaroli (1995) highlight a range of characteristics in terms of the person and the environment aspects of the transactional perspective, whilst reiterating that they cannot be considered as analysable separately. This highlights a number of details particularly relevant to our goals in this book. The person, for example, is considered as a "dynamically organised system" (ibid., p.153). This terminology is itself interesting in that it breaks down the body barrier, enabling easier comprehension of the person as an integrated aspect of a wider whole. Emphasis is placed on human activity as the organising and integrating factor in the system and this is seen expressly in terms of an integration of thinking and doing. The social context is considered to be an important influence on the way in which activity is oriented. This is significant because it indicates that human activity is not aimless, or motivated purely by individual need, but is a response to a continuous exchange between individual motives and the opportunities presented by the wider environment, which is assumed to consist of physical and social aspects. Characteristics attributable to the environment aspect of this conception emphasise that "The environment consists in a setting: that is an organised whole in space and time of physical aspects, social activities, and symbolic aspects and meanings" (Bonnes and Sacchiaroli, 1995, pp.159-160). This would suggest that the environment here is considered to be synonymous with the term

---

1 This does not necessarily imply acceptance of an entire unification in reality in the sense of a complete merging of human and environment to the extent that they are literally "one".

setting which has a specific definition implying a holistic entity of material and social aspects, as well as meanings arising from their interactions.

Theoretical origins of place

The term setting, as incorporated into transactional perspectives of the human-environment relationship, is well consolidated in environmental psychology. It has its origins in the ecological-psychology of Barker (1968) and derives from the term behaviour setting which emphasises the role of the environment in determining individual behaviour. Examples of behaviour settings cited by Barker include church, the grocery store, petrol station, school, Rotary Club etc. These examples define particular collectives which are distinguishable from one another both in terms of physical features and the kind of behaviour which is associated with them. Taking the example of a church, this is a behaviour setting which consists of: the kind of patterns of behaviour typical of a church, such as celebratory functions, singing, religious contemplation etc.; the distinguishable physical attributes, such as the presence of a pulpit, altar, pews etc.; and the times when the church functions. Each behaviour setting is thus a collective conception defined in terms of a kind of fit of behaviour, physical attributes, and time. There are links to be made here with the motivating influences behind Alexander's pattern theory (1977): broadly the idea that cities in particular can be understood as networks of patterns thought of as integrations of human behaviour with particular physical or spatial attributes. This idea of settings moves in the direction of holism and appreciation of context dependence in that settings are defined in terms of interrelationships of different aspects, and that their study ought to be based on observing what actually takes place, rather than what is provoked by external interventions. One of the limitations of this concept however is that it tends to ignore the subjective impact of different individuals in the setting (Bonnes and Secchiaroli, 1995). The assumption here is that individuals within the setting are interchangeable, and that their behaviour can be, more or less, determined

through control of the socio-physical context. This conception shares some degree of commonality with current approaches in landscape architecture and other environmental design disciplines in that there is an implicit assumption that significant aspects of human psychological functioning can be led by manipulation of the physical environment.

In recent years, the term place appears increasingly in environmental psychology. In some cases it is used synonymously with setting and in others with the more precise intention to develop a place theory. Conceptions of place are closely associated with geographical research and architectural design. According to Bonnes and Secchiaroli (1995) the central interest in architecture for places in particular, rather than the environment in general, has had a significant influence on the subsequent concern for the concept of place as an area for study in psychology. Early opportunities for collaboration between architects and other environmental practitioners and environmental psychologists were however hampered by problems of comprehension over the way in which place is conceived. Architects, for example, tend to focus primarily on particular locations whereas psycho-environmental processes, such as territoriality, privacy etc., were the principal focus in psychology. These conceptual differences exemplify a central difficulty in defining a conceptual framework for landscape architecture, which requires a marriage of physical space and psychological processes. To some extent these differences are reconciled in the work of Canter (1977) who is credited with developing much of the early work on place in environmental psychology. Canter proposes the term "place" to emphasise the need to orientate research in environmental psychology in the direction of wholes rather than simple assemblages of elements or variables. For Canter a place is a holistic entity which is the result of relationships between actions, conceptions and physical attributes. To fully identify a place it is necessary to know what behaviour is associated with it, what the physical parameters are, and also what conceptions people have of that behaviour in that particular physical environment (Canter, 1977). In this way the material world, human behaviour and individual psychological functioning are integrated to define place.

The theoretical foundations of place theory in architecture and design also include the conception of genius-loci or spirit of the place (Norberg-Schulz, 1980) which attempts to unify physical and spiritual elements in place. Drawing from the eighteenth century writings of Alexander Pope, Norberg-Schultz's discussion about place is located in the phenomenology of Maurice Merleau-Ponty (1962). Each place possesses its own spirit rooted in the natural environment and, in this sense, is reminiscent of Romantic notions of World Spirit because it assumes the existence of a pre-existing naturalness which is there to be discovered. Successful human intervention in the environment is supposed to depend on identifying and then responding appropriately to the specific genius-loci. Drawing specifically from Goethe, Brook (1998) extends this principle to propose a practical means by which a landscape may be read prior to prescribing development proposals. Norberg-Schulz attributes environmental problems and human alienation in part to a lack of appreciation of place dependency. Science and technology, he considers, are responsible for generating an erroneous belief that people can exist satisfactorily free from a direct dependence on places. Genius-loci attempts to define place in a way which transcends physical attributes by assigning spiritual significance with which human intervention must harmonise if it is to be considered right. It is important to recognise however, that the spiritual element arises pre-given from the place's intrinsic physical characteristics. Human-environment duality is preserved here, as is the idea of place as a static and objective entity with which there are either appropriate or inappropriate ways for people to interact. Human activity here is defined in terms of a response to place, rather than as an active component in the definition or realisation of place.

Tuan (1974; 1980) and Relph (1976) move beyond this to define place in entirely experiential terms; as a dialectical process between human functioning and natural order. People are assumed to acquire a sense of place through their intentions in relation to the physical environment of those intentions. Places are then, not just products of physical characteristics of the environment but "products of intentional human acts turned towards the 'creation of places'" (Bonnes and Secchiaroli, 1995, p.165). Human acts in this context significantly include gestures, either alone or in association with speech, as well as the making of things. Sense of place is produced and maintained as much by the ritual of communication through gesture and speech as it is through the creation of manufactured items. Tuan (1980) draws from anthropology to illustrate this point, citing cases from different cultures which highlight that communities are bound together by the continuous process of creation and recreation of places. "What unifies the far flung members of the Mbona cult and gives the cult centre its special aura is not the shrine, but the act of building it – not so much the final material product, as the cooperative effort and gesture" (Tuan, 1980, p.6). In this sense place is defined quite explicitly in terms of human expressive acts. Places can be brought into being as a result of cooperative activity, whether this is in the form of physically making something material or in the form of speech or gesture: by affirming significance through communication. Places can thus be made both by processes of manufacture (defined in terms of human cooperation, rather than purely material production), or by identifying and affirming significance in the pre-existing material world. Tuan emphasises the dynamic nature of place by suggesting that a place's stability depends crucially on the way in which people talk about it. "City people are constantly making and 'unmaking' places by talking about them. A network of gossip can elevate one shop to prominence and consign another to oblivion...in a sense, a place is its reputation" (ibid., p.6). This is a dynamic and human oriented conception of place, as opposed to the static and intrinsic spirituality of genius-loci.

These developing conceptions of place contribute to a growing emphasis on the holistic nature of the human-environment relationship in environmental psychology research. This is extended, in Proshansky (1983) particularly, into considerations about how place influences the development of the human self. Through focusing on the multiplicity of places that make up the structure of day-to-day life, significance is given to the sense of belonging in defining the relationship between individuals and their socio-physical environment. Proshansky, Fabian and Kaminoff (1983) consider that individuals define themselves in society, not just by distinguishing themselves from other people, but also in relation to the objects and spaces they are in contact with. Because places are crucially significant in the satisfaction of biological, social, psychological and cultural needs, they are therefore considered meaningful to the processes of self-identity. The impact on self-identity of phenomena such as the deterioration of neighbourhood, frequent changes of residence and technological transformations of the surrounding landscape are given as examples. This perspective is used to emphasise that there is no physical environment which is not at the same time a social environment and vice versa. Walter has also sought to emphasise the importance of human participation and expressive action to the achievement of places defined as the location of experience. Walter (1988) considers that a place has a topistic reality which gives primacy to the contribution made by peoples' feelings and emotional expressions in the making of places. Expressive space can be both *found* and *made*. *Found* expressive space is that which holds particular emotional or spiritual significance for individuals, *made* expressive space is that which has human emotional expression built into it, so that the result in physical form can be experienced as the embodiment of the thoughts and feelings of those who conceived and constructed it. This particular kind of building is called "pathetecture" (ibid., p.143) by Walter and means constructing emotion by building. Pathetecture is the process by which expressive space is made by material means and this principle can be exemplified by Alexander's poetic account of the development of a small residential settlement in Mexicali. "We have tried to construct a housing process…in which the houses which are made have, above all, human worth, in the simple, old-fashioned sense that people feel proud and happy to be living in them and would not give them up for anything, because they are their houses, because they are the product of their lives, because the house is

everything to them, the concrete expression of their place in the world, the concrete expression of themselves" (Alexander, 1985, p.16).

With the idea of pathetecture Walter seeks to establish that the conventional processes of architecture are only a stage in the larger process of pathetecture, so that the interventions of architects in the making of new places are a first step of a continuous and dynamic process of building, demolition and rebuilding structures, as well as decorating and redecorating surfaces. Pathetecture implies a way of bringing places into being through the cooperative and antagonistic relationships between people who make the physical form and those who use and share it: a relationship which determines the expressive quality of space. Places without this kind of expressive energy are dead places, according to Walter, likely to induce feelings of boredom, malaise, and violence. Rationally planned space "exclusively intent on providing a machine for living" (ibid.), provides an example. Walter goes on: "Towns may die for all sorts of reasons, but expressive vitality depends on how a place engages the imagination. A place is dead if the physique does not support the work of the imagination, if the mind cannot engage with the experience located there, or if the local energy fails to evoke ideas, images, or feelings" (ibid., p.204).

Arnold Berleant (1997) echoes these sentiments in his concern to establish the concept of living in the landscape as the basis for a new aesthetic of environment. In common with theoretical material discussed above, he takes living to mean more than the occupation and use of space by people. His scheme assumes a conception of the relationship between space and people in which the environment is an integrated whole consisting of physical, social and perceptual features. Collectively, these constitute conditions for life and thus, the environment is assumed to consist of human given attributes and conversely, people are given environmental attributes. Humans and natural processes are not conceived as pairs of opposites but aspects of the same thing: a unified human-environment. Berleant considers a landscape to be a particular type of environment distinguishable because of its particular human purpose. Each landscape has its own distinguishable perceptual, social and physical features. This integrated conception of the human-environment relationship is, for Berleant, the basis for aesthetic experience. It extends beyond the kind of disinterested contemplation associated with aspects of the Romantic movement and derives from engagement and participation. This is an active rather than passive orientation which acknowledges both physical and perceptual forms of activity. Environmental aesthetics for Berleant, is the study of environmental experience as opposed to the sum of quantifiable properties (a Cartesian concept), or related only to subjective feelings (a Romantic concept). Aesthetic experience is therefore grounded in human participation with their surroundings and Berleant stresses the significance of ordinary acts of routine life.

Section Two

The concept of experiential landscape

Introduction

Previously we have tried to sketch out aspects of thought about human-environment relations and have suggested that an element of philosophical immaturity might be at the root of limitations in landscape architecture's capability to respond more fully to human dimensions in its place-making activity. We assert that giving greater prominence to a more holistic attitude to human-environment relations in the intellectual development of landscape architecture might be fruitful and we have tried to highlight sources that might be explored in more detail with this in mind. We have also highlighted that developments in place theory in particular seem to offer potential for a theoretical interpretation of holistic human-environment relations by integrating human behavioural and psychological functioning with the spatial and material world. Although it is quite clear that this and related principles are as yet far from the mainstream of contemporary landscape architectural thinking there are grounds for some optimism. It is evident, for example, that there have been frequent attempts to explore the implications of a more phenomenological understanding of the nature of place in the realm of architecture and urban planning. There remains considerable potential in this for landscape architecture's theoretical and methodological development and we can see this

beginning in elements of so called socially responsive approaches to urban design in which landscape architects are increasingly influential contributors. Valuable efforts are being made to tease out ways this might be developed for more practical application: Llewellyn-Davies' *Urban Design Compendium* (2000) developed in association with English Partnerships provides an example. Of particular relevance here are messages implicit in this arena suggesting that certain spatial configurations may be beneficial to human experience of the external environment, the practical implications of which are hitherto not explored.

Up to now we have been concerned with theoretical grounding, an intellectual and academic justification for developing experiential landscape as a way to conceptualise people-space relations in the routinely encountered outdoors. At the heart of experiential landscape is a commitment to the idea that human experience has spatial dimensions and we have tried to present some justification for this view. Experiential landscape is, though, more than a field of academic inquiry. We are also interested in investigating how to apply the philosophical and theoretical principles that underpin experiential landscape in practice. Partly this means finding ways to understand the experiential character of outdoor settings through interpretation of spatial organisation and working out what components and procedures of design processes might help to make experientially better places. Space is arguably a fundamental medium for those who design outdoor settings and the sculpting and moulding of space and the material elements that define it are central to their purpose. The concept of experiential landscape responds with a conceptual framework setting out how certain categories of human experience can be interpreted spatially. This has helped develop and consolidate our ideas about how outdoor places can be understood holistically as four spatial types called centre, direction, transition and area, which combine in an infinity of ways to make places of different experiential character. Centre, direction, transition and area can be thought of as a kind of code representing the spatial expression of these experiences in the outdoors and, through knowing something of their properties and characteristics, makes it possible to read the experiential profile of existing settings and, although to a more limited extent, those still in the planning and design process. This model provides the basic structure upon which to begin to build the components and procedures required to apply experiential landscape principles in practice and this is what this section will sketch out. Before doing so, however, we want to say a few things about why the concept of experiential landscape is structured as it is.

Although there is a lot of complexity and difference in how this is expressed, a general convergence appears detectable across a diversity of sources to support the view that certain kinds of spatial configuration are associated with sustaining the fundamental human impulse to know where we are and what this means to us in relation to our wider surroundings. This appears to give primacy to categories of spatial configuration that can engender feelings of location, continuity and change. This is not to say, of course, that this is all people need to experience in their routine use of the outdoor environment to attain a sense of fulfilment. But it does appear that these sensations, in a sense, form basic foundations for how people orientate themselves, physically and psychologically, and from which they can then enjoy the sense of well-being that allows more sophisticated forms of place awareness to develop. So, although

the experiential landscape model may appear to some extremely condensed, there does appear to be some theoretical justification, stretching back at least as far as Lynch (1960), for it to give us a starting point to link human experience with spatial expression in ways relevant to design decision making. Following on from this, then, is the issue of how to interpret this in a way sufficiently digestible and practical in contemporary practice contexts. Without being able to do this it is very unlikely that these evidently important experiential dimensions will ever find themselves sufficiently embedded into design practice and may remain in the comparatively rarefied environment of academia.

This is a problem that environmental psychologists Stephen and Rachel Kaplan highlighted a few years ago in the introduction to their book with Robert Ryan, *With People in Mind* (1998). The problem as they saw it was that although enlightened design practitioners recognised value and relevance in the research findings of environmental psychology, they simply could not easily translate the research literature into usable recommendations. The Kaplan's solution to this was to appeal to the structure of Alexander's *Pattern Language* as a framework with operational potential and they proposed their own matrix of patterns and themes to present solutions for the design and management of everyday nature. In terms of digestibility, this is a much lighter touch than Alexander's epic work and an extremely useful and readable contribution. Although it was not meant to specifically address the urban outdoors, its quest to try to condense some quite complex concepts about the human-environment relationship into a set of principles relevant at the drawing board provides some inspiration for the way in which the structure of experiential landscape has evolved. Whilst acknowledging the risks inherent in over-simplification, the appeal of trying to compress a wide range of experiential diversity within just four overarching themes of centre, direction, transition and area is that it has the potential to provide a quickly memorable framework within which to weave a great deal of detail.

Another distinguishing feature of the experiential landscape concept that has crucial relevance in practice is that it offers the opportunity to take into account, and compare and contrast, the place perceptions of professionally trained members of project teams and actual users of the setting. During the development of the experiential landscape concept we have become convinced that the most useful understanding of place comes, not from privileging either professional training or public consultation, but by being able to bring both together in a collective view. There is sufficient evidence in environmental psychology and social science research to indicate that significant differences may exist in the way places are perceived by trained professionals and the non-specialist public. Salaman (1974) for example, argued for the idea of occupational communities consisting of trained professionals socialised into the beliefs and values of their particular profession that then assume precedence over client or public values. Subsequent research in the context of landscape architecture supports this idea and suggests that landscape architects emphasise physical and objective qualities in their judgement of landscape, whereas non-specialists tend to emphasise what places mean to them in relation to their daily living patterns (Clamp, 1981; Uzzell and Lewand, 1990). These differences have been taken to suggest that public and professional perceptions should both be considered in design decision-making processes.

Our own experience from pilot studies and experimental field work concurs with this. We have repeatedly found both trained professional and non-specialist site user perceptions seem to provide an important yet, taken separately, incomplete view about place perception for entirely different reasons. Trained environmental design professionals, for example, when looking at a site they do not routinely use, tend to respond to visual clues to identify where they perceive centre, direction, transition and area. It is important that they do, because the physical and spatial fabric delivers stimuli that influence users and we have to know about this to make appropriate design decisions. But this is not all that influences users and so it provides only a partial picture. Users tend instead to respond mainly to what associations places have for them

and quite often this relates to places that might be visually insignificant or effectively invisible from a conventional professional perspective. This is also important because it reveals details about daily habits and emotional associations that simply are not accessible through examination of a site's visible attributes. But, although the experiential landscape process can translate these responses into a spatial vocabulary, it again provides only a partial picture because it is sensitive to bias in the views of users who participate in the process and it can expose individual idiosyncrasy and personal preference disproportionately. Outside professionals and inside users view place differently and it is together that they contribute to producing a more complete picture of the experiential characteristics of a setting than would be the case with either one separately. This may well have implications for advocates of public participation in planning and design processes beyond the scope of this book.

Experiential landscape is an approach to open space analysis and design that stresses social relevance over appearance. One of the implications of this is that we tend to see a focus on small and sometimes visually insignificant, places. These can be pivotally important to the routine lives of individuals and groups but may be more or less invisible against the larger issues of many environmental improvement projects, or can in fact stand out because they are ugly when assessed against conventional aesthetic criteria. The experiential landscape approach can respond to differences in context to overcome this. These differences may arise for a multitude of reasons governed, for example, by the nature of the setting: people perceive place in a public city centre differently from the inhabitants of a residential setting, or it might be differences in user group. The approach to information gathering from primary school children has to be different from that used with adults, or people with learning disabilities, for example. Because of these, and other factors, it has been found a necessary part of the approach to design specific details of methodology in response to the circumstances of the context. For this reason the approach detailed in this section represents a generic approach. It constitutes the components and procedures that provide an overall framework applicable in all cases, but within which there is a requirement for context dependent refinement to make it fit the purpose. The root of this lies with the qualitative nature of experiential landscape research, the early development of which drew from Grounded Theory to help structure an appropriate methodological foundation. Grounded Theory advocates an approach whereby the area of study is the starting point for the research and the theory is allowed to emerge from the data. Qualitative methods of information gathering, recording and analysis are essential in experiential landscape because human consciousness is not static and people must be engaged on a level that will bring out nuances that may differ depending on the time and purpose of use that the place under investigation has. Also in this respect there are some structural comparisons with Alexander's *Pattern Language* in that it is supposed to represent a set of principles that have to be adapted locally in each and every case.

The net result of this is that, in general, experiential landscape tends towards a "bottom up" approach to open space analysis and design in that it often focuses on the fine grain detail of settings and then looks at how these work together to influence the experiential character of the wider setting. To an extent this capability is to do with another feature of experiential landscape. The spatial types, centre, direction, transition and area are scale independent and this means that it is possible to detect them at different levels of scale. So, for example, the spatial sensation of centre might be apparent at a very personal scale, say for instance at someone's garden gate where a routine encounter with a neighbour occurs. This indicates that a centre of the type social interaction exists here, identifying a significant location in the routine social life of that individual that may be no more than a few feet square. Equally, locational experiences can be much larger in size. Many would probably associate strong locational experiences with Trafalgar Square in Central London, for example, but at this public level of scale, smaller spatial sensations will almost always be recorded within it, creating a kind of nesting effect of spatial experiences at various scales. Again then, although experiential landscape has an apparently simple structure in its four basic spatial types, it can facilitate very complex scrutiny of place character in great detail and at different levels of scale. It is worth noting here that the scale independence and nesting characteristics apparent in the way that centre, direction, transition and area appear, present interesting geometrical challenges when it comes to thinking about how to design using the experiential landscape approach.

Experiential landscape is an attempt to investigate one way of operationalising these theoretical principles. It does this by integrating aspects of human experience with their spatial implications and developing a process for reading experiential character in existing and proposed open space settings. The material in this section will describe how this can be achieved with a special kind of layered map that represents graphically the distribution of different types of spatial experience. This has potential as an analytical tool augmenting conventional survey and analysis techniques with explicit experiential information. It also has potential in design decision-making and geometrical implications relevant to this are also discussed in this section.

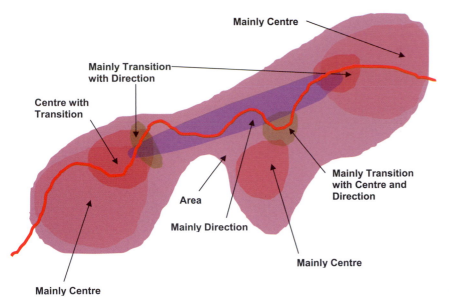

Mainly Centre

Mainly Transition
with Direction

Centre with
Transition

Area

Mainly Direction

Mainly Transition
with Centre and
Direction

Mainly Centre

Mainly Centre

Plate 1
Experiential landscape is an integration of CDTA

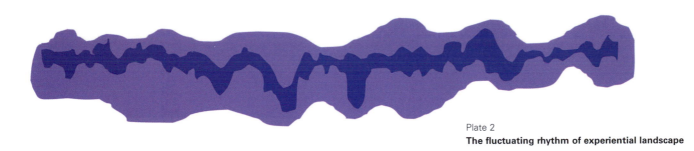

Plate 2
The fluctuating rhythm of experiential landscape

Plate 3
**Multi-layered musical anatomy
arises from the complex interplay
and blending of sound expressions
at different scales working together**

INTONATION

NOTES

MELODY

SYMPHONY

Experiential place	Type	Symbol	Description
Centre Subjectively significant location engendering a sense of here-ness and proximity.	Social imageability		Red open circle or polygon
	Social interaction		Orange open circle or polygon
	Restorative benefit	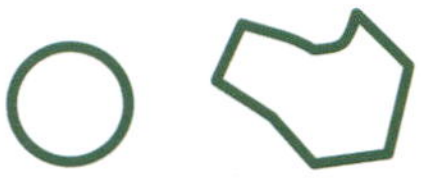	Green open circle or polygon
Direction Subjectively significant continuity engendering a sense of there-ness and future possibility.	Movement		Green dashed line. If bi-directional then no arrows, if single directional then arrow marks direction, if pauses mark pause with an asterix
	View	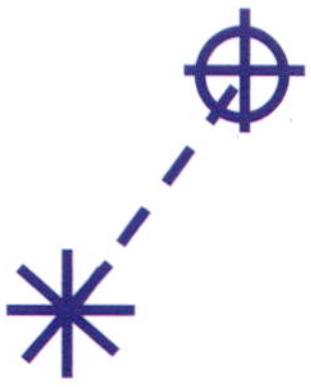	Blue asterix denotes standpoint, blue "target" denotes objective, dashed line denotes view line
Transition Subjectively significant point, or area, of change engendering a sense of transformation in mood, atmosphere, or function	Threshold		Two thick red parallel lines
	Corridor Segment Ephemeral		Red polygon, hatch in one direction and add: Tc for corridor, Ts for segment or Te for ephemeral
Area Subjectively significant realm engendering a sense of coherence and containment.			Purple open polygon

Plate 4

Table of CDTA symbols and themes

Plate 5

An experiential landscape map for an individual

Plate 6

A composite experiential landscape map

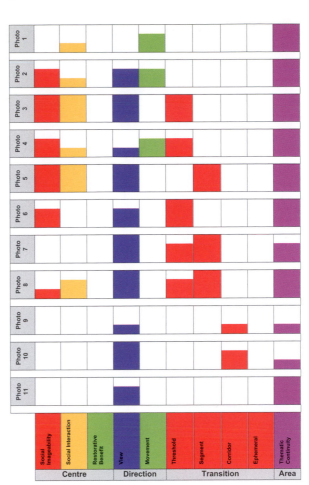

Plate 7

An experiential landscape map of The Piggeries

Plate 8

An experiential landscape map of Friary's Court

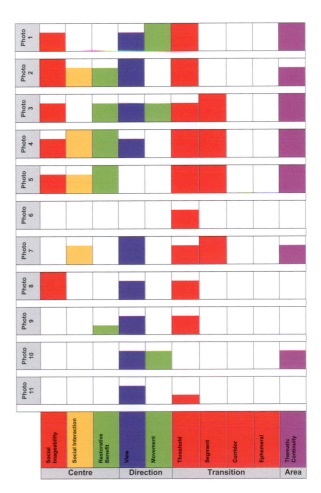

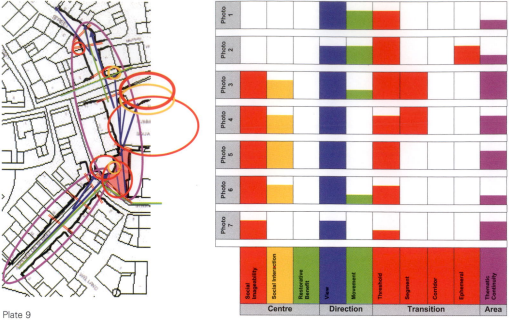

	Centre			Direction		Transition				Area
	Social Imageability	Social Interaction	Restorative Benefit	View	Movement	Threshold	Segment	Corridor	Ephemeral	Thematic Continuity
Photo 1				■	■	■				■
Photo 2					■	■			■	■
Photo 3	■	■		■	■	■	■			■
Photo 4	■	■		■		■	■			■
Photo 5	■	■		■		■				■
Photo 6	■	■		■		■				■
Photo 7	■			■		■				■

Plate 9

An experiential landscape map of Poundbury

Plate 10

Experiential landscape maps of Kirby Hill arising from the research team survey

Plate 11

Area

Plate 12
Centre: social interaction, restorative benefit and social imageability

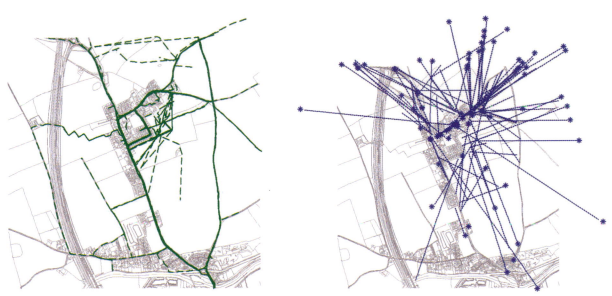

Plate 13
Kinetic and sensory direction

Plate 14
Transition

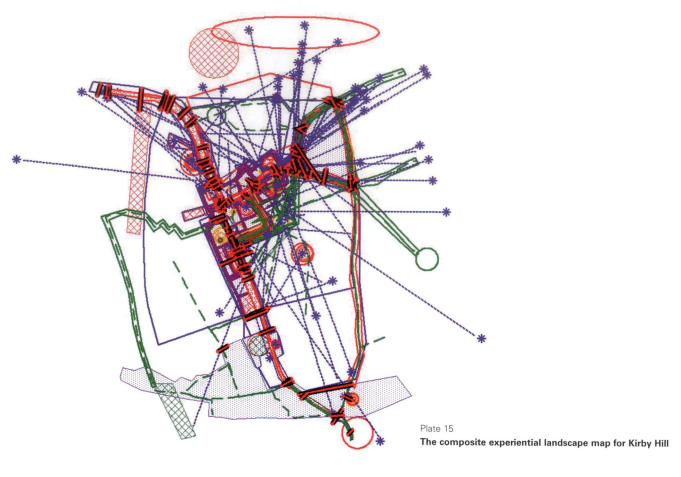

Plate 15
The composite experiential landscape map for Kirby Hill

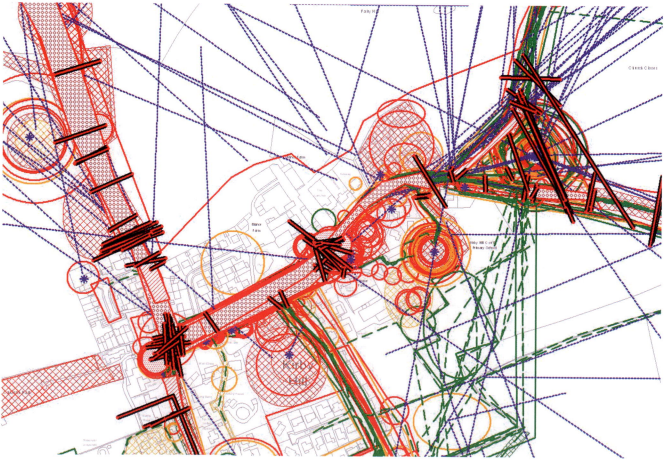

Plate 16
The experiential character of the village core

Plate 17
**Kirby Hill's identity is not a matter of boundary but of variations in
intensity that permeate into the surrounding landscape**

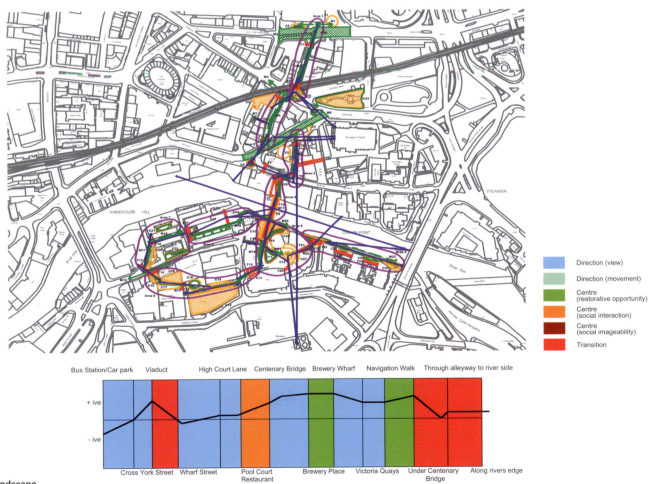

Plate 18
**The experiential landscape
map for the journey**

Our journey

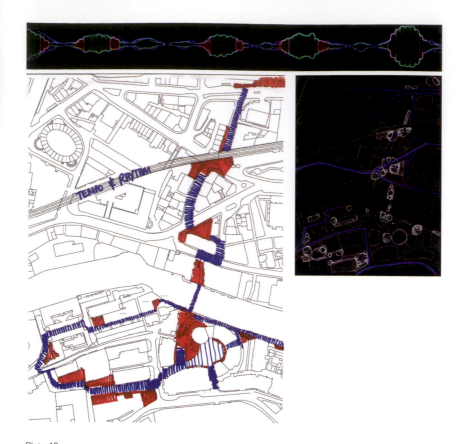

Plate 19
David's concept diagrams for achieving a better balance, rhythm and pattern of directions and centres

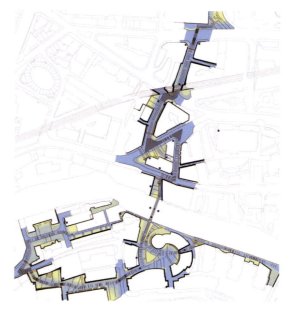

Plate 20
Refinement of the concept showing how the pace of movement varies in response to spatial and functional criteria

Plate 21
Exploring how the overall concept can be interpreted experientially for the detailed site

Chapter 4

Experiential and spatial dimensions

An experiential dimension

"Without understanding how our daily routines form and inform the goodness of our designs, the likelihood is that we at best perpetuate our own value laden opinions, and at worst our momentary whimsy, on the everyday lives of an unsuspecting public" (Bob Scarfo, University of Maryland in *Several Authors*, 1992, p.166).

This chapter begins the process of developing the concept of experiential landscape by looking specifically at experiential issues and then exploring how these may be interpreted in spatial terms. Trying to determine an experiential dimension for people-space relations is no easy task because it involves confronting an almost infinite breadth of human psychological and behavioural variation influenced by a wide range of personal, social and cultural factors, as well as by physical and spatial attributes of the environment. This becomes especially problematic when we start to try to understand this in ways meaningful to the practicality of shaping new settings. As we saw in the previous exploration about the development of theories of place, this is partly because of the intrinsic conceptual difficulty involved in thinking about how to design something that we are asked to accept consists of human perceptions as

well as spatial and material elements, a problem made no easier when professional training has evolved to focus on the spatial and material form and fabric. It boils down to simple practicality. Materials and space are relatively stable and tangible entities amenable to being moulded and changed in ways that the comparative intangibility of human psychological functioning does not.

We are not claiming that the concept of experiential landscape is a panacea for this problem. It is meant to provide a beginning for a journey towards an alternative way of looking at the outdoor environment by emphasising it as an experiential whole rather than a material and spatial composite. If we begin here and try to set out a conceptual framework for the experiential landscape along with some operational procedures for its application then we will at least have presented something with theoretical worth and practical value that can accommodate and encourage subsequent development and refinement. For this reason we decided to begin by trying to identify categories of outdoor experience important to achieving and sustaining human well-being at a fairly fundamental level: we want to know firstly what people need to experience rather than what might be nice to experience.

It seemed important, for example, to look first at what happens to people during their day-to-day movement around and about the streets and spaces that make up their routine everyday settings, rather than on places they might make special visits to: on holidays or days out for example. When people have days out, say to the local park, the beach, a walk in the woods for example, they are generally making a conscious decision to do something they will enjoy, specifically because it is diverting, beyond the scope of their everyday life. Such special places obviously matter to people, but what of the everyday mundane world they return to: the world of the school run, the journey to and from work, the walk to the local shop and post box, the dog walking route, the street corner encounters and the neighbourly chat over the front garden gate? This is the world where experiences may occur at a much more subliminal and subconscious level but that can make the difference between a fulfilled life and one that is not. This is particularly the case for people who, perhaps for economic, health, social or cultural reasons, for example, do not or cannot regularly access special places to give them respite from the ordinary. For this reason we will try to deal with what experiences matter most to people in relation to their routine contact with the everyday outdoor world. The question then is what exactly is this and what are the spatial implications relevant to the design of such settings? Despite variations in methodological detail and disciplinary emphasis, consistencies can be found in research, particularly in cognitive models (Uzzell, 1991), to provide a basis for understanding experience in relation to spatial design. For our purposes here we suggest that this can be interpreted for open space design by looking at patterns of place experience that broadly fall into three distinguishable categories related to how people:

- attach significance or value to certain locations;
- orientate themselves;
- develop awareness of their homeground and come to be able to distinguish between different neighbourhoods, city quarters etc.

Attachment of significance

People attach significance and value to outdoor settings for many different reasons. Often this can be motivated by highly personal circumstances, to do with memories and associations, good or bad, or the familiarity that builds up over time through the routine use of certain locations for particular purposes. It might be stimulated by the way a place looks or smells, or because of sounds or certain sensations that make it stand out as distinguishable or different in some way from the general background of daily life. The 'what' and the 'where' that becomes prominent in the life of one person may not be noticed at all by others as being in any way significant. The processes of place attachment perhaps draw attention to the difference between space and place most because the same physical location may become highly important to some and be completely ignored by others. For those to whom the location matters, for whatever reason and however subliminally felt, that space becomes a place in their lives and a part of what it is for them to be fully human. The same space might equally well mean different things to different individuals and groups and this could change at different times of the day, week or year. In this case such a space could be said to be many different places, possibly at the same time for different individuals, or at different times according to variations in patterns of use. The space along the roadside outside a primary school in a residential area may be an intense and important place of routine social contact for the parents of children attending school twice a day, five days a week. Nearby homeowners may equally well feel a strong sense of place here at these times, but for entirely different reasons because of the noise and nuisance caused by the build up of people and concentration of vehicles. This roadside space is a strong place because of its significance to many. But the sense of place is not for the same reasons and is not so intensely felt all of the time. Within this complexity we can identify three underlying themes which seem to usefully categorise how particular outdoor places may become prominent in people's lives. These include: the social imageability of places (Stokols, 1981); the capacity of places to offer restorative opportunities (Kaplan, Kaplan, and Ryan, 1998); and social interaction and territoriality (Altman, 1975; Martin, 1997).

SOCIAL IMAGEABILITY

Places are memorable for their social associations (Stokols, 1981) as well as their physical form (Lynch, 1960). As places become increasingly layered with social meanings, the interdependence of social and physical components is assumed to increase, binding groups to particular places. Certain settings may contribute particularly to place attachment of this kind. Some, for example, become significant through functional necessity. Regular visits to shops and other local facilities can, often subliminally, make these places landmarks in the routine pattern of everyday life. Others become significant if they are compatible with personal or collective goals, or because of valued physical features or social functions (Stokols, 1981). Thus people may form attachments to places which satisfy particular motivational needs or desires, or which exhibit fine design and distinctive environmental quality, or those which are meaningful, for marriages, burials, or recreational pursuits, for example. These characteristics constitute a totality of social imageability implying that places become especially significant when they have particular physical or social value, are able to satisfy specific needs, and are regularly visited (Bonnes and Secchiaroli, 1995).

RESTORATIVE PLACES

The need for people to be able to retreat from stimulation to relax and recuperate is widely recognised to be important, and places which include nature (Kaplan and Kaplan, 1989) or water (Carr *et al.*, 1992) have been found to be particularly conducive. Research has also suggested that restorative places are those that offer people certain experiential opportunities. These include: the sensation of being away, either physically or psychologically by enabling the mind to wander; extending the scope of what is normally experienced; engendering a sense of fascination or psychological engagement; and compatibility with one's expectations and inclinations (Kaplan, Kaplan and Ryan, 1998). Restorative benefits can be assigned to places without the necessity for actual physical or visual contact. For example, places offering quiet retreat are found to be valued if they are perceived to be accessible and nearby, even if they are infrequently used (Kaplan and Kaplan, 1989).

SOCIAL INTERACTION AND TERRITORIALITY

Places where people congregate routinely or where they pass one another regularly and perhaps exchange casual greetings can become significant in routine daily life. Whyte (1980) noted that places stimulate conversation between strangers if they have features or activities that encourage comment. In neighbourhood settings this often happens close to the dwelling and overlaps with territorial concerns: gardens with low boundaries, for example, are traditional for neighbourly socialising. Martin (1997), in a study of American back-alleys, observed that successful settings tend to be those that strike a balance between "revealing-ness", to encourage social contact among neighbours and territorial monitoring, and "hidden-ness", to provide for privacy and withdrawal. Territorial associations can be powerful influences on people's place attachment and apply in both private and public realms. Altman (1975) specified three different types of territory according to the psychological centrality a space holds for individuals. Primary territory may be the dwelling or private garden, for example, where territorial occupation is often demonstrated through acts of personalisation; an experience important to achieving fulfilled lives (Kaplan and Kaplan, 1989; Bentley *et al.*, 1985). Conversely, people can identify territory in public spaces: a favoured table in a street café, or regularly used seat on a bus, for example. Here, a sense of temporary ownership may grow with frequent use and prolonged occupation. Public places may be valued because they present opportunities to people-watch. Research shows that spatial and social monitoring is important to achieving personal satisfactions (Kaplan and Kaplan, 1989; Carr *et al.*, 1992). In between primary and public are secondary territories, such as private clubs, where individuals can experience exclusivity of occupation as part of a group (Altman, 1975).

Orientation

People need to develop a sense of familiarity about where they are in relation to what is around (Lynch, 1960; Bentley *et al.*, 1985). They also need to extend beyond the familiar to extend physical and cognitive competencies and benefit from the stimulation afforded by considering options, wondering and imagining, experiencing mystery and the possibility of discovery (Kaplan, Kaplan and Ryan, 1998). Locating the familiar and being sure that exploration will not result in becoming lost requires orientation skills and three categories of place experience can contribute to this.

MOVEMENT

To orientate, people need stimulation as they move around. This is more likely when choices have to be made, when imagination is exercised and attention attracted (Kaplan, Kaplan and Ryan, 1998). Beneficial settings, in this respect, may have high levels of permeability offering choice of routes, diversity of experience, and encouragement to explore (Bentley *et al.*, 1985; Rudlin and Falk, 1999). Achieving permeable settings is increasingly associated with grid-based layouts with networks of perimeter block development instead of relatively impermeable and self-contained cul-de-sacs (Bentley *et al.*, 1985; Baxter, 1998; Rudlin and Falk, 1999; Llewelyn-Davies, 2000). This increases the potential for alternative routes and modes of mobility and can more easily contribute to the development of street identity, important to engaging the interest and attention of passers-by. Curves and bends which introduce a sense of mystery and anticipation by hiding and then gradually revealing what is ahead engage the imagination and have been found to be preferred by people, particularly when they include points of interest along the way to aid navigation and attract attention (Kaplan, Kaplan and Ryan, 1998).

VIEW

The presence of strong visual devices, such as landmark features, vistas and views, are important because they help emphasise a sense of direction as well as providing orientation aids (Lynch, 1960; Kaplan, Kaplan and Ryan, 1998; Llewelyn-Davies, 2000). This relates particularly to the experience of walking, during which people tend to scan what lies ahead to identify a series of intermediate goals en-route to a more distant destination (Alexander *et al.*, 1977; Bentley *et al.*, 1985). According to this point of

view, walking is an incremental process that requires the presence of objects or views that can act as temporary navigation aids, breaking the journey into a linked sequence of shorter walks. This sense of sequence appears to be a particularly important influence on how places become memorable (Cullen, 1971). A varied sequence of long and short views, terminated with landmarks, and along which are variations in shape and size of space, heighten awareness of a setting by emphasising a series of revelations, strengthening the experience of progression and continuity (Cullen, 1971; Kaplan, Kaplan and Ryan, 1998; Rudlin and Falk, 1999).

CHANGE

Sensations of anticipation, mystery, continuity and sequence are associated with physical features which mark entrances, changes of level or direction, or which pinch space into holes, gaps or corridors to define frameworks which connect places physically or visually. Periodic experience of change illuminates the contrasts that bring settings to life, strengthening psychological engagement by heralding a shift of atmosphere, mood or function, and marking the passage from here to there (Cullen, 1971; Alexander *et al.*, 1977). The experience of change and transformation is particularly important to Alexander's holistic conception of the urban environment. To be psychologically beneficial, points of change should work, not only as punctuation to join different spatial realms together, but also as sensations which engender feelings of arrival and gradually induce a sense of change (Alexander *et al.*, 1977). Places where change is experienced are often where choices need to be made. They encourage people to pause and reflect on where they have been, where they might go next, and can be landmark features in their own right, aiding navigation or becoming significant social places at which to meet.

Neighbourhood awareness

Knowing one's own neighbourhood is an important component in people's territorial repertoire. There is an intrinsically subjective element to how an individual might perceive their neighbourhood but two components of place experience may help strengthen a sense of neighbourhood identity.

PRIVATE-PUBLIC AWARENESS

People feel and behave differently, towards one another and their surroundings, according to the levels of privacy they perceive (Sommer, 1959; Hall, 1966). The development of theory establishing the influence of degrees of privacy on routine human behaviour is generally attributed to Edward Hall (1959, 1963, 1966). The synthesis of his findings is the concept of proxemic space which establishes a typology of zones to express different categories of human relations: intimate, personal, social, and public (Hall, 1966). Similar principles have been explored in architecture and argue for settings to be organised to heighten the experience of gradual progression from private to public realms (Chermeyeff and Alexander, 1963; Alexander *et al.*, 1977). Proxemics is based on anthropological observations that suggest humans have innate tendencies to band together in mutually supportive, and usually small, social groupings. This has been extended with the term distemic space to explain how culturally distinguishable neighbourhoods become apparent in cities (Greenbie, 1981). Proxemic and distemic space define two spatial realms that function in a complimentary manner to maximise human psychological health. The former describes the homeground that satisfies basic needs and provides security, and, when this is achieved, the latter provides challenge and enrichment. Greenbie argues for a rich mosaic of proxemic environments, or diversity of neighbourhoods, enfolded within a wider realm of shared distemic space (Greenbie, 1981).

THEMATIC CONTINUITY

Neighbourhood identity may also be strengthened if there is discernible commonality to distinguish it from the rest of the surroundings. Fine grain variation and detail contribute character and interest in neighbourhood settings by means of, for example, "an endless variety of components: texture, space, form, detail, symbol, building type, use, activity, inhabitants, degree of maintenance, topography" (Lynch, 1960, p.67). The neighbourhood also requires thematic continuity within

these variants to establish overall sense of rhythm, pattern and coordination to give it distinguishable identity (ibid.). Lozano (1974) has discussed this principle as a balance of variety and diversity where variety refers to subtle variations in otherwise coordinated sets, and diversity refers to a range of different sets, implying a greater degree of differentiation. In residential settings especially, touches of personalisation can contribute to the balance of variety and diversity, and therefore the differentiation of neighbourhoods. Research suggests that personal expressions in neighbourhoods are unlikely to be completely random or chaotic but may conform, however loosely, to some level of cultural or group norm. There is evidence to suggest, for example, that the appearance and content of front gardens can be influenced by mimicking and adapting what nearby neighbours have done (Kaplan and Kaplan, 1989; Zmyslony and Gagnon, 1998). Such neighbourhoods offer familiarity and attachment and are distinguishable from surrounding neighbourhoods that display their own characteristics and unifying textures.

This brief and concisely presented review of research begins the process of giving structure to the way in which we can understand something about fundamental experience in the outdoors. It is not intended to provide a comprehensive overview of outdoor place experience: we are not suggesting that this is all people need to experience in routine life. Simply that without opportunities to access at least these experiences routinely then some kind of diminishment in life quality is likely to be the consequence. From this review we can also begin to see that spatial implications are implicit in these experiences and we will move on now to look at this in more detail (Table 4.1).

Spatial dimensions of experience

"Any functional action has particular spatial implications" (Norberg-Schulz, 1971, p.8).

In what sense is it meaningful to talk about human experience having spatial implications when, intuitively, it does not seem to have the tangible

Table 4.1 An experiential dimension for routine contact with the everyday outdoors

Attachment of significance

Social imageability: functional use, goals and motivations, physical features, social meanings.

Restorative benefit: being away, extent, fascination, and compatibility.

Social interaction and territoriality: communication, primary, secondary and public territory.

Orientation

Movement: choice, imagination, and attention.

View: landmarks, views and vistas, sequence.

Change: direction and level; entrances, exits and gateways; atmosphere and function.

Neighbourhood awareness

Public and private awareness: private, semi-private, semi-public, public.

Thematic continuity: rhythm, pattern, coordination in texture, space, form, detail, symbol, building type, use, activity, degree of maintenance, topography.

shape and form of space as we might understand it in an architectural sense? That human experience can be thought to have spatial dimensions has philosophical roots in the work of phenomenologist Maurice Merleau-Ponty. One of the consequences of his exploration into the phenomenology of perception was to draw conclusions about the interrelated nature of human existence and the spaces within which it is played out. "We have said that space is existential; we might just as well have said that existence is spatial" Merleau-Ponty, 1962, p.293). The justification for this rather remarkable statement comes from Merleau-Ponty's primary interest in our bodily habits and skills. Much of what we do in the world, particularly at a routine and mundane level, generally involves bodily skills that operate without our having to pay conscious attention to them. We can perform all sorts of complicated tasks without having to consciously direct ourselves to carry out the relevant component acts. Driving a car, negotiating obstacles, playing a musical instrument, performing a sporting activity, all actually require an enormous number of different body movements to come together to do these things effectively. Once learned though, these activities become habitual and it is as though they are performed on automatic pilot, so to speak. Indeed once this habitual state is achieved, paying conscious attention to the details of what your body is doing can be sufficiently distracting for the task to go wrong. Most

musicians, for example, know about finger memory and how this can be upset by thinking about it whilst playing. To get it right many of the bodily skills involved in our routine daily activities have to be performed subconsciously (Figure 4.1).

The significance of this is that such skills only become apparent in a suitable environment. Remove the violin from the violinist and the fingers lose their memory, for example. In this case the violin is a part of the environment the violinist needs for the occasion of playing a tune and during the playing it is also part of the activity: an extension of the body. In a phenomenological sense then, when witnessing the activity of music making, the idea that the body and the violin are separate becomes blurred because the phenomenon of the live musical experience cannot exist if they are. This is reminiscent of our earlier account of the way Hans George Gadamar illustrates the phenomenological nature of understanding in his philosophical hermeneutics by talking about the structure of game playing. In much the same way that a game's rules exert constraints on its players, but at the same time require the interpretation of the players for the game to become fully realised, the same holds for the relationship between violin and violinist. Players and rules must coalesce for the game to be experienced and so too must violin and violinist for the music to be experienced. We can extend this principle into

4.1
Remove the violin from the violinist and the fingers lose their memory

those habits are expressed. For Merleau-Ponty this kind of fit between bodily action and its environment is crucial to our ability to make sense of our actions and the world around us.

These ideas have been brought into the architectural arena by Christian Norberg-Schulz (1971) in an attempt to bring structure to an understanding of space as a dimension of human existence and we will consider some of his principal themes here in relation to the experiential issues discussed previously. It is worth noting that a concern about how we should design to take account of the importance of fit between human functioning and its context is central to the life's work of Christopher Alexander. In fact Alexander's biographer, Steven Grabow, refers to the conceptual similarity with Norberg-Schulz's perspective on human-environment relations in explaining some of the origins of Alexander's thinking. More recently Hillier and Hanson have claimed that social potential can be quantified through analysis of spatial structure and the way it is connected together. Social interactions are thought of by Hillier as interdependent with the spatial organisation in which they occur. "Society must be described in terms of its intrinsic spatiality. Space must be described in terms of its intrinsic sociality" (Hillier and Hanson, 1984, p.26). This conclusion follows almost literally the assertion of Merleau-Ponty, quoted above, that the existential and spatial dimensions of human life are in effect mutually defining. Returning to Norberg-Schulz however, there is potential in some aspects of what he described as existential space schemata to relate to the experiential concepts established earlier. Norberg-Schulz asserts that existential space has three constituent elements assumed to exist at different levels of scale: "*centres* or places (proximity), *directions* or paths (continuity), *areas* or domains (enclosure)" (ibid., p.18). This concept is abstract and limited in that it deals with human experience in space at a rudimentary level. But, the patterns of place experience outlined earlier coupled with wider aspects of socially responsive approaches to environmental planning and design, in which the essence of Norberg-Schulz's work can be detected, offer the potential for a fuller expression of the concept.

an environmental context by looking at the relationship people have with certain places, a kitchen or vegetable garden for example. These places form contexts for our actions, but just like the violin, they also become part of the activity. The complex range of bodily activity involved in preparing and cooking food not only depends on the layout and content of the kitchen but is also expressed through the kitchen's existence. Kitchen and cook coalesce in an expression of food creation the experience of which transcends the mere existence of cook and kitchen as separate entities. Similarly the vegetable garden is a context within which certain bodily actions are simultaneously developed, sustained and expressed. In this case those to do with nurturing the growth of food plants.

By focusing attention on the relationship between our entrenched bodily habits and skills and their dependence on the surroundings, Merleau-Ponty is literally pointing to a spatial dimension at the heart of what it is to be human. It implies that people and their settings create a kind of totality where different contexts activate different habits and thus become a part of the way

The starting point for Norberg-Schulz's existential space schemata lies with his assertion that humans have innate tendencies to externalise centres, or locations, in the environment as points of reference from which to become aware of where one is in relation to the rest of the surroundings. Centres are therefore given a primacy as the most basic elements reflecting Norberg-Schulz's view that human spatial perception is subjectively centred (ibid., p.20). This is very similar to the way Kevin Lynch had earlier talked about the significance of the subjectively locational sensation of "here I am" (Lynch, 1960, p.18) which people associate with certain places in the city. An extension of this, as a person's ability to know their position by distinguishing here-ness from there-ness, can also be found in Cullen's views about good townscape (Cullen, 1971). On a more abstract level, the concept of centre "as a psychological entity which is perceived as a whole" (Alexander, 1993, p.32) is particularly important to Alexander's vision of the nature of order in

general and he has described how the subjective feeling of centre can be interpreted geometrically and applied using a prescribed set of procedures to create a structure called a field of centres (Alexander *et al.*, 1987, p.23). Creating a field of centres in this sense essentially means developing urban settings that can be experienced by people as a complex web of interconnected locational opportunities at different levels of scale. An example of somewhere that Alexander thinks represents this kind of spatial field is the Alhambra Palace in Granada of which he says, "the plan is a marvel of centres formed in a thousand combinations, and yet with beautiful symmetrical local order at every point in space" (Alexander, 2001, p.187). Centres are essentially subjective impulses stimulated by and projected onto the material surroundings. They are distinguishable from one another but interconnect to form a composite spatial structure. In Norberg-Schulz's schemata, this is held together by the element direction (Figure 4.2).

4.2

The Alhambra Palace: a complex field of centres (after Alexander)

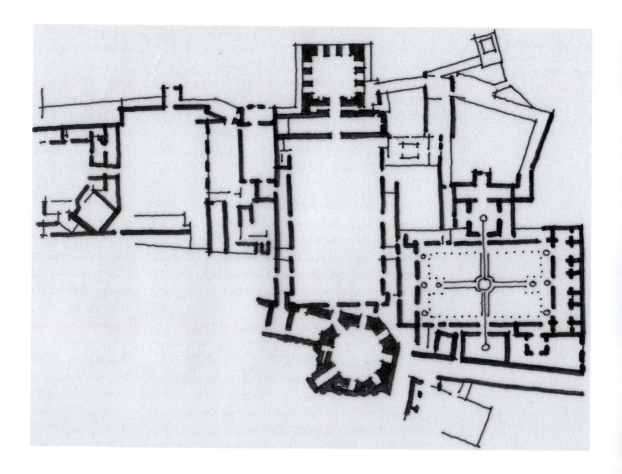

Existential space contains direction as the awareness of continuity so that the centred sense of location, or the known, combines with the sense of the unknown, or future possibility. Direction has its own subjective dimension in that progression is made towards personally significant goals, and if conditions allow, by means of personally chosen routes. It has distinctive character, given by the perceptions and events that happen along the way and so is understood as more than simply a functional element facilitating mobility from here to there. The importance of a sense of direction to the experience of progression and continuity, and its role in developing a sense of place has long been established in urban planning and design thinking (Lynch, 1960; Cullen, 1971; Bentley et al., 1985). Relationships of distinguishable spaces and the paths, landmark features, vistas and views that draw them together contribute beneficially to psychological engagement (Kaplan, Kaplan and Ryan, 1998) and remain significant to the development of socially relevant urban environments (Tibbalds, 1992; Rudlin and Falk, 1999; Llewelyn-Davies, 2000). These argue for a wider understanding of direction than that provided by Norberg-Schulz: as a spatial element that is not simply directional but also sequential and multi-faceted. The sense of direction appears to be sustained by a succession of incremental experiences, involving kinetic and visual sensations together, linked by periodic points of change, or transitions (Alexander et al., 1977; Bentley et al., 1985; Llewelyn-Davies, 2000).

Norberg-Schulz describes the property of transition, not as a discrete element in his spatial schemata, but as a property that along with his conception of direction binds together other elements to form a cohesive sense of place. He explains this as an area of tension at the edge of a centre suggesting that the sense of direction effects centres in a sense by bulging them outwards. According to Norberg-Schulz the centre "is stretched towards the outside, at the same time as the outside penetrates the border, creating an area of transition" (Norberg-Schulz, 1971, p.25). The experience of transition as embodied into the physical form of towns and cities is present in Lynch's (1960) ideas about nodes and edges which can be locations at which changes in character, style, function and atmosphere occur. It is important also to Cullen (1971) as an important spatial component that gives structure and sequence to the sense of serial vision he believes gives us the fundamental dynamic of townscape experience. The Kaplan's (1998) have also argued along similar lines as a result of their own research in visual preference testing, that the potential of openings, gateways and partitions to guide the eye and control view encourages psychological engagement and exploration. The experience of transition as psychological transformation has particularly comprehensive expression in Alexander's concern to explore the designed environment as an unbroken spatial continuity (Alexander et al., 1977; Alexander, 1979). Stepping from one realm to another is too abrupt, insufficient to facilitate necessary adjustments to mental attitude and mood. It should, instead, be a gradual experience. For example, the pattern "entrance transition" (Alexander et al., 1977, p.548) calls for physical space to be configured to enhance the transformation from street behaviour to gradually induce the sense of intimate relaxation associated with being inside. There is reason in these wider perspectives to suggest that transition ought to be considered as a spatial element of equal significance to the other three in Norberg-Schulz's schemata, rather than simply as the glue that binds them together.

The third spatial element Norberg-Schulz defines is area, or domain, understood as the relatively unstructured ground against which centres and directions appear as more pronounced figures. Area has a unifying function representing the totality of the stable image of the environment for an individual as a recognisable region of common texture within which personally significant centres and directions can be discerned. A distinction is therefore to be made here between experience of area, as a general sense of overall coherence and more localised experience which consists of specific senses of location and extent conceptualised as centre and direction. This abstract concept can be understood in the context of other writers in terms of the awareness of district or neighbourhood. For example, Lynch (1960) identifies districts as relatively large areas

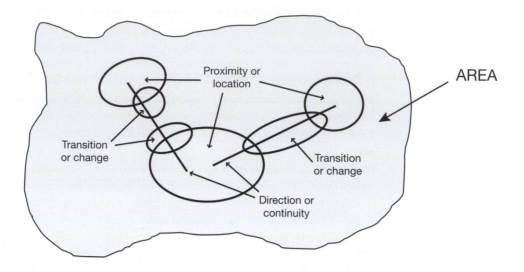

of cities "which the observer can mentally go inside of, and which have some common characters" (ibid., p.66). Such districts are assumed to aggregate in larger clusters to form whole cities. Alexander adopts a similar point of view at the neighbourhood scale suggesting that neighbourhoods are distinguishable in terms of identifiable character and discernible boundary (Alexander *et al.*, 1977).

When we consider Norberg-Schulz's concept in the light of other examples from environmental planning and design theory we can begin to see the potential to construct an abstract image of people's relationship with space that can be interpreted in terms of place. It suggests a tripartite concept of place comprising the simultaneous awareness of where one is in relation to what lies beyond. This awareness can be represented spatially in terms of a holistic relationship of centre, direction and transition. These are conceptualisations for the spatial dimension of place experience. Diversity of place experience is perceived as pronounced against a less structured, but discernibly coherent, area that can be equated with neighbourhood or district (Figure 4.3).

This abstraction has potential to give a spatial structure to the experiential dimension outlined earlier. For example, centre, as subjectively significant location, can be related to the experience of place attachment revealing the possibility for a range of centre types depending on their significance to social imageability, restorative benefit, or

social interaction and territoriality. Similarly, the three categories of place experience that contribute to orientation (movement, view, change) have spatial dimensions in the elements direction and transition, and, finally, private-public awareness and thematic continuity, which help induce neighbourhood or district awareness, can be interpreted spatially as area. Experiential and spatial dimensions can thus be conceptualised in terms of four fundamental elements (centre, direction, transition and area) and these are summarised in the following table (Table 4.2).

Table 4.3 then shows how these spatial and experiential dimensions can be brought together. This now shows a development from Norberg-Schulz's existential space schemata establishing that the spatial elements can be related to specific categories of experience fundamental to routine contact with the everyday outdoor environment. It also highlights that subsets of each can be conceptualised to relate to different types of spatial experience. For example, in terms of the component centre, which expresses spatially the experience of location, there are three distinguishable ways that people can come to attach meaning and significance to particular locations: because they are imageable, either physically or in terms of social associations assigned them; because they are associated with restorative experiences; or because they are where significant social contacts occur. Similarly, the experience of direction has two distinguishable aspects: one stimulated by

Table 4.2   **Spatial dimensions relevant to experience of routine contact with the everyday outdoors**

Centre

Subjectively significant location engendering a sense of here-ness and proximity.

Direction

Subjectively significant continuity engendering a sense of there-ness and future possibility.

Transition

Subjectively significant point, or area, of change engendering a sense of transformation in mood, atmosphere, or function.

Area

Subjectively significant realm engendering a sense of coherence and containment.

visual factors and the other through movement (Table 4.3).

Before moving on from this to consider the details of experiential landscape there are some other characteristics of outdoor place experience we would like to highlight that have implications for spatial organisation. To begin with it is worth pausing to note here the use of the words significant and associations, rather than valued, appreciated or preferred, for example. Whilst in design terms we would obviously be trying to make places that are beneficial to people and we would hope that this would be expressed in terms with positive connotations, it is important to recognise that place experience is not necessarily always positive. Places can become embedded in people's lives for all manner of negative reasons just as they can for positive reasons and this has to be taken into account somehow in attempts to uncover the experiential characteristics of existing settings. For example, it is quite possible to conceive of places having quite a profound influ-

Table 4.3   **A provisional concept of experiential landscape**

Spatial dimension	Experiential dimension
Centre	*Attachment of significance*
Subjectively significant location engendering a sense of here-ness and proximity.	Social imageability: functional use, goals and motivations, physical features, social meanings.
	Restorative benefit: being away, extent, fascination, and compatibility.
	Social interaction and territoriality: communication, primary, secondary and public territory.
Direction	*Orientation*
Subjectively significant continuity engendering a sense of there-ness and future possibility.	Movement: choice, imagination, and attention.
	View: landmarks, views and vistas, sequence.
Transition	
Subjectively significant point, or area, of change engendering a sense of transformation in mood, atmosphere, or function.	Change: direction and level; entrances, exits and gateways; atmosphere and function.
Area	*Neighbourhood awareness*
Subjectively significant realm engendering a sense of coherence and containment.	Public and private awareness: private, semi-private, semi-public, public.
	Thematic continuity: rhythm, pattern, coordination in texture, space, form, detail, symbol, building type, use, activity, degree of maintenance, topography.

ence on someone's life because they are associated with anti-social behaviour in others. Such places may actually be avoided for this reason so that no physical contact with them happens anymore. But nevertheless there is an experience projected onto a part of the physical environment here: one of disapproval, apprehension and perhaps fear. Such a place can be said to be significant and to hold associations for individuals in relation to its social imageability or interaction, but in this case this is so for negative reasons. The positive and negative side of place attachment will be picked up again subsequently in the context of techniques developed for recording and mapping spatial experience.

Another characteristic that has important implications relates to the holistic nature of

outdoor place experience. The categories of place experience we have highlighted do not occur to people independently of one another as though they were discrete and separate facets of life encountered exclusively one after the other. Instead, it seems more realistic to understand place experience as a whole phenomenon. Conscious people going about their routine business in the outdoor world have continuous experiences. The categories we have discussed are simply a way to organise, or classify, how that whole experience may change in character according to the circumstances prevailing. For example, an individual may feel a sense of restorative benefit at a particular location that is also significant for its opportunities for social contact. It is also extremely unlikely in the real world that

4.4

A place with a good balance of centre, direction, transition and area

this will ever happen in total isolation from some or all of the experiences we have related to orientation and neighbourhood awareness. Outdoor place experience is then not a simple question of either-or, but more a seamless composite where one or more kinds of experience may temporarily predominate over others. The categories we describe here provide a means to understand the complex and changing nature of place experience, not that one or another kind of experience occurs to the exclusion of others (Figure 4.4).

Chapter 5

The vocabulary of experiential landscape

The table at the end of the last chapter combines experiential and spatial dimensions to provide the fundamental basis from which the experiential landscape concept can begin to be explored in the field. We begin this chapter by looking more closely at the components, centre, direction, transition and area, as an emergent vocabulary potentially capable of describing the characteristics of experiential landscapes, highlighting their particular characteristics and more importantly how they work together as a whole. Translating the theoretical aspects of experiential landscape into a practical form involved a wide range of field activity in professional practice and in research and design studios, many of which involved students of landscape architecture and urban design in the United Kingdom and overseas. This provided opportunities to apply and test different elements of the experiential landscape concept and develop methods and tools in various contexts. These activities amplified the theoretical foundations of experiential landscape and began to explore in more detail whether the abstract components of centre, direction, transition and area could be recognised in the physical world, initially by trying to discover if there were particular properties and characteristics for each that could be particularly associated with these experiences. A wealth of material gradually accumulated over a period of about five years from field and studio investigation and began to illuminate how we could use CDTA as a language to describe the structure and nature of experiential landscape (Figures 5.1, 5.2, 5.3).

In what follows we will look at each component of the experiential landscape vocabulary in turn, first outlining in general some of the key characteristics to emerge from our investigations. These begin to add structure to the concept by differentiating between generic properties for each component and properties that seemed indicative of particular types. For example, a general sensation of direction almost always seemed to become pronounced when something occurred to shift attention away from where one was to somewhere else. It is almost as though properties of the surroundings acted to generate a kind of psychological extrusion replacing a sense of here with a pull towards a sense of there. We were able to identify three distinct experiences that seemed most often to generate this sensation, either individually or in combination. We categorised these as: linear containment, route, and anticipation. But bound together within this were further properties that appeared to differentiate between directional sensations stimulated mainly by sight and sound

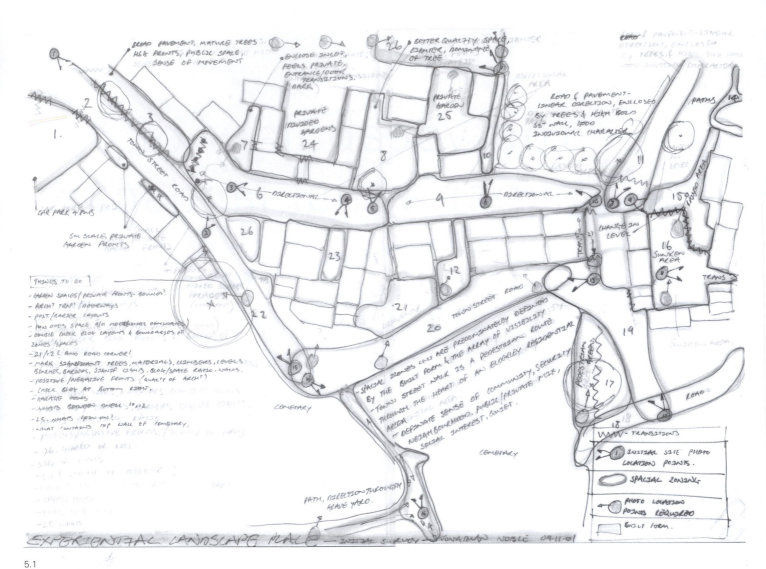

5.1

Mapping field observations in Leeds

5.2

A postgraduate student research team investigating the properties of centre in a residential area

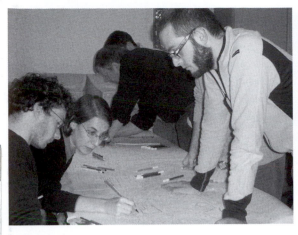

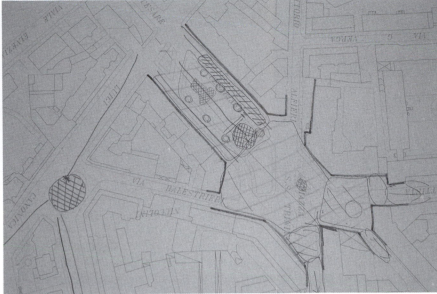

5.3
Students in a pan-European workshop investigating the experiential characteristics of public open space in the China Town quarter, Milan

phenomena and those stimulated mainly by kinetic phenomena. So, for example, a strong sense of direction could arise in situations where something prominent elsewhere, usually something visible but possibly a sound, over-rides the impact of nearer distractions. In this case the sensation of direction is generated by something that one may not necessarily go to but that emphasises, possibly momentarily, the awareness of there over here. Alternatively, a sense of direction can arise through actual motion as people walk about during daily routine. It is interesting to note that in this case it is not every available route taken that registers as a sense of direction, it tends to be the ones that stick in the mind. This could be because of routine and frequent use, association with particularly memorable activities, or with features or encounters along the way. From this we have drawn the conclusion that it is meaningful to differentiate between kinetic and sensory types of direction and that certain environmental qualities can be associated with each.

We begin the discussion with centre, looking first at the qualities we have associated with the generic sensation of location before moving on to look at each of three distinguishable types of centre. A table at the end of each section summarises the key principles. We should point out here that the development of an experiential landscape vocabulary based on the CDTA model is not in any sense an attempt to determine a finite list of environmental qualities for these conceptual components. There are two main reasons for saying this. The first is that our findings here are based on observations we have carried out during the course of our studio and field based research, practice applications and by drawing from relevant literature. We believe that this gives the concept sufficient solidity to be both theoretically valid and practical, but we are fully aware that there will be more that will add to, and possibly challenge, what we present here. The second is that we do not in fact believe it is possible, in principle, to arrive at a fully determinate and closed language simply because what induces sensations of CDTA is to an extent entirely personal. What we are presenting here is indicative rather than prescriptive, a conceptual framework from which things develop and not an absolute solution.

Centre

Some of the environmental attributes that seemed to induce the predominant sensation of location we call centre were fairly predictable. For example, centre sensations were frequently asso-

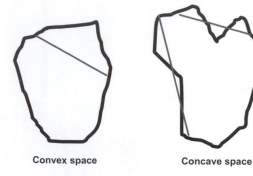

Convex space   Concave space

**Convex and concave space
(after Hillier and Hanson)**

ciated with locations that had a discernible sense of enclosure and especially so if they appeared in the visual field as generally convex in shape. The geometrical property of convexity means that the containing surfaces of a space face into it in such a way that if a line was to be drawn between any two points in the space it would never go outside (Figure 5.4).

Hillier and Hanson (1984) have associated convex spaces like this with social potential in residential settings and we used an adaptation of this to explore the spatial characteristics of the sensation of centre in several residential settings including Poundbury, Dorset. Each cell on the plan represents where, within the streets and squares of Poundbury, the defining surfaces reflect inwards giving each a discernible sense of enclosure, even though this may be very subtle in places. The accompanying photograph shows one of the residential pedestrian streets as an example. It illustrates how the façades of the houses here

gently angle inwards on the right, accentuating the overall sense of enclosure (Figure 5.5).

A more detailed inspection of the sense of enclosure apparent in this location reveals, however, a more complex spatial structure. Consider in particular the impact of subtle detail in the façade alignment where the white houses are on the right, coupled with the slightly protruding façade about half way down on the left where the steps to the front door are, and the tree position and the associated change in surface treatment. These are very subtle variations within the overall sense of enclosure and coordination, but reveal that the totality of this space is actually constituted from three distinguishable cells. No account has been taken here of the way this space is actually experienced by its residents and visitors. It does show, however, that if we focus purely on the property of convex space, three potential centres appear recognisable within its overall spatial structure which may become reflected in the way the space is perceived and used. The occupants of the white faced houses on the right, for example, might well form particular attachment to the space in front of their houses. This is likely because of normal territorial impulses, of course, but the fact that their houses are white whilst most of the others are red brick, the proximity of the trees, the change in ground surface, the slightly protruding façade opposite along with the step detail, distinguish this segment of the street to an extent that might intensify it as territorially different from the rest of it. This is speculation, of course, but if the territorial

**Convex space in a Poundbury
street**

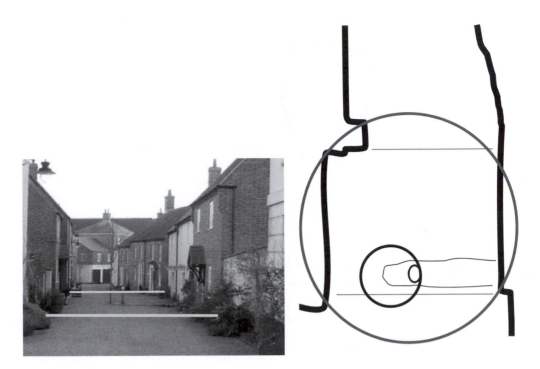

5.6

**Potential system of centres
induced by subtle architectural
and landscape details**

impulses, or to put it another way, the sense of ownership and attachment, felt by the house occupants are subliminally heightened by this means then it has been achieved by very small and subtle attention to detail and this we believe is significant (Figure 5.6).

This perhaps points to a much less predictable environmental attribute relevant to how we understand the experiential dimensions of centre. This is that, at one level the street in Poundbury could be thought of as one centre, in the sense that it has an overall sense of enclosure and coordination, and is likely to be experienced as such by residents and especially passers-by. But at another level, this larger centre seems to be comprised of three smaller ones. These are already distinguishable from a detailed examination of spatial and physical features present, but may become even more pronounced in the perceptions of residents through habitual use: uses that may have in part been stimulated by these particular spatial and physical circumstances. To this extent then, centres can be thought of as entities that in a geometrical sense are folded within one another. There is an implication from the experimental field work done as well as from exploration of theory to suggest that

sensations of location, or place attachment, may at least partly be associated with the degree of enfoldment apparent in centres at particular locations. Occurrences of place attachment may be more intense where centres are made up from smaller centres of different levels of scale acting together to define the larger whole. Returning momentarily to the figures of convex and concave space, we can now see how the principle of paying attention to small-scale landscape and architectural detail can have the effect of transforming a broadly concave space into three convex spaces, potentially increasing experiential richness (Figure 5.7).

5.7

Concave space is now three convex spaces

Other attributes that seemed associated with the sensation of centre include the existence of transitional features and views. At first this seems odd because these appear to be associated with experiences of change and direction, other components in the experiential landscape framework, and not with the sense of location. It appears however that, although it may seem counter-intuitive, the sense of our proximity in the environment actually diminishes if we cannot experience where we are in relation to our wider surroundings. Like a cellar, settings that offer total containment without glimpses of a world beyond and a means to access it will quickly become claustrophobic and disorientating. Centre is, then, not about strong containment to the extent that other experiences are shrouded out. This results in a sense of isolation rather than location. Rather it seems that awareness of centre is more a question of emphasis. We must be simultaneously aware of direction and transition to locate where we are in relation to what lies around, but what makes the experience of centre is simply that the locational sensation is predominant over the others.

An example of this is the balcony of my hotel room in Malta where I wrote notes for this section. Over the course of my week's stay here, this location took on an experiential significance for me as a strong centre because of social imageability and restorative benefit. Imageable because of the

temporary territorial claim I developed with it as a place in the shade where I could write each day. Restorative because of the shade, the association with thinking, reading and reflection; the relaxation from the holiday; the peace of mind from knowing that my daughter was safe and having a fun time with friends; the warmth, but not too much warmth, and the constant background sound of the sea. The physical containment of the balcony walls and the table in the corner add physical and spatial components that support the sense of centre. The reason I sat where I did though was partly because it felt right to sit with my back to the niche in the corner of the bedroom window and wall, but also because there was a view (Figure 5.8).

This view introduces the experience of future possibility, an experience associated with direction, because it looks towards a near distant settlement. The feeling of direction is further enhanced by the sense of movement implied by the curvature of the road and the repetition of the roadside palm trees; also by the horizon as a subtle eminence capped by buildings. Transition is also apparent in the way that the balcony wall on the right of my view and the railing help to enhance the view by framing it and giving foreground detail heightening the sense of distance and extent. Area is apparent in the dryness of the landscape, the warm slightly clammy air, the sparse and scrubby vegetation, and the unifying

5.8

A predominant sense of centre on a Maltese hotel room balcony

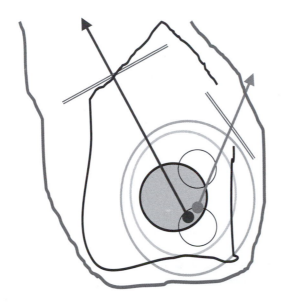

A type of experiential landscape map (Dobson Cluster) recording the experiential character of the balcony showing that the full CDTA range is present but that the sensation of centre is the dominant one

5.10

An experiential symphony of CDTA in a Prague streetscape

larger scale as an experiential symphony of CDTA. The emphasis with which each is felt subtly changes in unbroken and continuous fluidity. Almost everywhere strong locational sensations are woven together in a complex mosaic by gateways, gaps, arches and colonnades, offering access, glimpses and views to what lies beyond. The totality of these parts generated a coordinating and reassuring whole, or area, expressed in Prague's distinctive architectural forms and spaces (Figure 5.10).

Another of the principal attributes of settings that seemed to deliver prominent centre experience was that settings that appeared locationally significant, as opposed to isolating, tended to be close to routes that encouraged passers-by. The presence of people sitting and waiting, watching and talking, eating and drinking either individually or in groups tended to generate strong locational sensations, sometimes, it seemed, almost irrespective of other environmental qualities. It appeared as though the awareness of people at ease, rather than moving about, imbued where it occurred with an intrinsic sense of here. Where people paused others seemed attracted to

influence of the block-like architectural styling and its limited range of sandy coloured rendering (Figure 5.9).

The near labyrinthine configuration of small squares and courtyards, passageways and streets that characterise the streetscape in parts of Prague's old town exemplify this holism on a

5.11

The sensation of centre can grow from the casual gathering of people

do likewise. People attract people and in this sense the sensation of centre appeared to grow out of the social interaction or casual gathering of people (Figure 5.11).

These human and environmental qualities appeared to be active influences, either individually or in combination, on the extent to which people felt sensations of location as they moved about their surroundings. We felt they gave us a basis from which to categorise experience of centre in a generic sense in the following way.

A centre is a subjectively significant location engendering a sense of here-ness and proximity characterised by:

– being mainly convex in shape and contained;
– being made up of smaller centres;
– having views beyond;
– having transitional features;
– being on a route that encourages passers-by.

Not all of these have to be evident to generate a sense of centre for someone, but in very general terms the more of these properties that were present the stronger the sensation of centre was likely to be.

As well as these environmental features however, other attributes appeared that were

more specific and these were used to distinguish different types of centre. For example, centres that appeared significant because of their social imageability tended to be those near or actually at facilities that people routinely visited to use, such as local shops, banks, post offices, restaurants and bars, tea shops etc. The most successful locations in this respect seemed to be places where there is a wide mixture of uses. Mixed use tends to generate choice and it is the appeal of choice that attracts people as well as the expectation that a variety of needs and desires can be met together. Mixed use environments are often characterised by variety in architectural forms, spaces and landmark features and this variety of forms will have different perceptual significance to different people. The same objects, buildings and spaces will attract different meanings and social values according to the habits of individuals and groups. Accordingly it appears that further environmental characteristics can be identified that may be particularly relevant to the experience of centre. For example, to define a specific type of centre memorable for physical or social reasons. This can be summarised as follows.

Social imageability (memorable locations)
– Presence of facilities (shops, post-box etc.).
– Pronounced physical features (monuments, trees etc.).
– Visual variety and complexity.
– Social meaning (ceremony, work, play).
  (Figures 5.12, 5.13)

Another distinguishable type of centre is that which appears prominent in the routine lives of people because of opportunities presented for social interaction. Ever since Jane Jacob's seminal work, *The Death and Life of Great American Cities* (1961), the literature has frequently asserted that successful urban places tend always to be those that attract and can encourage spontaneous interaction between people. Again this type of centre has implications at different levels of scale in the sense that social interactions can be experienced at quite large scales, such as in this large green urban square (Figure 5.11), or at more of a neighbourhood scale, like in this city courtyard.

5.12
This corner of New York's Greenacre Park has a social meaning for many of its regular visitors as a place for refreshment, socialising and relaxation. The waterfall, trees and enclosing green walls give it a distinctive and memorable visual character as well as a localised sense of enclosure

5.13
Distinctive ornamental detailing can also contribute to making locations memorable illustrating that the sense of centre is scale independent

But equally well, a favourite spot in the square may have a particular significance of its own for an individual, family or social group, for example (Figure 5.14).

Scale independence is a characteristic of centres generally and this is expressed in the generic property which highlights that the strongest centres tend to be those that are made up from smaller centres. However, there appears to be an interesting difference between types of centre in this respect. Whilst there are obviously exceptions to this, centres significant because of social imageability tend in general to be those that have some level of visible prominence whether at large or small scales. Those significant for reasons of social interaction are often not visually prominent or exceptional. Nevertheless they may be extremely important components in the routine social life of individuals and, as in the example of the small communal yard in this residential development in Chapel Allerton, Leeds, might actually be the main place where social contact with neighbours occurs. Most of the residents in this community are elderly and this yard is where occupants of the adjacent houses put out their rubbish and hang out their washing. The yard owes more to functional expedience than aesthetics but although it might not have a noteworthy visual appeal, its particular functionality brings neighbours together spontaneously and frequently. To its elderly users, some of whom may not be able to venture far, this may heighten the significance of the yard from simply satisfying functional needs to satisfying social ones, making it a prominent and important centre of social interaction in their lives (Figure 5.15).

To summarise then, environmental attributes we have found to be especially associated with centres significant in people's lives because of social interaction include the following.

Social interaction (meeting)
— Significant convergence of routes.
— Presence of features for waiting.
— Seating in social groupings.
— Presence of features encouraging comment.
— Revealingness (low garden boundaries etc.).
— Places of arrival/departure.

5.14
Three centres at different levels of scale

5.15
Potential social interaction centre in Chapel Allerton, Leeds

A final type of centre focuses on locations that become significant to people because they hold restorative connotations. That outdoor settings have a capacity to benefit human health and well-being has become well established by research, particularly in the field of environmental psychology. Christopher Day puts it this way. "If you've ever been somewhere that renewed energy, bathed you in calm, inspired you, you will know that places can actually be *health-giving*" (Day, 2002, p.182). Throughout history outdoor settings have frequently been created to engender restorative benefit in people, for example, by being spiritually uplifting or by stimulating benefits to physical and psychological health. In this context the term restorative refers to the potential of outdoor settings to deliver a general sensation of revival or renewal mitigating the stress and mental fatigue which can arise from prolonged exposure to some aspects of urban environments. As the Kaplans pointed out (1998), most people appear to become routinely fatigued because of the need to continuously manage increasing amounts and competing sources of information. The term information overload has long since crept into the lexicon of contemporary Western culture, highlighting that maintaining a focus on what one needs or wants to do whilst trying to screen out surrounding distractions often requires significant effort. The greater the effort expended the quicker that mental fatigue will result, generating the need for restorative and refreshing experience. When places are found by people that can, for them, deliver this kind of respite they can

assume a particular significance because of the associations with pleasure and relaxation. Once again this can be experienced at a wide range of scales. People will associate restorative experience with locations that are very small where escape and contemplation might be focused on oneself as an individual. Equally, much larger places might stand out as significant as a totality because they are associated with restorative experiences in a more general sense, as oases offering retreat from busy city life (Figure 5.16).

As a consequence of our theoretical review and field observations we can begin to appreciate some of the characteristics of outdoor settings that seem particularly associated with restorative potential. In general these emphasise the importance of material elements and spatial configurations that can draw together the physical and mental worlds stimulating the mind to wander, to contemplate and wonder, and find satisfaction in the realisation of expectations. This tends to happen where people can feel they are separated from unwanted distractions such as confusing or attention grabbing features like signs, adverts, shop displays and crowds, for example, and where they feel safe from actual or perceived dangers engendering a feeling of security and retreat from stimulation: places where one's guard can be allowed to be let down. Although restorative experiences tend to be more readily associated with places of retreat, they also need to be visually and physically accessible so they feel welcoming. Often this means that restorative places in urban settings are usually close to main points of circulation. Opportunities for physical and psychological comfort are also important attributes. Physical and micro-climatic shelter as well as opportunities to sit, lie and maybe sleep all help to induce a sense of tranquillity and offer a chance to do nothing. The sense of tranquillity also appears to be strongly associated with contact with nature in some form, so physical and visual access to flora, fauna, water, sky, and natural sounds such as wind, leaves rustling, bird song, moving water etc., are all valuable stimulants of a restorative experience. Complete passivity is not always necessary however and so opportunities to interact with the environment, through physical and psychological engagement with the space and

5.16
Centres of restorative benefit at different levels of scale

5.17

The kinds of places that may become significant to people for the restorative benefit they can bring

contents are important. This might involve opportunities to make temporary spatial claims through the provision of moveable chairs, for example. This kind of interactive experience appears to be important in helping to generate a gradual attachment of significance over repeated visits through the building up of overlapping memories (Figure 5.17).

The environmental characteristics of centres' significant for restorative benefit can be summarised thus.

Restorative benefit
– Separation from distraction.
– Comfort and shelter.
– Provision for rest.
– Presence of nature (trees, water, natural materials).

– Stimulating features (psychological engagement).

Putting this altogether we find that we have an emerging model describing a set of provisional environmental characteristics for centre as the spatial expression of the experience of location. It shows that there are environmental characteristics associated with centres in general and there are also additional characteristics that are particular to different types of centre. The different types represent different ways in which people come to attach significance and value to locations. This model is summarised in the following diagram (Figure 5.18).

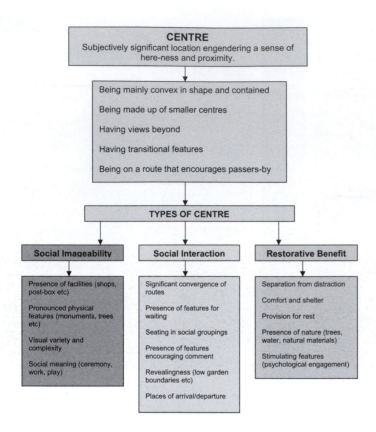

CENTRE
Subjectively significant location engendering a sense of
here-ness and proximity.

Being mainly convex in shape and contained

Being made up of smaller centres

Having views beyond

Having transitional features

Being on a route that encourages passers-by

TYPES OF CENTRE

Social Imageability	Social Interaction	Restorative Benefit
Presence of facilities (shops, post-box etc)	Significant convergence of routes	Separation from distraction
Pronounced physical features (monuments, trees etc)	Presence of features for waiting	Comfort and shelter
Visual variety and complexity	Seating in social groupings	Provision for rest
Social meaning (ceremony, work, play)	Presence of features encouraging comment	Presence of nature (trees, water, natural materials)
	Revealingness (low garden boundaries etc)	Stimulating features (psychological engagement)
	Places of arrival/departure	

5.18
The conceptual model for centre

Direction

The discussion about the development of centre characteristics highlighted that centres do not exist in isolation to other kinds of spatial experience. In fact the very sensation of location seems to depend on the simultaneous awareness of a realm beyond the immediately proximate. Our ability to comprehend the sensation of here-ness requires that we can place this in relation to the surroundings, otherwise the sensation tends towards claustrophobia. Gordon Cullen understood this relationship when he said in his exploration of the structure of townscape that "no sooner do we postulate a HERE than automatically we must create a THERE, for you cannot have one without the other" (Cullen, 1971, p.10). Awareness of there is encapsulated by the experience of direction.

Our explorations showed that the sensation of direction can be conceptualised by three interconnecting categories of experience which link together the here and there. The first one we have

called linear containment. This refers to a general sense of containment that draws attention to a spatial continuity and this is influenced most by attributes of the enclosing surfaces. Linear containment is what presents the awareness of the possibility of continuity and presents a way of realising that possibility. In a sense this gives the directional sensation its own sense of here, but this time with a linear rather than locational emphasis. The second one, which we have called route, extends beyond the awareness of a potential continuity to the actual act of going from here to there. In this category, environmental attributes that predominate are those that relate to ease of movement, the clarity of the primary route and its relationship to people's intentions and how this is supported in particular by floorscape. Finally there is the category of directional experience that provides the motivation for moving from here to there. There has to be the incentive provided by generating a sense of anticipation: that there might be something desirable or perhaps as yet unknown that encourages us to want to access, or possibly just contemplate, realms beyond. Environmental attributes that seem most to stimulate the sense of anticipation include what we can see and hear, and what we can imagine. There appears to be a need for things which catch our attention, but also for the setting to give the impression of holding something back, encouraging a sense of mystery and the tease of future possibility.

Before looking at these categories of experience in more detail we should first consider again the question of emphasis. In the discussion about centres we highlighted that an excessive sense of location can be induced in situations where there is little or no simultaneous awareness of direction and transition. At extremes this may lead to isolation and claustrophobia, and may even undermine the sensation of location as a consequence of the disorienting effect of not being able to sense where one is in relation to the wider surroundings. So, just as too much centre may have a negative impact on the experience of location and proximity, the same seems to be true for direction. In this case however, this appears to highlight a difference between the sensation of direction and the quality of the experience of direction (Figure 5.19).

5.19

A fulfilling direction experience must have some centred and transitional attributes

If we consider the two pictures here, it seems clear that the left one presents quite a strong sense of direction but few people would probably see this as a place likely to provide a good quality of experience. The picture on the right also has many of the attributes of direction but seems to offer a more fulfilling experience: it just looks more interesting. This appears to be partly because, as well as the presence of directional attributes, there are also those that relate to centre and transitional experiences. The conclusion from our investigation of this is that, just as a fulfilling centre must have directional and transitional attributes, a fulfilling direction must have some centred and transitional attributes. This implies that the principle difference between centre and direction is not mutual independence as discrete spatial entities but a question of what emphasis of centre, direction and transition appears manifest at particular locations. In the case of centre, the presence of direction and transition appears to contribute to a sense of orientation, whereas in the case of direction the presence of centre and transition seems to contribute to the enhancement of the quality of experience.

The picture on the left is an example of a situation where the perspective effect of the floorscape, coupled with an apparent absence of anything engaging in the foreground, extrudes awareness to the distance with such dramatic force that it completely overwhelms the sensation of here. It is not, of course, that the sense of here has gone, just that the sense of direction speaks much more loudly in this context. The photograph on the right is also an example of where there is a predominance of the sensation of direction, this time because of the linear containment of the narrow street, the perspective impact of the floor material and, to some extent, the focal effect of the light at the end of the street. However, here the extrusion effect on awareness appears far less powerful. This seems partly because the perspective effect, although clearly evident, is less dramatic, and partly because the slight recess in the building line to the right side helps to compete by maintaining our awareness of here. Where the building line returns to narrow the pavement this creates a slight sensation of transition marking the point where the shop frontage is left. In this example it is as though the smooth and uninterrupted directionality evident in the left photograph has been replaced with a rougher, grainy quality that weakens the directionality a little with a competing awareness of centre and transition. But if too many of the attributes associated with centre and transition are present then these can oppose the essential attributes of direction and weaken it to a point where it is no longer the predominant sensation. For example, façade continuity is an important attribute stimulating the sensation of direction. However continuity taken to the extreme of monotonous uniformity, like that in the left photograph of one of the less charming parts of Barcelona, is unlikely to deliver a sufficiently fulfilling experience. It is better if the overall sense of continuity is punctuated with visual complexity and variety along its length. These are attributes associated with centre because they contribute to attracting and holding attention and therefore are likely to induce locational sensations. Too much visual complexity, though, may become so distracting that the sensation of direction becomes shrouded out, whereas too little

leads to an experience that is monotonous and uninviting. The ideal, rather like this street in York, appears to be a question of subtle adjustments in the balance of CDTA rather than of emphatic insistence on one to the expense of the others (Figure 5.20).

Summary

The experience of direction can be understood then to consist of a combination of sensations related to how we come to an appreciation of the relationship between a here and a there and how we make the transition between them mentally and physically. Linear continuity represents the experience of a kind of containment through which we become aware of a sense of direction and can identify its route. This seems to relate quite closely to centre in that it can be conceptualised as a sense of location that has become stretched out and elongated making a kind of conduit rather than a specifically proximate experience. Environmental attributes that stimulate this sensation seem to focus on the way that

5.20

It is better if the overall sense of continuity is punctuated with visual complexity and variety along its length

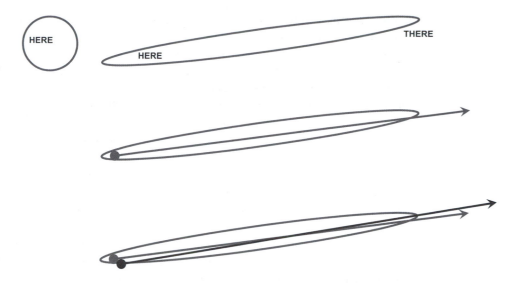

5.21
Linear containment can be thought of as a sense of location, or centre, which has become elongated to form a conduit

5.22
Route now combines with movement determining the means by which to get from here to there

5.23
Anticipation provides the incentive to engage with the realm beyond

5.24
The conceptual model for direction

containing surfaces emphasise what is ahead: by developing a visual rhythm perhaps emphasising perspective, and by not drawing too much of our attention to specific locations along them, for example. In some instances actual physical containment might not exist at all. A sense of perceptual containment can arise in situations where, for example, a strong visual focus attracts the attention to such an extent that the visual field appears to contract, diminishing awareness of what lies in the periphery of vision (Figure 5.21).

The route aspect of direction introduces a more dynamic or kinetic experience relating to the prospect of traversing the divide between here and there. Environmental attributes that relate to this are those which reveal an actual path upon which to travel should one wish to take it and that it is clear, accessible and distinguishable from adjacent, and relatively speaking, minor routes (Figure 5.22).

Finally, anticipation stimulates the prospect of future possibility providing the incentive, accentuating awareness of a there. Environmental attributes that relate to this are those that can stimulate a sense of mystery and anticipation, an encouragement to explore. In this respect visual stimuli appear to predominate but equally a distant sound or smell might induce the same effect (Figures 5.23, 5.24).

DIRECTION
Subjectively significant continuity engendering a sense of there-ness and future possibility

Stimulated by the perception of:

Linear containment *(awareness of the possibility of continuity and how to realise it)*
Route *(the actual act of going from here to there)*
Anticipation *(the incentive or motivation for going)*

CONSTITUENTS OF DIRECTION

Kinetic	Sensory
Enclosure	Exploration and mystery
Rhythm	View, smell, sound
Non-engaging facades	Deflective facades
Ease of movement	Linearity of floorscape
Clear primary route	

Transition

The sensation of transition is what allows us to experience differences between adjacent places. At the most fundamental level a transitional sensation is what occurs at the point where adjacent places that have distinguishable characteristics collide. This implies that transitions are in some sense an inevitable consequence of what happens at the boundaries of places: a by-product of the way spatial arrangement happens in the world. This appears to be the view taken by Norberg-Schulz (1971) when he describes transitions as the glue that binds together other spatial components to form a coherent whole. Whilst this adhesive analogy is useful in conceptualising the nature of transitional experience, it overlooks a more complex picture because it tends to suggest that transitions are perhaps rather fleeting, spatially insubstantial entities that do little more than mark boundaries. Another way to look at transition is consider what it contributes to the development of a spatial language.

In the previous discussion about centre and direction we emphasised that these spatial experiences do not manifest themselves as discrete, independent entities, somehow arranged side-by-side for us to pass through. Instead they seem to appear to us as a seamless continuity of place experience that we are an active part of and that changes in emphasis in a fluid and dynamic way according to the environmental attributes present, their scale, and the meanings and associations that people project onto them though routine use. This kind of continuity seems very much like the way that written language works. The different feelings and emotions experienced as one reads a novel for example are stimulated by variations in the arrangement of a relatively small range of letters and other symbols: relative, that is, by comparison to the practically infinite breadth of their potential psychological impact. Our understanding of written language depends to a very large extent on the presence of punctuation marks. These break down an otherwise seamless flow of letters and words into manageable and comprehensible packets and they also show us what emphasis is to be given to different passages as we read. Richness, rhythm and fluidity, or the poetic quality of the text, depends on the existence of different kinds of punctuation. If we only had full stops to use, for example, reading would be a very jerky, mechanical and probably a generally unrewarding experience.

Transition is the punctuation of spatial language. Just as with punctuation in text it allows us to experience spatial continuity as sequences of comprehensible passages by intervening in the continuity at intervals to provide rhythm and structure to the whole. Sometimes this may be abrupt and dramatic, perhaps contributing to a sense of excitement and stimulation, like moving through the relatively narrow doorway of a gothic cathedral before the immediate revelation of its majestic interior, for example. At other times it may be much softer and more subtle, encouraging the passage between places to be experienced gradually, inducing a calmer and more fluid adjustment in mood. So, just as there are different kinds of punctuation mark to generate comprehension in text, so there are different kinds of transition that help comprehension in the spatial realm. Our investigations have identified four distinguishable types which we have called threshold, corridor, segment and ephemeral.

Threshold

A threshold is probably the simplest form of transition because it occurs in an instant defined usually by quite an abrupt contrast on either side of it. Although it is spatially the smallest transition it can create the most impact because of its immediate and abrupt nature. Thresholds tend to be characterised by marked changes in material, texture, colour, form and shape, level and direction, for example. The gateway illustrated below delivers a very strong threshold experience because it combines many of these attributes in a small, but visually distinctive, spatial concentration (Figure 5.25).

Corridor

A corridor is spatially more expansive than a threshold in that it delivers its transitional experience gradually rather than abruptly. It usually takes the form of a restricted and directed passage connecting two or more spaces. In many ways corridors possess quite strong directional qualities. However, their generally small-scale, relatively short distance, clearly defined entrance and exit, and lack of internally interesting features that might hold particular attention, all work to emphasise the sensation of passing through rather than of a more general sensation of continuity. Environmental attributes that characterise corridors include linear continuity of materials and framed views. They also generally have a tangible human scale coupled with a sense of safety (Figure 5.26).

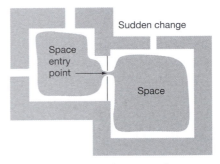

Sudden change

With a narrowing down between walls,
perhaps with a gate

5.25
Threshold

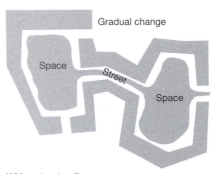

Gradual change

With a street or linear space

5.26
Corridor

Segment

A segment defines a type of transitional experience of a more complex kind than threshold and corridor. One of the defining features of a corridor is that it links together two or more spaces but does not have any particular locational qualities of its own that might encourage interaction with it in its own right. A segment recognises that sometimes a strong sense of transition might be accompanied by a sensation that there are also locational qualities present as well, making a kind of hybrid between transition and centre. Segments are usually formed from the overlapping of two adjacent spaces and as such possess characteristics that appear as a continuity of both, making a place with its own particular qualities. This is different from a corridor which joins two spaces that would without it be physically independent from one another. A strong segment might have a central focal point, choices of direction, and attributes that encourage psychological or physical engagement within it. Segments are often the spatial entities that soften the stark linearity and hard unbroken edges between spaces, instead allowing adjacent spaces to integrate and flow into one another. Arcades, colonnades, street cafés, porches and landings that protrude from buildings to link with adjacent open space are places where segments are likely to be experienced (Figure 5.27).

Ephemeral

An ephemeral transition recognises qualities of the environment that can generate strong transitional sensations but are not permanent features. These include in particular the transient effects of sun and shade patterns, variations in temperature, and wet to dry in rainy weather. There are also seasonal features, particularly changes in vegetation at all scales due to flowering properties that introduce seasonal changes in colour and scent, emergent leaves in spring, the gradual development of autumnal shades before falling off to reveal winter branches. The photograph opposite shows an example of how the transition between an open glade and woodland is enhanced by the contrast of sun and shade (Figures 5.28, 5.29).

Area

The last component in the experiential landscape concept is perhaps more general and less tangible than the other three and it has a different role. In this chapter we have discussed how experiential landscape is conceptualised as a holistic collective of centre, direction and transition and area. Each component has its own particular experiential character relating to specific aspects of routine outdoor experience and we have detailed how these components are themselves constituted in finer detail. CDTA are the building blocks of experiential landscape place and different kinds of places become manifest in the world as a consequence of how these components weave together. All are present everywhere but to varying degrees of emphasis and scale which, rather like the ripples, swirls and eddies that make the underlying forces of a river current visible, reveal localised characteristics of place experience

5.27
Segments tend to occur where there are adjacent spaces with a softer edge between them

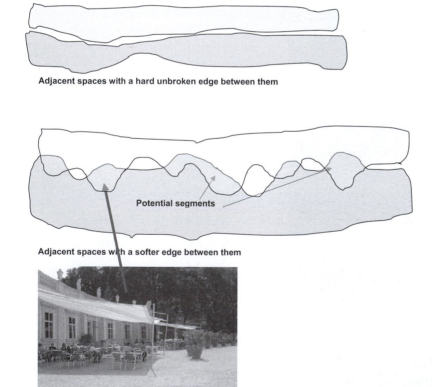

Adjacent spaces with a hard unbroken edge between them

Potential segments

Adjacent spaces with a softer edge between them

The contrasting quality of light gives
a sense of progression

5.28
Ephemeral

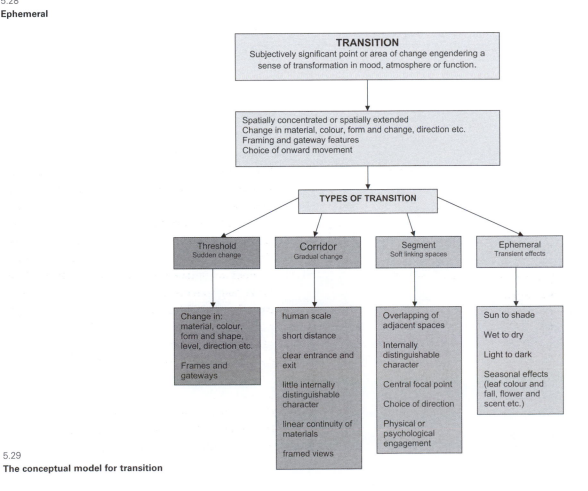

5.29
The conceptual model for transition

within the overall continuity that defines the experiential landscape (Figure 5.30).

For example, this photograph of the North Yorkshire town of Knaresborough, the same view more famously used in Christopher Alexander's *Timeless Way of Building*, can be understood as an experiential landscape. It is the visible manifestation of an unbroken field of place experience at different levels of scale and characteristic. But, at the same time, Knaresborough is obviously more than this. It has qualities and characteristics as a whole that transcend the sum of its constituent parts. It appears to display an internally consistent quality that gives it its own unique and recognisable identity, a common texture that can be stepped inside of and experienced as a whole. This is what the component area defines. Area is at one and the same time the product of combinations of centre, direction and transition, and a recognisable entity in itself as a whole. Area is a quality of the experiential landscape as a whole, whereas centre, direction and transition are qualities of the smaller experiential landscapes places which coalesce to form it. Area is the quality that

gives an experiential landscape its sense of identity and is part of what makes it possible to distinguish Knaresborough from New York. Within this overall coherence there is a great deal of fine grain variation apparent at all locations: this is what makes Knaresborough experientially rich rather than monotonous. But the variation does not exist to a level that destroys the sense of overall coherence, pattern and rhythm. Area then is the property of our surroundings that transcends the collective impact of fine grain variations with a larger scale sense of coordination, or thematic continuity, so that we can experience a wider sense of being somewhere rather than somewhere else. It is both made up from centre, direction and transition and simultaneously forms the background against which they work together in an internally consistent fashion. Sienna and Florence exhibit area-ness, or thematic continuity, that is similar but not the same, whereas by comparison New York has an entirely different sense of area. All provide a recognisable, enveloping sensation within which other kinds of sensations work (Figure 5.31).

5.30
The North Yorkshire town of Knaresborough

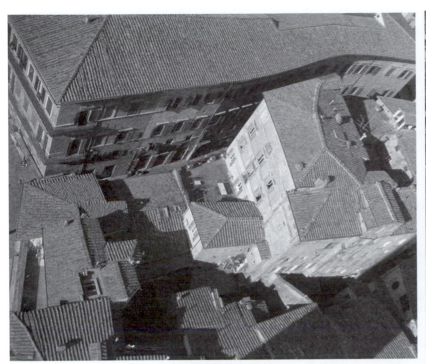

5.31
The organic qualities of Florence and Sienna streetscape deliver similar sensations of area whilst the characteristic gridiron layout of New York has quite a different one

5.32
A range of distinguishable areas can be experienced in the alleys that radiate from the main high street in Kendal

---

AREA
Subjectively significant realm engendering a sense of coherence and containment

↓

Thematic continuity
    Rhythm, pattern
    Co-ordination in texture, space and form, detail and symbol, building type, use and activity, degree of maintenance, topography.

Degree of privacy
    Private, semi-private, semi-public, public

Made up of integrations of centre, direction and transition in continuity

Made up of other areas

5.33
The conceptual model for area

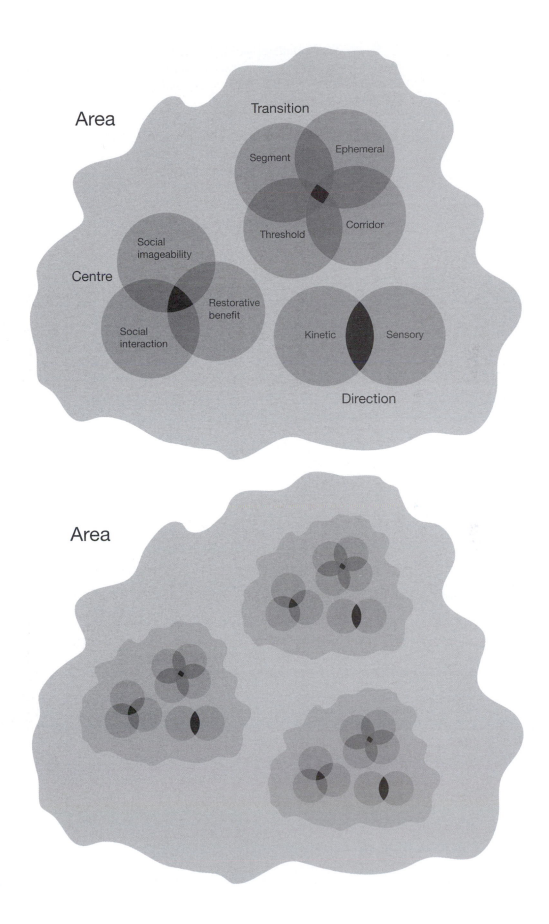

5.34
The holistic relationship of CDTA

Area also has a similar characteristic to centre in that areas can be experienced within areas. So just as the sense of location can be strengthened if there is a range of locational experience in roughly the same place (in other words that strong centres tend to be made up from smaller centres), so areas also aggregate to form larger ones. This may appear in terms of distinguishable urban quarters, for example, relating to cultural, functional or social issues, or it might be related to perceptions of degrees of privacy and public-ness. In the Cumbrian town of Kendal, for example, a range of distinguishable areas can be experienced in the alleys that radiate from the main high street. Some are semi-private residential places, others have a primarily retail purpose and are more public. They all coalesce however to give structure and character that together define the wider identity of Kendal as a recognisable town in its own right (Figures 5.32, 5.33, 5.34).

Chapter 6

Reading the experiential landscape

Introduction

An experiential landscape is not an objective phenomenon in the sense that it already exists out there in a predetermined form waiting to be discovered. Revealing and then interpreting it is a primarily qualitative pursuit. Ask 10 trained and experienced landscape or urban design professionals to record their place perceptions of a particular setting and you will get 10 different results, even if instructions given to them about how they should interpret the concept of place perception is very precise. There is likely to be some common ground governed by their shared professional background and expertise, but there will be many significant differences. This also applies if you ask the same of 10 inhabitants of the same neighbourhood, although here our experience shows that the differences far outweigh any commonality because the relationship that people develop with their home surroundings is so intensely personal. The central point is, though, that it makes no sense at all to ask which of these is right and which is wrong, and it makes no sense to ask which is better, more valuable, more significant, more important etc. We simply do not have any way available to us of giving sensible, reasonable answers to those questions. The reality is that they are all right because, just like a fingerprint, place perception is something that is unique to the

individual and is driven by a raft of personal predisposition, preference and prejudice, influenced by cultural, social, educational and professional factors, and much more besides (Figure 6.1).

So what are we to make of this in terms of how we reveal and read the experiential landscape? The approach developed is based on the idea of layering information drawn from individuals and given a graphical representation, and then by inductive reasoning searching for what appears to be significant from the mosaic of visual information produced. This requires interpretative skills that can be quickly acquired and which have intellectual foundations in a branch of qualitative research that deals with coding and categorisation procedures. Particularly helpful in this respect are the general principles that underpin grounded theory. Grounded theory is a methodology for qualitative research originally developed in the 1960s for use in the social sciences. Whilst this remains the principal field of application it has since been successfully applied in other related fields. Fundamentally it provides for the development of theory through the systematic collection and analysis of data through conceptualisation and categorisation procedures based on questions asked, and the identification of comparisons and differences in data which is usually derived from field observations and inter-

6.1
These two plans show the results of early experiments carried out to develop mapping techniques for layering with GIS computer software. The map at the top reveals the pattern of the experiential landscape for 10 residents in this area. The one on the bottom is the same area but in this case represents the experiential landscape recorded by 10 postgraduate landscape architecture students

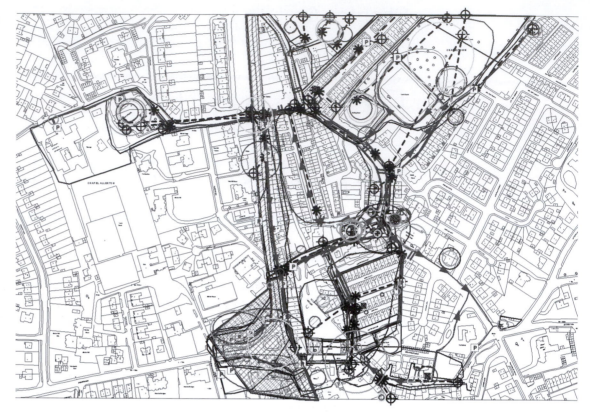

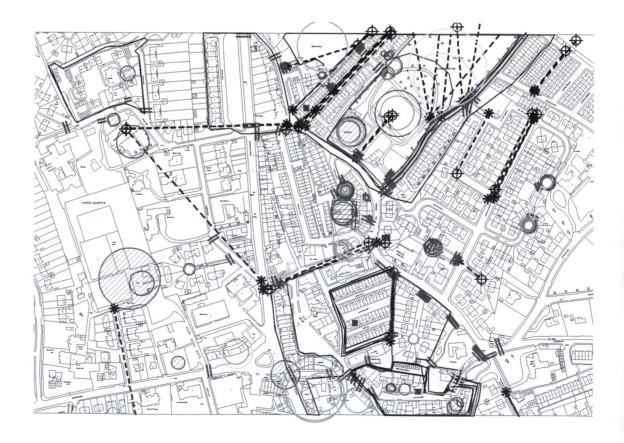

views. Conclusions are therefore inductively derived from the specific field of study. Grounded theory scholars will quickly realise that the methods we describe for applying the concept of experiential landscape in no way constitutes a grounded theory study in the conventionally understood sense. Instead it builds from techniques derived from grounded theory as a basis from which to develop a structured approach to gathering relevant information, recording and then interpreting findings. What follows is a general account of these three stages of the experiential landscape approach. The first deals with gathering the information from which experiential characteristics of a setting can be induced. The second stage is concerned with recording the information and specifically how it is coded in terms of CDTA and given graphical expression as experiential landscape maps. The final stage is about how these maps can be interpreted.

Information gathering: specialist training and user experience

In virtually every practical situation concerned with the study or redesign of an existing outdoor setting, there will be an individual, or more likely a team of individuals, with relevant training and experience initiating and leading the work. The big question is, and this is one that has been exercising the minds of nearly everybody concerned with design and management of the outdoors for years, what is the proper role of these people in the process? There is neither the time nor space here to review the merits of the myriad arguments about the extent of professional interventions versus the merits of public participation. The gist of it though lies with the moral authority a person can claim, who does not live in or use a setting, to make judgments that will affect change in that setting. Contemporary society, in general, bestows that authority on individuals and groups by virtue of specialised training. Speaking momentarily as an educator of landscape architects, it is important, useful and right that this should be so, and this is because of two things. The first is that most people thus educated generally possess unusually acute spatial awareness, and the second is that they are trained to take an overview of a situation, placing details in wider contexts; spatial, cultural, disciplinary, for example. These are valuable attributes when it comes to understanding the concept of place in the outdoor world, but they will never be sufficient because they simply cannot access the minds of those who use a setting. A professional's eye view of place in settings unfamiliar to them arises from theory and concepts learnt and experience of their application, it might also include a certain amount of personal intuition. But a setting's users' perspective arises from authentic lived experience in that setting and this is quite different when it comes to place perception. This is not to say that the place perceptions of professional outsiders are wrong, they are not. They simply highlight different aspects and so, in terms of a full picture of quality of place in a setting, are incomplete. In this sense the moral authority of professionals in planning and design situations should be thought of as conditional. This means either accepting the status of their findings as limited, in fact crucially limited, or accepting an obligation to strengthen their authority by incorporating the user perspective.

The experiential landscape approach is people oriented. It depends first and foremost on being able to accumulate information about the way people perceive their surroundings loosely in terms of three experiential themes of place attachment, orientation and neighbourhood awareness. To achieve this we need to know something about what aspects of the lives and surroundings of people lead them to identify and perhaps come to value particular objects, features or locations in their daily routines. We also want to know what, for them, stands out from the general background, perhaps because it has some sort of visual prominence, for example, or because it might have a particular meaning or emotional attachment. This information may point to particular locational attachments, or it might equally begin to reveal orientation devices that people use consciously or subconsciously to navigate. Identifying frequently used routeways and what happens, or is seen or heard, or felt along them adds further dimensions of detail which can hold clues again about special locations, or about patterns of movement. It can also help to reveal where particular experiences of change occur, either very locally in terms of small changes in direction, level, mood, atmosphere, or function, for example. Or it could be something much stronger that might signal where someone feels they have transcended what they might intuitively feel to be their homeground, the place of familiarity, safety, or personal control, and have entered a more public, shared realm where different rules and feelings apply. Sometimes this might be quite abrupt and immediate, startling almost, or sometimes it might grow very gradually, or happen in incremental stages. All of this holds clues about how people come to perceive their place in the surroundings of their daily routines. It makes up the internal geographies of individuals defined by the way that certain parts of the homogenous background shared by all come to prominence because of associations given to them, for whatever reason, by that individual. This is very much an experiential geography but one that is intimately bound together with elements of the material and spatial world routinely encountered. Such internal geographies have very real but hidden dimensions and it is the purpose of experiential landscape to try to make explicit this otherwise implicit order so that it can be explored, a bit like how an X-ray image reveals hidden dimensions of anatomical structure, but with one crucial difference: anatomical structure has a determinate form but is hidden from view, the experiential landscape is fundamentally indeterminate and is actually generated by the process of revealing.

To achieve this, the experiential landscape approach develops from the principles of cognitive mapping, a technique pioneered several decades ago in environmental psychology whereby people's mental image of their surroundings is exposed, often so that it can be compared with the physical arrangement of the actual surroundings. It owes much in terms of inspiration to Lynch and Rivkin's paper, "A Walk Around the Block", first published in the journal *Landscape* in 1959. This was probably the first time, certainly in the context of urban planning and design, that human emotions were associated with spatial characteristics arising from

analysis of people's direct perceptions of an ordinary streetscape. One of the more profound hypotheses to emerge from this simple study was that "the individual must perceive his environment as an ordered pattern, and is constantly trying to inject order into his surroundings, so that all the relevant perceptions are jointed one to the other" (Lynch and Rivkin, 1959). This implies two important things about place perception that are central to experiential landscape. One is its intrinsically holistic nature in that people seem instinctively driven to see localised places as part of a larger coherent whole. This impulse is supported where some sense of overall coordination is evident in a setting, whether this is visual or functional, for example. The second is that where there is no explicit sense of coherence to a setting, then order is injected into it through habitual use and familiarity which allows people over time to pull it together into a whole by means of associated meanings. This latter form of order does not have an immediately accessible visual form that can be appreciated, say by city regeneration experts or environmental design professionals, but it is nonetheless profoundly real and equally at risk from inappropriate interventions. One of the aims of developing a way to operationalise the experiential landscape concept is to try to make this hidden form of order visible.

This figure symbolises the approach we have developed to try to achieve this. It shows a range of ways to obtain information that reveals different aspects of the relationship between people and the places they use. In general it is intended to be a practical response to the realisation we alluded to earlier, that perceptions of place in the outdoor environment are quite different depending on who you are and what your relationship with the setting under investigation is. This principle underpins most approaches to participative design and the important thing here is what this means in terms of developing as full an understanding of place experience as possible. In this figure we differentiate between sources of information, which contribute differently to a full understanding of place experience. Some sources are from outside specialists, representing those with training in spatial design who do not

Semi-structured interviewing

Conversation

Role play

Anthropological tracking

Non-participant observation

Professional reading of site

6.2

The experiential landscape increases in clarity and resolution by gathering information in a range of different ways

routinely use or inhabit the setting, and others from internal users, representing those who do use the setting routinely. The figure shows that the optimum situation is one in which place perceptions of both can be obtained. It also shows that the best way to gather the necessary information from internal users is by means of semi-structured interviews where this is possible and we will detail what we mean by this later.

There is another important issue, however, that has emerged from our experiences in field and studio work and this is how frequently difficult it is, for a wide range of practical reasons, to achieve this optimal situation. The key question here is if, for whatever reason, it is not possible to interview enough, or possibly any, internal users, does that mean that you cannot say useful things about the experiential potential or characteristics of the setting you are concerned with? Our answer to this question is no. You can say useful things, it is just that you only get a partial picture and if you have to rely only on information generated by external specialists it is likely to be very partial indeed. Like the image at the bottom of the figure what you get is a faint impression of the experiential landscape. It lacks resolution because it is generated from place perceptions of people cultured in a specialised way of looking at the external environment who do not have personal

or emotional attachments in that setting. It also lacks stability for the same reason: change the outside specialists and the image of the experiential landscape they generate will not be the same. But even if it is not possible to interview the setting's internal users, successively better resolution and stability can be acquired by using other methods that give insight into aspects of the way people use the setting. These include non-participant observation, anthropological tracking, role-play and conversation and we will talk about these methods and the contribution they can make to increase the resolution of the experiential landscape later.

The essential point here is that the experiential landscape is something that has no determinate form: it simply comes into being and increases in resolution and stability as a consequence of the information from which it is derived. As we shall see later, it is in fact doubtful that a fully complete impression of experiential landscape can ever be achieved, because it is by definition, partly experience, and that aspect of it depends on who is doing the experiencing, and this will change for different individuals and indeed for the same individuals over time. The experiential landscape is only that which emerges from the information derived from those who participate at a particular time. Clarity of resolution and stability of image will grow the higher up the figure one is able to get (Figure 6.2).

First, we will focus on how outside specialist place perceptions are obtained and what specific contribution this makes to the experiential landscape approach and then move on to look at the processes used for revealing those of the settings users, highlighting where relevant what the relationship is between them.

Outside specialists

The role of the outside specialist in the experiential landscape approach essentially has two aspects. The first is that an experiential landscape map produced as a result of a professional survey has proven to provide a useful benchmark against which to structure and steer a subsequent user group survey. The second aspect is that there are various circumstances in which it might not always be possible to access a user group from

6.3

The experiential landscape is only that which emerges from the information derived from those who participate at a particular time. Regular patterns of occupation may not always be apparent to outside specialists

whom to draw meaningful information. The most obvious example is for projects that are still in the planning and design stages, but this might extend in some circumstances to those in the formative stages of a phased construction, or those that are completed but for which occupation or use is yet very immature. In these situations it is still possible, worthwhile and useful to obtain insight into the experiential potential implicit in the proposed spatial structure of the scheme. It is just that this can only be done to a relatively limited degree because it cannot incorporate patterns of place perception that develop through established use and occupation (Figure 6.3). Nevertheless it is still important and valuable to do so and we show examples of this kind of work in chapter eight: "reading the experiential landscape in residential settings". It can be accomplished in the following ways.

At the most basic level a professional experiential landscape survey can be considered a scoping, or reconnaissance exercise carried out to give an initial impression of patterns of experiential character for the setting under investigation. This involves the professional team recording where they perceive CDTA to be from observation of the spatial and material properties of the site, or graphical and virtual imagery if the site is not yet built. This can be done collectively as a group, but

better still individually so that the findings of each individual can be collated into a collective view, and we will explain how this happens later on. This latter tends to provide a more complete picture, whereas the former often reflects the inevitable compromises arising out of discussion and negotiation. It is important to realise that the professional team is relying on their understanding of the properties and characteristics of outdoor space that are associated with the spatial sensations inherent in CDTA, the basis of which is given by the experiential landscape conceptual framework. The resulting experiential landscape map, in essence, represents a set of theoretical principles projected onto the site in question via the interpretative skills of the professional team. This bares some similarity, in principle rather than detail, with Hillier and Hanson's work in the mid 1980s in which they show a relationship between the social functioning of residential settlements and their spatial configuration. By analysing maps of settlements to reveal patterns of spatially contained locations and lines of vision they proposed a way of quantifying a social logic of space. In practical terms, our own experimental field work shows that an effective way to gather the necessary information about a site from which to then produce the experiential landscape map is

Experiential Landscape Place Research
Field Record Set

SCALE: 1:1250.

PROJECT:

LOCATION: little London.

DATE: 3/5/01.

SUBJECT: field micl

STATUS: KT + IUS.

VENUE: Walk rowl.

CONDITIONS: rain

1) *Evidence of n'hood but discrete & separated by areas of un-correlated* ... *islands in isolation. but separated by great distance. There is potential for the cluster to become a more defined n'hood.*

2) *Transitions - most implied not strongly defined + exit in isolation rather than join between centres or areas.*

SUBJECT
PROJECT

CENTRE - POSITIVE *Social Imageability*

Ref	Locn	What	Significance
Csp1	Street Corner	bench / street cover.	physical features. Stand out for rest of background :- i) corner ii) others. people watching pedestrial iii) presence of bench + small lawn trees to frame it + offer sense of security iv) strong presence of vegetation to wall guy day domestic feely. v) wall offered security sense of enclosure when combined with trees.

site visit 1hr.
Mapp 1 1/2 hrs.

6.4

Early field observation methods proved to be cumbersome and a distraction to a more intuitive approach

by touring the site in a series of pedestrian journeys and recording a commentary of observations along the way. This is supplemented by photographs and written and graphical notes on a plan of the site as required (Figure 6.4).

In the early stages of our work to investigate the practical implications of experiential landscape we devised a detailed checklist detailing spatial and material properties our research had associated with CDTA with the intention of giving the survey tours enough guidance to make certain that observations made were sufficiently comprehensive and rigorous. In practice however, it quickly became apparent that whilst this worked quite well, it was immensely laborious and quite unnecessarily rigid. Experience gradually revealed that, instead of visiting the site with an armoury of clipboards, proforma sheets and other data gathering paraphernalia, this was best done in a more informal and relaxed way. This worked well because of the relative simplicity of the CDTA model. Although each of these spatial components holds quite a lot of complexity, differentiating between the different types of component and their constituent types, we found through a series of workshops and short training sessions that the essence of the model can be assimilated very quickly especially by those with spatial design training. Releasing research teams from the necessity to complete field records in the form originally devised allowed the mind of the observer to focus much more on the details of the setting. With practice, guided by general themes relating to CDTA, it rapidly became almost second nature to record the required information. The experience of doing this is very much like tuning in to a different way of looking at a setting: a kind of guided intuition which allows the trained

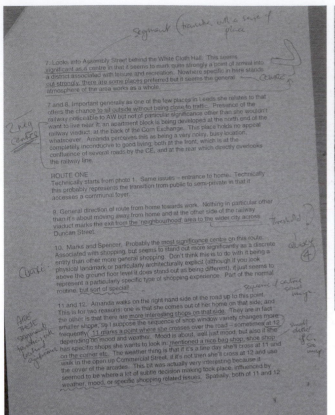

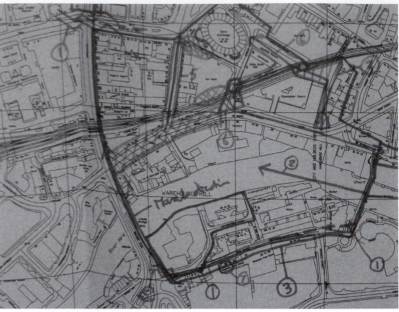

6.5

A partial transcript is made from voice recorded field observations and then coded to make experiential landscape maps which show the distribution of CDTA

observer some freedom to record what seems to stand out as important, by focusing on spatial volumes and material composition and thinking about the sort of sensations they appeared to engender. The voice recorded field observations then constitute the basic data for subsequent interpretation. This involves making a partial transcript, like the one in the figure above, which is then interpreted, using coding and categorisation procedures derived from the principles of grounded theory, to conceptualise the content in terms of CDTA. This information is then given a graphical form and mapped to show the pattern of CDTA that individuals perceive (Figure 6.5).

As we discussed earlier, experiential landscape maps produced this way give only a partial picture of the experiential character of a setting because they do not take into account user experience. But, in situations where access to user experience is not available, they still have considerable value in raising awareness of the experiential dimensions of spatial organisation in

a setting and can significantly augment conventional survey and analysis approaches as a consequence. The experiential landscape can however be given a better level of resolution by watching what people do.

Non-participant observation (Figure 6.6)

This technique involves the passive observation of the activities of groups or individuals with the intention to "understand practices, interactions, and events which occur in a specific context" (Flick, 1998). It provides access to the cultural mechanisms of a place as well as the spatial relationship that the site users have with their surroundings and can give detailed insights into the social lives and relationships of people. Observations are usually best carried out throughout a day to appreciate the intricacies and changes of patterns of use that occur in response to diurnal and activity based influences. Observations are usually recorded by taking notes, in text and diagrammatic form, sometimes

supplemented by photographs, which focus on behavioural tendencies and their spatial orientation. Symbolising observations graphically on plans is important and this coding framework provides the means to simplify recording and analysis of the process (Romice and Frey, 2003). The process helps to identify experiential charac-

teristics from the observations made and fixes these at the locations where they take place (Figure 6.7).

Take this street scene in Vienna, for example. To the outside specialist the water sculpture may appear to be a landmark, contributing mainly to the street's directional attributes. However, there are other dimensions revealed by watching what happens to the sculpture as people pass. On a warm June day, this girl is one of many observed stopping and putting her hand in the water before she goes on her way. Now the sculpture a not just a visual device on the street, it also appears to be a more significant location to local passers-by, generating a more pronounced sense of centre because it is a place to pause, or gather, and to stimulate conversation among people. It is also evident that it is delivering some restorative benefit with its sound, and cooling sensations as well as simply being fun!

Anthropological tracking

Another kind of observational approach involves watching for traces of people, rather than people themselves. The so-called desire lines that tend to develop in soft surfaces provide a familiar example of this because they leave visible evidence that the real patterns of pedestrian movement do not quite correspond with the designer's intentions. In this Milan square, the desire line draws attention to the attraction of a metal service cover which, for reasons unknown, appears to be a popular gathering point beneath a tree just out of shot (Figure 6.8).

A more subtle example can be seen in the picture opposite of the park entrance on Beacon Hill, Boston where the stone pier with curved railings emphasises the transition from the street into the park. On the floor here there is a lot of discarded chewing gum, cigarette ends and on the first stone course are two drinks cartons. What this tends to suggest is that, in addition to its evident transitional contribution as a park entrance, this location is a well used rest point. The curved stone wall beneath the railings is at a height and has enough top surface available to offer a seat in a sheltered recess by the park entrance with an excellent view of the activities along Beacon Hill. An observation of this kind argues for a richer experiential character at this location than at first might seem the case. As

6.9
Signs of occupation at the park entrance on Beacon Hill, Boston

well as being a strong transition, a threshold in fact, there is also sufficient evidence here to suggest that it may also, for some at least, be quite a complex centre: a sheltered vantage point to pause and wait for friends, to smoke, chew and drink (Figure 6.9).

Conversation (Figure 6.10)

It is too easy to overlook the value of casual conversation as a means of gaining insight into the way that public places are used because it seems rather unstructured and perhaps scientifically haphazard. But it is not always possible to explore in more detail observations made by the approaches detailed above by more systematic participant interviews. It is usually possible in public places, though, to ask someone, if of course it is safe and appropriate to do so. Returning to the Milan desire line we illustrated above, the tree where people gather is now in the right hand side of the picture. It is revealed from conversations on site that this is a regular gathering point for the distribution of drugs, and that the tree offers some degree of privacy as well as acting as a meeting point. It is conveniently sited to the bench on the

6.8
A well-trodden route in Milan

for social interaction, as the place where routine social contact occurs. The anti-social nature of the activity makes no difference to the sensation of centre subliminally experienced by its users. For other, more law-abiding members of the public who may have been witness to this activity, the sensation of centre may be equally strong, but this time in a negative sense, as a place to be avoided associated with illegal activity and potential threat.

Returning to the park in Boston MA (Figure 6.11), from an outsider's perspective it might be assumed that this place has a strongly directional character given mainly by the blockwork pattern in the floorscape, complimented by the avenue of trees, rhythm of the railings, and the focus provided by the steps at the end. There is also a sense of potential centre suggested by the seating and expectation of occupancy by placing a litter bin next to the group in the foreground. It is intriguing that no one ever seemed to occupy these seats, choosing instead to sit a few yards away. Here there is a similar collective of elements: a path, some trees and benches, yet this time the benches are nearly always occupied. Speaking to one of the bench occupants revealed that he preferred sitting here for several reasons: there was more room, the path was wider and you didn't feel like you were in the way of people walking along. You also felt you had some

6.10

A seat, but also a convenient step that partly explains the popularity of a nearby tree for the distribution of drugs

other side of the wall and this appears to act as a convenient place to more easily climb over the wall, conduct their business and then move off via the service cover and down to the street. Again, this information points to a complex experiential character here. The wall and bench are transitions and their existence here is to some extent why this location, over all the other apparently similar possibilities around, has been chosen for this purpose. For the dealers and their clients the tree and service cover makes a significant centre: for its social imageability given by the collective physical prominence of the bench, wall recess, service cover and tree, and because of the functional associations assigned to the place; and also

6.11
Unoccupied seats

6.12
Occupied seats

Role-play

In situations where user information is not accessible from personal contact, we have found that it can be useful to supplement information derived from other methods by adopting the technique of role-playing. Role-play, as a technique to give trained professionals a local or lay perspective, particularly in community oriented environmental improvement projects, is often used in training programmes for public participation, for example, The Neighbourhood Initiatives Foundation's Planning for Real approach. Our own experience in this respect has been developed through experimental design studios with students involved in landscape architecture higher education. For example, during a studio project designed primarily to develop and trial aspects of methodology for mapping the experiential landscape, half the student group involved acted as professional landscape architects briefed to undertake an experiential landscape survey of a residential site while the rest acted as residents who would be interviewed as participants in the process. The purpose of role-play in this context was to encourage the students to try to experience the environment through the eyes of fictitious locals. This process has obvious limitations because it is impossible to set aside entirely one's own personality, experiences and preferences but to make it as realistic as possible each of the resident students was assigned a character profile that was representative of people who might live in and use the area. To help them, analogy was made with actors assuming a character role for a play or film. The "actors" were each given a name, age and a detailed profile of their character's principal personality traits: likes and dislikes; leisure interests; occupation and place of work; family and friends. Each character was assumed to live at a real address that the students could locate in the site area. This helped them to ground their character with a sense of realism given by being able to imagine themselves living in an actual location

6.13
A runner's routine and the significance of a lamp post

privacy and shelter offered by the tree, and the trees in totality made a pleasant sense of cover. In experiential terms, then, this helps us to distinguish the experiential character of these two places. In the first, there is a sense of centre but weak by comparison to the strength evident in the directional attributes. This sends signals that it is a place to pass through and not a place of repose. The second place by comparison seems to offer a more balanced sensation of direction and centre. The man sitting on the bench also reported that he often saw the jogger, who had just passed by, always check his

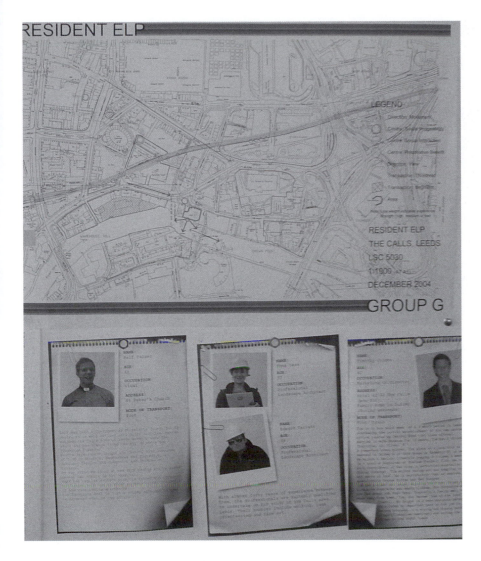

6.14

Using role-play to simulate the routines of site users

This may not be practical in every situation but it is clear from this work that the information arising from a process of role-playing adds considerably to the detail and depth of the experiential character revealed about the setting. This is simply because it forces a situation in which participants have to look at the setting through the eyes of someone likely to use it, or live there and although entirely fictitious, raises to the forefront of consciousness an attitude to the setting that would most likely have been otherwise overlooked. It helps to begin to supplement the theory led place perceptions of professionals that mainly tend to be influenced by what the setting looks like, with something a little deeper: the perspectives of those with a life in the setting, even though it is a made up one. In the absence of real users this approach can significantly improve on the professional perspective on place perception, particularly if some attention is given to assigning roles that can be located at a real address in the setting, as a dwelling or work place for example, and that the personality profile is a realistic one for that particular setting (Figure 6.14).

Semi-structured interviewing

This particular technique is a method frequently used in qualitative research when it is necessary to allow participants to range as naturally and freely as possible in their responses to questions whilst at the same time maintaining some underlying structure to the session. The way this usually works is to have predetermined topics that guide conversation allowing new questions or insights to evolve as the discussion develops. In some of the early pilot work a semi-structured interview framework was devised around a series of questions that tried to focus the conversation on each of the four spatial categories separately. The main reason for this was that we felt the subsequent analysis would be easier if the interview had already packaged, so to speak, responses into these categories. In practice we quickly realised that this was hopelessly naïve and betrayed a significant ignorance about the nature of effective interview practice and about the nature of place experience. We came to understand that it is pointless to try to dissect a person's routine environmental experience into discrete packages

and, more importantly, meant that they could develop a sense of a daily routine and pattern of movement to and from that address. Most of the students developed a graphical storyboard to help articulate this. The technique helped them to enrich their character and their daily life with details of where they might routinely meet with neighbours, walk their dog if they had one, sit and contemplate etc., gradually adopting the small details and idiosyncrasies that make up a particular human personality in relation to daily routines. Having become immersed in their characters these students were subsequently interviewed by one of the "professional" students and the details of their daily routines mapped in the experiential landscape format.

corresponding to the spatial types we were concerned with because place experience is an intrinsically complex and overlapping phenomenon. We had to adopt an approach to interviewing that was better tuned in with how people moved about their surroundings and so themed conversations gradually evolved that allowed participants to recreate mentally what they did and felt in as natural a way as possible.

The essential thing to note in terms of gathering the required information from users is that the experiential landscape concept determines an overall framework of content, or themes, for the semi-structured interviews, but that this is actually never used in this form in the field. This is because, in every case and for various reasons, the actual content of the interviews has to be adapted to suit the specific circumstances of the context. At the most fundamental level the purpose of the interview is to guide a participant to talk about their routine daily experiences of the outdoor environment in a conversational style. Guidance is given to steer them to think in different ways about locations that stand out for them for various reasons, about routes they routinely take and those they avoid, things they see along the way, places where they feel that a sense of change occurs, and about whether they can identify any kind of overall pattern or coordination. Table 6.1 summarises the overall interview framework for the experiential landscape concept and shows how the various questions and prompts are

Table 6.1 **The generic experiential landscape semi-structured interview framework**

Centre	Social imageability	Find out about places often visited, when, where and why.
		What they like to do and where do they go to do it.
		Are there places that has some sort of special appearance and if so what do they like about them.
	Social interaction	Where do they find they are most likely to bump into people.
		Where would they go and do things as part of a group.
		Are there particular places in public they regularly choose to use.
	Restorative benefit	Are there places where they go to think about things, if so where, and why do they go there.
		Where do they go to escape from their everyday routines.
		Where do they think there is a special place that they can engage with.
		What are the places that please them.
Direction	View	What particular views, features or landmarks do they notice and from where.
	Movement	When they walk around, which ways do they choose to go, in what direction and why do they go that way.
		Do they regularly stop or pause along the way.
Transition		Where do they feel there is a change in atmosphere and what is it that prompts this feeling.
		Are there any noticeable changes in level or entrances, gateways, exits, gaps and corridors that they notice.
Area		Where are there definite areas, and what is it that makes them feel that these areas are different to each other.
		Where are the places that they feel are theirs.
		Are there any places that are not theirs but they feel an attachment to and at what point do they start to notice other people but still feel a sense of the place being theirs.
		Where do they feel that they begin to be in a completely public location.

Table 6.2   **Semi-structured interview guidelines developed for adult and child participants at Kirby Hill**

Adult	Children
1. What bought the participant to live in the village?	**1. What would they normally be doing today?**
2. About routine activity:	**2. Routine activity:**
How do they normally travel in and around the village – car/foot/bike? Does this vary on weekdays, weekends, other times e.g. times of day etc.?	Do they go to the village school and if so by what route?
At what point do they think they have arrived in Kirby Hill?	Do they go anywhere else in the village and why? – friends etc.
At what point do they think they leave Kirby Hill?	Walk/cycle?
Where do they think they have arrived at their immediate neighbourhood?	**3. Imagine and remember:**
Where do they think they have arrived home, and are there any places or features that they feel are theirs?	Notice what? – on all routes
Do they always leave/come to the village using the same route? If the route varies:	Points of arrival at these places?
Why does it vary?	Notice on way back – same/different?
Does the place where they feel they exit or arrive change with the route they take?	Do they stop or pause anywhere – if so where and why?
Where do they normally go to in the village?	Do they regularly meet people or notice people on the way – if so where?
What route do they take and why?	**4. Nearly there yet?**
What do they notice in particular?	At what point do they think they have arrived in Kirby Hill?
Do they feel any sense of change: mood, atmosphere in any particular places in the village?	At what point do they think they leave Kirby Hill?
Do they feel there are any definite areas within the village, and if so what makes them feel different to each other?	Where do they think they have arrived at their immediate neighbourhood?
Do they stop or pause anywhere – if so where and why?	Where do they think they have arrived home, and are there any places or features that they feel are theirs?
Do they regularly meet people on the way – if so where?	Do they always leave/come to the village using the same route?
Are there any particular landmarks or features they particularly notice, inside and outside the village:	Night time different?
In the village	**5. Favourites**
Outside the village	Favourite place in village.
Do they always go the same way around the village?	Like doing best?
Are there any places they regularly go to – if so where and why, what do they do there?	What is the best thing about living here?
Are there any places that they think have a special appearance, meaning or are there any places they go to 'get away' or be alone?	What is special about living in Kirby Hill? e.g. e-mailing a pen pal.
Are there any places they do not like or would not go to?	**6. Worst**
Are there any features, landmarks or objects that they do not like, if so why?	Are there any places they do not like or would not go to?
3. Where do they feel that the centre of the village is?	Are there any features, landmarks or objects that they do not like, if so why?
4. What do they feel gives the village a separate or distinct identity from Langthorpe or Boroughbridge?	Anything don't like about the village?
5. What is special about living in Kirby Hill?	
6. Why do they live here?	
7. Is there anything else they would like to say about their experiences of living in Kirby Hill?	

related to each of the spatial components CDTA and their subtypes (Table 6.1).

This provides an overarching framework adaptable to fit the circumstances of each particular situation. This makes it possible to respond more appropriately to different users, children as opposed to adults, for example, to different types of setting, and to different project objectives. The outcome of the professional experiential landscape analysis has also proved to be an extremely useful guide when it comes to adapting the semi-structured interview content. This is because it reflects the perspective of trained individuals working within a certain theoretical framework and as such is capable of exposing potentially interesting characteristics about a setting that might warrant more focused investigation through the user survey. For example, in the Kirby Hill village identity work that will be detailed in section three, the professional experiential landscape map revealed characteristics in the clustering of CDTA that suggested an incremental sensation when approaching the village from the south. There appeared to be obvious implications here for the way the village boundaries might be perceived and, since this was something that was relevant to the project brief, meant that the semi-structured interview could be steered to try to tease out local perceptions that might illuminate this more completely. Table 6.2 summarises the guidance notes for the semi-structured interviews at Kirby Hill to illustrate this in two ways. The left column shows the guidance developed for interviewing the adult population and the right a further refinement developed for interviewing children in the village (Table 6.2).

The interviews are conducted in pairs so that one can focus on leading the dialogue while the other takes notes. It is best to do whilst looking at a large plan of the setting under consideration and it seems to help the participant orientate if they can locate where they live, or work, or find other features that connect them with the site. Since quite a lot of the interview basically involves taking a mental journey around the setting, the plan is also very helpful in terms of tracking these routes and can act as a prompt in itself, jogging memories about certain locations or features because they can be seen on the plan. The overall

purpose is to conduct a conversation with a participant around a series of predetermined themes to gather sufficient information about the nature of their routine contact with the setting to be able to ultimately code responses in terms of CDTA and identify what it is that generates them (Figure 6.15).

Information recording

The information gathering stage yields voice recordings and transcribed text, along with supplementary notes, diagrams etc., that record details of the place perceptions of the professional project team according to the theoretical principles of experiential landscape and, preferably, the same recording the interview responses and other information from user participants. This raw material needs to be interpreted in terms of CDTA and this is achieved by coding parts of the transcript in relation to their correspondence with how CDTA are defined. The interpretive skills necessary can be quickly acquired and in general this has proven to be a relatively straightforward matter because of the way observations and interview processes are structured to be amenable to simple coding. For example, consider this short passage from a participant interview.

> "...I always go round that way with the dog. Usually a couple of times a day and if I'm not in a rush, or if it's fine weather, say, I might sit on that corner (points to a wall on corner of Church Street). Quite a few folk are often out with dogs the same time as me, or dropping the kids at school, and I might have a chat with Mary or Bill if they're out and about. Sometimes I don't see anybody but I like the view of the river anyway from here. Reminds me of that horrible, mucky pike my lad brought back once. He used to like fishing there when he was younger..."
> (Figure 6.16)

This short passage is rich with information about how this lady's routine experiences are intimately bound to particular locations and we can interpret this in experiential landscape terms in

Outside specialist. This is a real place. It is somewhere in an ordinary neighbourhood that some locals visit regularly, others do sometimes, others hardly at all. For some it is an important place, for others less so. The perspective of an outside specialist is rather like this image. We see, note and analyse that which our specialist training tells us we should. Our true grasp of the experiential reality of this place is obscured. Just like looking at it through frosted glass we can see some things, but not much.

Non-participant observation. There is a fish and chip shop nearby. We can watch people buying food, some of whom walk a certain route into this small park to sit on the bench and eat. But not many do, most move on, probably because it's winter and cold. The park slopes up to a house on the horizon that seems to act as a focal point. The few that use the park look in this direction. These observations begin to reveal a little more clearly something of the experiential life of the park and its inhabitants. For some, but not many, it seems associated with movement direction, centre (social imageability, restorative benefit) and sensory direction.

Role-play. Using our imagination to become one of the fish and chip shop customers, we can imagine a scenario. During warmer months it is a distinct possibility that the significance of the park would become more locally pronounced as a place of lunchtime retreat. The fish and chip shop serves a small local working population and, with this in mind, other benches would be occupied by individuals and small groups, talking, eating, relaxing. Other centres thus become potential features of this emergent experiential landscape.

Anthropological tracking. There is other evidence of human activity around the base of the trees by the bench on the left-hand side of the picture. Broken glass, compacted earth and trodden down plants bear witness to the footwork of those straying from intended pathways. Further examination shows that the object of the desire line is a larger tree ring-barked to a major low branch. Further directional and centred experiences, implicit in these observations, begin to resolve into view.

6.15
Bringing the nature of experiential landscape into focus
(continued overleaf)

6.15
continued

Semi-structured interviews. These observations help to steer the direction of semi-structured interviews carried out with some of the park's users. This is what a couple of lads had to say: "I play with me friends in the park, tig and climbing trees and stuff, I like the views when you go up that hill and you have a look. I like the hill, 'cause I like to look out for the views and stuff"; "I like it 'cause its just like there's space to run and have fun, like when your like tired they have benches that you can sit, they have benches and that, you can sit on and eat yer chips, you don't have to sit on the ground."

Another attaches more significance to the tree: "Ma special place is like there's a really big tree, I like it up there 'cause there's a really good view, there's a little diddy tree and then there's a really massive one, and I'm the only one that can climb it. That trees me favourite place because it's big and got a good view, and I'm the only one that can climb it, its ma tree, I like it 'cause I'm the only one that can climb it."

For this boy the park seemed to have both a real and imagined significance articulated though a regular dream: "I usually imagine when I'm asleep, have a dream when we've got the park, it belongs to me, and there's a big metal frame over it where no one can get in, and then there's a door and a key thingy, a number and you type numbers in it. I'd keep the place as it is now, except have a really big climbing frame … I'd let me friends in, but they'd have to come to me for the key, and every now and then the roof would open and let water in for the trees, or if that didn't work, or it didn't rain there would be some sprinklers on the roof … I'd keep the park where it is now, its good where it is, I like the good view, so wouldn't want to move it."

Would he like to own this tree?

No he wouldn't! He only owned it when he was in it. "when I'm at the top of the tree it feels great, because I like climbing, I think I'm the only one that can climb it, it's a challenge, you have to swing yourself up, its just as good climbing it as getting to the top, but at the top its just such a great view."

This example illustrates the way in which the experiential landscape shifts and evolves in character and emphasis with the application of different methods of information gathering. At one level it has some centred characteristics, but is predominantly directional, given by the route into the park and the strength of the view up the hill. At another level it holds far richer and more complex qualities transcending reality and imagination in the dreams of one of its occupants increasing the intensity of centred sensations because of social associations among children, focused on the imageability and restorative benefit of the tree.

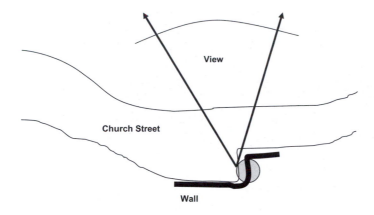

6.16

A diagram of a routine resting place rich with personal significance

the following way. To begin with, the participant has identified a particular type of directional experience to do with movement because of the regular use of the route for walking the dog. This defines a component part of an experiential place in the life of this lady of the type movement direction because this spatial experience stands out for her partly as a consequence of frequency of use. But there are also other experiential qualities here. The wall corner is particularly significant and in quite a complex way. It is obviously a centre for her because she chooses to pause here and thereby gives it a locational significance as part of her routine: it delivers to her a locational sensation. But the real interest lies in why this sensation exists and there seem to be three aspects. First, the significance of this spot is partly that it holds social associations for her being the place where

she seems to routinely encounter acquaintances, marking the location as a centre of the type social interaction. Second, is that this location also seems to engender a rather reflective mood. It is a spot associated with relaxation when there is no pressure on time, with fine weather, and also with memories of her angler son in his younger years. This indicates that the corner of the wall is also delivering a degree of restorative benefit to the lady and so we can say that as well as being a centre as a location made significant because of social interactions, it is also made significant because of the pleasure it delivers in terms of relaxation and reflection. The third aspect relates, not only to the sensation of centre, but to direction and this time due to view because it is clear that part of the lady's choice to sit here is because she can see the river. This aspect strengthens the sensation of centre still further because it adds to the list of pleasurable associations contributing to why she sits there. But it is now also the point from which she experiences a sense of extent and continuity because of the visual draw of the river. The findings from this small example can be summarised in tabular and diagrammatic forms. These form the basic tools with which experiential landscape observations are recorded (Table 6.3).

This table summarises the key experiential components drawn from coding this particular passage from a semi-structured interview. It describes a particular location in a person's

Table 6.3 **Summary table of the resting place experiential character**

Spatial type	Subtype	What	Why	Intensity W, M, S
Direction	Movement	Church Lane and St John's Walk, west to east and back	Routine dog walking	Moderate
Centre	Social interaction	Wall corner	Frequent people meeting	Strong
	Restorative benefit		Relaxation and reflective mood (family associations, contact with nature, good view)	
Direction	View	Wall corner to river	Mid-distant panorama to river	Moderate

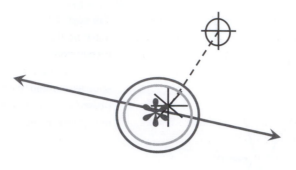

6.17

Dobson Cluster for the resting place

neighbourhood with a place character defined by a composite of four distinguishable spatially related experiences. We can say that it is an experiential place contributing significantly to the diet of directional and locational sensations in the life of this individual, and that the locational significance is quite strong, partly because it is significant for a variety of reasons. By interpreting the variants of CDTA using simple symbols this information can be expressed diagrammatically, providing the foundations for mapping the experiential landscape place characteristics of settings. This kind of diagram is called a Dobson Cluster[1] and is the basis for understanding the different nuances and characteristics that experiential landscape places have. This is the fundamental tool through which the experiential landscape place characteristics of existing settings can be read and from which new ones can be designed in a more experientially aware manner (Figure 6.17).

Essentially the arrowed line represents bi-directional movement: meaning that it holds its significance for this individual there and back. The bold asterisk locates a place where a routine pause occurs along the way. This represents the location of the wall corner and it is important to note the build up of intensity shown by the overlapping of symbols here. The light circle records its significance as a centre because of its association with social interaction, and the darker circle records the restorative associations for the centre. The lighter asterisk relates to the experience of view direction and locates where the view is from. But at the same time this also adds to the graphical build up that represents where the wall corner is and so makes its own contribution to the visual

intensity that evidences this spot as particularly important to this individual. The broken line shows the direction of view and at the end of it is a symbol to target what is being viewed: in this case part of a river.

This diagrammatic way of expressing experiential place character is fundamental to the operationalisation of experiential landscape. It is the key to the way the complex and often very subtle relationship between human experience and its spatial expression can be made visible and therefore available to design decision-making processes. Each of the symbols represents a record of how a particular kind of experience is projected onto space by an individual. Each symbol has its own text record of its unique details arranged in the format show on the above table and, through the use of the GIS software used to collate experiential landscape maps, can be revealed for any given symbol at a mouse click. Where appropriate this can also be supplemented with photographic and other forms of visual information. The full set of symbols developed for experiential landscape mapping is shown in the table that follows (Plate 4).

It is worthwhile to note at this point that places can become significant in the lives of people for bad reasons as well as good. The interview passage used in this example is all about experiences that contribute to the outdoor life of the participant in positive ways. This is not always the case of course. Some locations can be highly significant in the experiential life of individuals because they are associated with irritation, fear, threat, or bad memories and sadness, for example. It is not uncommon to find in fact that the same location in a setting can appear to be significant for many users but for some it might have positive associations whilst others loath the place: the point is that it is no less significant because of the loathing. One example of this from a recent project turned out to be at the mouth of the village primary school. This is obviously a prime gathering point in the village at least twice a day during weekdays and many people interviewed reported very positive associations here mainly to do with the social opportunities afforded whilst dropping off and collecting offspring. The same location proved to be significant for others however because they

---

1 Named for Claire Dobson of elprdu who developed the analytical technique during a Masters degree research

associated it with varying degrees of irritation and inconvenience generated by the hoards of school run vehicles. These differences are recorded in the "why" column of the table but it was also felt useful for them to have a different graphical representation so that differences between positive and negative responses to place could be more visible.

To summarise then, partial transcripts of the voice recordings of place perceptions for professional subjects and setting users can be coded with relative ease to reveal their implications in CDTA terms. In essence this allows a spatial interpretation to be given to accounts of the way a particular setting, as a whole and in its parts, is perceived and used. By giving each of these spatial categories a graphical expression, their location can be identified on a map of the setting resulting in a mosaic-like image superimposed over the site plan. In relation to professional perceptions this provides a form of language to relate observations made about certain attributes of a setting's spatial configuration to its experiential potential. For setting users, the technique enables often very personal and anecdotal information about the way individuals use and assign meanings and associations to their routine surroundings to be given expression in spatial terms. Collectively, this allows dimensions of the life of outdoor settings normally hidden from view to be visualised as experiential landscape maps consisting of patterns of symbols spread out across the site. Not only does this locate different kinds of spatial experience relevant to individuals, but more crucially it also reveals the extent to which they are connected together or disparate, whether there are concentrations of experience at particular spots, and whether there are parts of the setting that appear to offer little in experiential terms, for example. By looking at combinations of symbols as Dobson Clusters in the way outlined earlier, the maps also reveal in some detail the character of place at particular locations and at different scales in terms of the presence and emphasis of certain spatial components over others (Plate 5).

The individual experiential landscape maps are not in fact an end in themselves but the means by which experiential characteristics for the setting are revealed when they are combined together as a composite. It is not so much the detailed content of the individual experiential maps that matter most but the way in which they provide the layers through which to see the wider picture. To this extent at least, any idiosyncrasy that might creep in through the way information is interpreted tends to become subsumed within the stronger patterns that emerge in the collective view. The layering of individual experiential landscape maps is achieved using GIS computer software. This allows diagrammatic, text and photographic forms of information to be collated and analysed in a multitude of different ways and this versatility is very important to the way in which experiential landscape maps are read and interpreted (Plate 6).

Interpreting the experiential landscape

The central purpose of producing a composite experiential landscape map is to reveal in diagrammatic form the spatial distribution of certain kinds of human experience across a setting. Contained within the distribution and density of the symbols from which the pattern is composed is information about the spatial configuration of experience for a collective of individuals representing the experiential anatomy of the participant community. By this means we can begin to understand something of the experiential quality and character of the setting and specific locations within it and we can then use this understanding to inform subsequent planning and design processes.

As with other aspects of the qualitative nature of the experiential landscape concept and its operational procedures, analysis of maps is much more a matter of informed interpretation than measurement of factual data: more a reading than analysis. We have found that it is much more useful to focus on the visual characteristics apparent in the mosaic-like patterns generated in experiential landscape maps, rather like searching the visual field of the experiential landscape map to look for clustering and concentrations, linkages, weaknesses in symbol distribution, for example, rather than amounts. To guide this reading we have found that it is useful to focus on the following general themes, as indicators of experiential potential. This helps to give some structure to the process without it becoming unnecessarily mechanistic:

- Quantity: indicative of amount of experiential potential (Figure 6.18).
- Balance: indicative of any bias in the overall balance of CDTA (Figure 6.19).
- Distribution: indicative of whether experiential potential is evenly distributed across a site or concentrated in certain locations (Figure 6.20).
- Connectivity: indicates whether CDTA is likely to be seamlessly linked or if there are "dead" spots (Figure 6.21).
- Intensity: indicates how strong or concentrated CDTA sensations are (Figure 6.22).

This is more like the experience of interpreting visual nuances in abstract paintings than objective scientific scrutiny. But, although at first impression this may sound like a rather strange and imprecise approach it is a relevant and necessary response to the holistic nature of outdoor place experience. As outlined earlier place experience cannot be satisfactorily understood in terms of discrete chunks set side-by-side. Instead, the nature of outdoor place experience is more like a seamless continuity that people can never step outside of because they are a fundamental part of how place is defined. The particular characteristics of place experience vary throughout the continuity and, rather like the eddies and ripples that make visible different characteristics in the flow of a river, the mosaic patterns evident in experiential landscape maps make visible variations in the place experience of a setting at a particular time for a particular participant population.

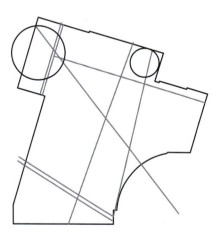

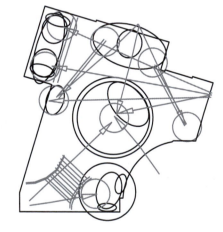

6.18

Quantity: indicative of amount of experiential potential

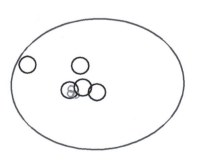

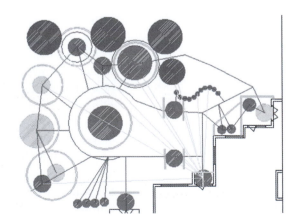

6.19

Balance: indicative of any bias in the overall balance of CDTA

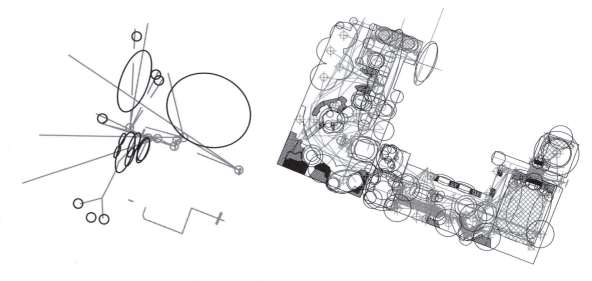

6.20

Distribution: indicative of whether experiential potential is evenly distributed across a site or concentrated in certain locations

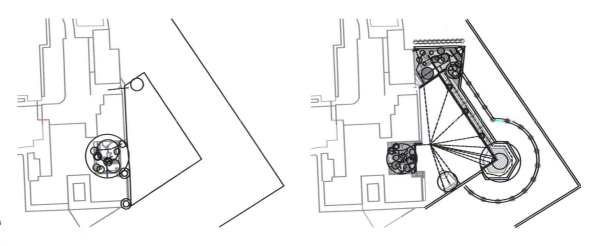

6.21

Connectivity: indicates whether CDTA is likely to be seamlessly linked or if there are "dead" spots

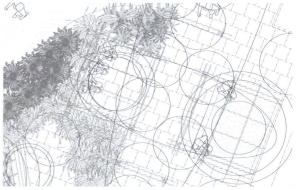

6.22

Intensity: indicates how strong or concentrated CDTA sensations are

These two maps, for example, show how GIS software allows us to isolate specific spatial types from the composite experiential landscape maps to give a visual display of the mosaic of any one of the symbols recorded across the setting. This technique helps us to more easily see whether certain kinds of spatial experience predominate over others without doing any actual counting. The left one is a composite map recording instances of restorative centre in a village analysis. The right one records view direction. Several observations can be made. First, it is clear there are far fewer symbols and this indicates, for the participants involved, that the experience of view direction contributes significantly more to the experiential character of the village as a whole than restorative centre. This provides a useful insight into an aspect of the experiential character of the village, but much more can be gleaned by simply examining the distribution of symbols and their intensity, or concentration, at particular locations. By this means we can see that restorative experience in the village appears most concentrated mainly in two locations and that the majority of the directional experience due to view appears to emanate from these locations also and that views to the north appear more prominently. These two maps then begin to reveal parts of the village that seem

to be experientially richer than others. Continuing to layer the maps produced for the remaining spatial types will add further detail and make it possible to determine not only where experientially rich and poor locations are but also what their experiential characteristics are in terms of the type and balance of symbols evident there (Figure 6.23).

Deconstructing the composite experiential landscape map to reveal the distribution patterns for each spatial type presents one way to read details of the experiential characteristics of specific locations. In particular it helps to make sense of composite maps that can be visually very complex and sometimes it can be difficult to access the necessary information, particularly in places where there is a very high intensity of symbols. Nevertheless it is important to recognise that variations in intensity of symbols as well as the type of symbols present represent a record of the experiential character as a whole. So although reading the experiential character of a setting by treating CDTA as discrete spatial entities existing independently of one another is useful in a practical sense, it is potentially misleading in a fairly crucial way. This is because of the holistic nature of place experience highlighted earlier. The sensation of centre, for example, can never actually be

6.23
Composite experiential landscape maps showing restorative centre and sensory direction

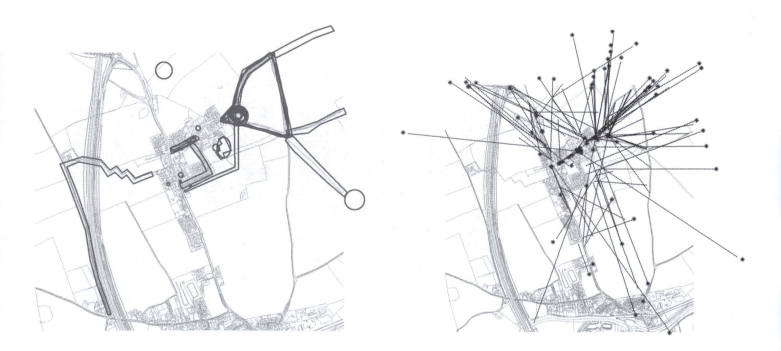

experienced in isolation of other spatial components in normal environmental contact. About the only way this can be envisaged would be to imagine being confined inside a sphere, something like a large ping-pong ball for instance, where there would be no visible means of exit to introduce a transitional possibility and no corners or variations in light quality, for example, to induce a sensation of direction. But this is so alien from authentic lived experience that it is not worth worrying about. Instead, just about every reasonably conceivable setting likely to be encountered in normal life circumstances can be described as a composite of CDTA and this is the case at all levels of scale (Figure 6.24).

For example, this setting is delivering an emphatically directional sensation induced mainly by the powerful perspective effect created by the pergola, its supporting pillars and the shade pattern on the ground. The exit point at the end of the tunnel adds to this sensation by providing a focal point drawing the eye to a distant location. But this opening also introduces a sensation of transition because it brings to the setting an awareness of passage from one location into another. Interruptions to the continuity of plant containers to the left side also suggest the presence of transitions because they may be possible exit points to the left side. The alcove effect these

create may also be suggestive of centres and the linearity predominant in its material composition and the light blue colour introduce a strong thematic continuity, or area. So the experiential character of this place at this location can be said to deliver a strong sense of area, is very strongly directional but contains awareness of transitional and to a lesser extent, centred, sensations also. As well as appreciating this place as a holistic ensemble of CDTA at varying intensities we can also imagine how an experiential sensation of a different kind might gradually unfold as we move further on. At the point where the picture is taken the transitional sensation seems relatively weak, overwhelmed by the strength of the direction inducing features, but this is likely to intensify as one gets closer to the point of exit, smoothly transferring the balance of experience from emphatically directional to emphatically transitional. So we can see then that CDTA cannot meaningfully be considered in isolation of one another but in fact describe different aspects of a holistic entity. Just as the three sides of a triangle can be distinguished individually in the sense that each can have a different length it is not possible to remove one altogether, no matter how short, and still have a triangle: it is the very existence of three sides together that define the triangle. This holistic characteristic of experiential landscape can be articulated graphically by means of Dobson Clusters which can be used to examine the experiential characteristics of a setting in different locations and at different levels of scale.

The following three maps provide an example of what can be read by examination of the Dobson Clusters. To begin with the pattern of symbols generated for the whole setting is itself a large Dobson Cluster. This example shows a setting of considerable experiential complexity but it is immediately apparent that there appears to be a significant concentration of mainly social imageability centres and view direction roughly in the middle, a major concentration of transition to the east side of this cluster, and beyond this a triangular formation of mainly restorative benefit centres. There is also a prominent sequence of transitions apparent running roughly north–south to the west side. Although there is a lot more

6.24
An emphatically directional sensation

detail, the point here is that these are the most prominent features visible in the mosaic pattern and this allows us to define the essential experiential characteristic of the setting as a whole. A short summary of this, focusing on the strongest features apparent at this level of scale, would be as follows.

This setting has a distinctive central core characterised mainly by strong sensations of location and view, particularly to the north and east. There are strong locational sensations associated with restorative experiences to the east of this core with strong transitional sensations that bisect the two locations. To the west side is a prominent movement direction characterised by frequent transitional sensations in sequence. (Figure 6.25.)

The presence and location of an experiential core in the setting and its essential characteristics are thus made visible by the composite map.

6.25

The experiential landscape map of Kirby Hill, North Yorkshire

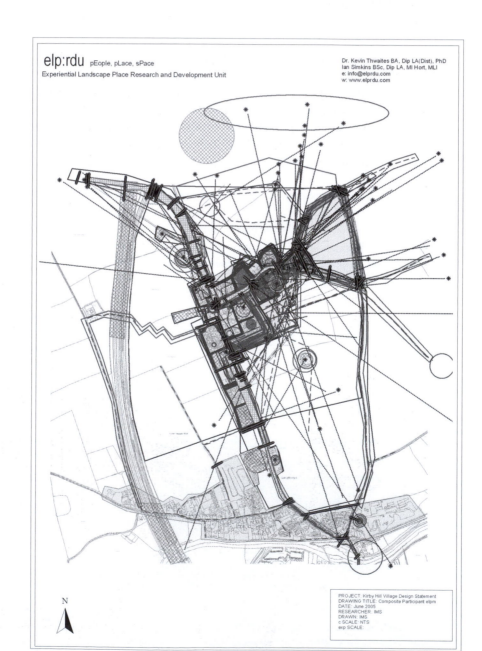

Zooming into this area allows examination of the location in much more detail and highlights an important feature of the GIS based experiential landscape mapping technique. This is that the zooming process does not just take you closer but it actually reveals additional dimensions of detail. This is very important because it gives visual access to localised variations and refinements in experiential character. For example, the closer view now shows that the intensely centred core area is itself actually a composite. This is made up from distinguishable social imageability centres concentrated roughly in the middle and to the south side of a lane, whilst two strong clusters of centres which include more prominent social interaction associations have become more visible. Four strong transitions are now apparent and the one to the east can now be seen to be more spread out by comparison to the others which are tightly concentrated. This latter is indicative of prominent localised features induc-

ing the transitional effect, whilst in the former case the overall transitional character of this part of the setting appears to be composed of numerous transitional experiences present across a wider region. It has also become clearer now that the view direction which contributes prominently to the experiential character in the region appears most strongly focused on a particular location just to the west side of the large composite transition (Figure 6.26).

Zooming in again allows us to elaborate yet further the experiential character at a very specific location. Here we can see more clearly that at the western extremity is a strong centre significant for social imageability and social interaction, and that just to its east side is a complex and very localised transition that works in two directions indicated by the criss-crossing of the symbols. We can also see that a string of social imageability centres have emerged into prominence to the south side of the lane and that there is a strong movement direction

6.26
Zooming in reveals additional dimensions of detail

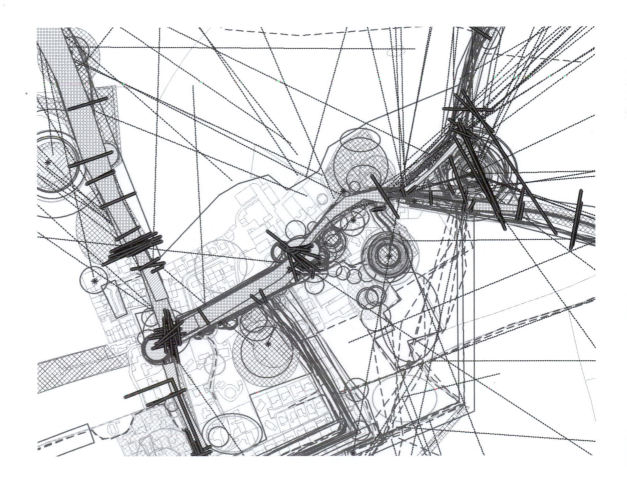

that dog-legs where the transition occurs (Figure 6.27).

Summary

This chapter has detailed the principles by which the experiential landscape character of settings can be mapped and read using a simple range of graphical symbols. We have described how data can be derived from both professional and user group place perceptions and how this can be coded to correspond with the CDTA model. GIS computer software enables experiential landscape maps of individuals' place perceptions to be layered together forming composites. These composite maps are the principal goal of the experiential landscape process and provide the way in which a wide range of information about the experiential characteristics of the setting and locations within it can be read. The composite maps make

visible otherwise hidden, but nonetheless real, dimensions of place experience. A special feature of them is that they provide a means by which the holistic nature of place experience can be visually articulated so that variations in place character, expressed in terms of integrations of CDTA, can be identified in different locations and at different levels of scale within a single map. The seamless and continuously evolving sequence of change in place character, along particular routes in a setting for example, can be identified and described in detail by this means also. This gives anyone interested in planning, design and management of the outdoors the tools with which to appreciate the spatial implications of aspects of human experience that become projected onto the surroundings through routine use and the association of meaning and value. As such experiential landscape offers potential to augment more conventional processes of site survey and analysis with a means to reveal human dimensions of open

6.27

Again, increasing detail at a specific location in the village shows a strong transitional and centred character

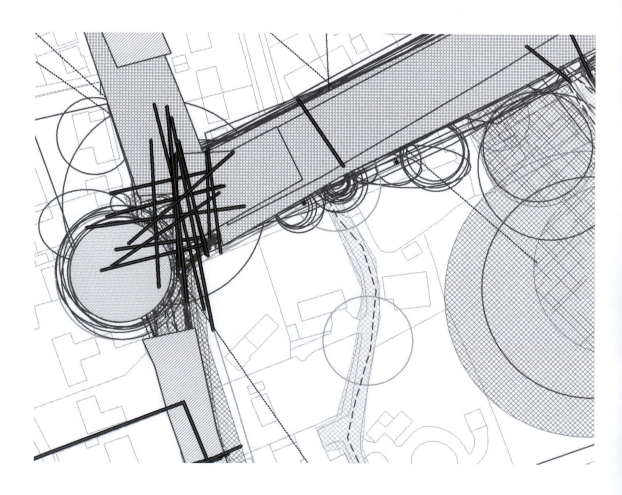

space use and perception in a manner conducive to assist design decision-making.

In the next section we will begin to turn our attention to the creative potential of experiential landscape by offering some reflections on the geometrical implications of designing with the experiential landscape concept. This will focus in particular on the importance of crinkling and will introduce a new word, experiemics, to conceptualise the holistic nature of experiential landscape design as it applies to scale.

Chapter 7

Reflections on geometry

Previously we have explored some of the principles and methods that enable us to read the experiential characteristics of outdoor settings. This chapter develops from this by reflecting on the geometrical implications of experiential landscape and its implications for design. At its most fundamental, geometry, as it is conventionally understood in environmental design disciplines, is concerned with juxtapositions of points, lines and surfaces. Although a complexity of cultural, social, economic, aesthetic and technical issues influence how we decide to shape our world, this fundamental geometrical awareness forms the basic building blocks from which new places are usually conceived and visualised. Our starting point here is to look at the picture of the world presented from an experiential landscape perspective and then ask how its particular nature might come to bear on our approach to geometric considerations.

Jane Jacobs said this about the way she believes order in cities is manifest.

"This order is all composed of movement and change, and although it is life, not art, we may fancifully call it the art form of the city and liken it to the dance – not to a simple-minded precision dance with everyone kicking up at the same time, twirling in unison and bowing off en-masse, but to an

intricate ballet in which the individual dancers and ensembles all have distinctive parts which miraculously reinforce each other and compose an orderly whole" (Jacobs, 1961, p.50).

It is not an order composed of material components and the spaces in between, but an order apparent in the collective actions of people as they go about their daily routines, routines by means of which the places of ordinary everyday experience are defined. This is not a static, sculptural kind of order, but, like music and dance, characterised only by movement and change: dynamic activity that comprises an orderly whole. Jacobs, in all but name, is describing an urban experiential landscape here, eloquently highlighting characteristics, movement, change, distinctive parts that compose wholes, which challenge our conventional geometrical approaches to design.

So what are the characteristics of experiential landscape that have geometrical implications and how can we understand the geometric structure of place experience in ways relevant to design? Chapter five outlined details of the spatial dimension of experience by trying to articulate that as we move through our surroundings we experience, in unbroken and sequential continuity, the ebbing and flowing influence of four integrated but distinguishable spatial experiences. These, in infinity of combinations, characterise our awareness of place and we have described how this normally hidden dimension of human existence can be made visible through mapping. Centre, direction and transition coalesce in different emphases and at different scales to form the larger spatial experience of area which provides our sense of overall coordination and coherence and through which we can recognise different urban realms and, for example, distinguish our own homeground from that of others. Areas themselves then coalesce into larger scale areas that allow us to distinguish one town and cityscape from another. This interweaving of centre, direction, transition and area, represented by our CDTA model, in different emphases and scales collectively defines a seamless spatial and experiential continuity, and this is what we have called the experiential landscape. It is not simply a stage upon which we play out the activities and emotions of routine life, but a living entity defined in terms of those activities and emotions as integral to where they occur. This conception brings significant challenges to how we perceive geometry mainly because the geometry that we conventionally understand is meant to be outside of us and devoid of any emotional or subjective content.

This conundrum is neatly articulated by Kim Dovey (1993) in terms of a difference between geometric space and lived space. What Dovey means by geometric space is the mathematical abstractions originating with Euclid that give us a model for understanding the world and which allows us to make geometrical representations of real-world situations. Euclidian geometry has since become so powerful a model that its representative status has become elevated to such an extent that it is now widely perceived as the one true arrangement. The problem with this is that it tends towards a real-world view in which it becomes possible to detach the authentic experience of people from a setting which itself is reduced to a set of value-free measures and coordinates. From an experiential point of view this presents an extremely limited perspective. As Merleau-Ponty explains, "Space is not the setting (real or logical) in which things are arranged, but the means whereby the positing of things becomes possible" (Merleau-Ponty, 1962, p.243). What he is talking about here is that space cannot be regarded merely as a receptacle within which things are contained, but more like the power, or force, which enables things to connect. This brings about a substantial shift of awareness from geometric space as a finite, static container, to a lived space which seems a more elastic phenomenon: a pliable and dynamic entity that bends, stretches and moulds at different scales in response to action.

This essentially phenomenological perspective not only embraces human functioning into its view of place in the outdoor world, it actually requires it to bring a full definition. This makes it almost meaningless to ask how to design an experiential landscape in a conventional sense because a part of it resides in the life patterns and psychological activity of individuals and groups and this is outside the realm of conventional approaches to design. Instead it may be more meaningful to talk about trying to create the conditions within which experiential opportunity can be optimised. This seems to imply a different geometrical attitude from that which is concerned primarily with the fabrication of spatial and material components. We can begin this by summarising the structural characteristics of experiential landscape that have geometrical implications. The experiential landscape:

- integrates experiential and spatial dimensions of human existence;
- is a holistic, field-like structure: an unbroken continuity composed of localised perturbations of place character;
- is characterised by fluid changes of emphasis in centre, direction, transition and area that determine experiential landscape place character at specific locations in the field;
- has an enfoldment and nesting of CDTA at different levels of scale.

Integrated human and spatial dimensions

Experiential landscape conceptualises the outdoors in terms of holistic relationships of centre, direction, transition and area (CDTA). Centre, direction and transition are three distinguishable, but inseparable, components that combine as experiential landscape places to determine the characteristics of particular locations within the wider experiential landscape. Area gives a sense of coherence and coordination to the experiential landscape, either as a whole or to regions of it. Each of these four related but distinguishable elements of experiential landscape are defined in terms of both spatial and human dimensions. In design this implies a need for geometrical ordering systems that extend beyond consideration of point, line and surface as objective abstract entities external to human functioning.

The experiential landscape is an holistic field-like structure

Connectivity, continuity and sequence are all important concepts in defining the overall structure of experiential landscapes. They are not conceived as though they are a collection of independently existing set piece settings merely linked together by paths and other routeways. This seems too abstract and mechanistic to sufficiently define the way place experience happens at a phenomenological level. Instead the experi-

7.1

These bar charts represent the changing emphasis of CDTA at each of the locations along the journey A-B and show how the seamlessly changing experiential place character can be recorded along its length

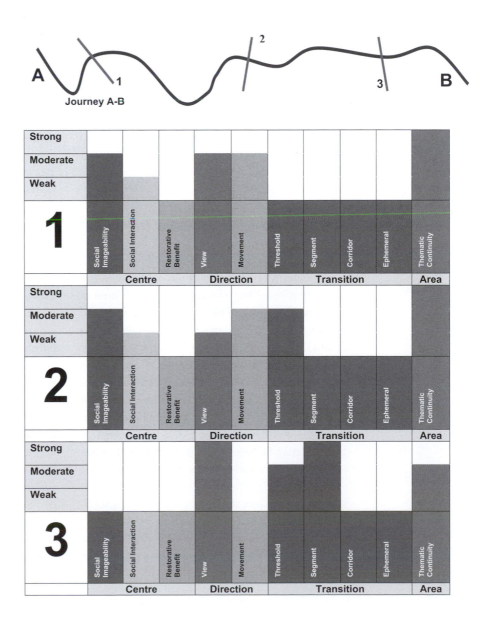

ence is more fluid and continuous with the most incidental and mundane of spaces contributing equally to the total diet of the experiential repertoire. Although still rather a crude approximation given the complexity involved, it seems more valid to conceptualise experiential landscape as a continuous, seamless field of experiential potential. This field is defined by, and varies locally according to, how different emphases of CDTA manifest at different locations. These localised variations can be thought of as distinguishable perturbations within the field continuity.

Experiential place character is determined by fluid changes in CDTA emphasis at specific locations

The experiential landscape is constituted from experiential landscape places. The characteristics of experiential landscape places depend on whether and to what extent there is an emphasis of one component over another at a particular location. The ebbing and flowing of this emphasis along a particular journey, for example, can help to visualise how the experiential landscape place character changes seamlessly at intervals along a particular journey (Figure 7.1).

CDTA can be detected at different levels of scale

CDTA are scale independent. They are spatial experiences that can be detected at virtually any scale that can be comprehended by human subjects. We have also highlighted that centre and area are in fact partly characterised by being made of smaller centres and areas and that they themselves contribute to the resolution of centres and areas at larger levels of scale. This appears to relate to the different ways people perceive their surroundings at different scales. For instance, at the individual level of small things, the sense of location may be heightened by activities that can be performed directly by the hands, by handling or manipulating objects for example. For small groups it might be stimulated more by social activities such as sitting and talking, eating etc., whereas at more public levels of scale, the sense of location might be stimulated by an awareness of larger visual forms, perceptions of privacy within an otherwise public realm etc. The geometrical

implications of this tend to draw emphasis to processes of enfoldment and nesting rather than mere assembly.

These are four characteristics of experiential landscape that have geometrical implications challenging to Euclidian geometry. We can now move on with these characteristics in mind to explore the kind of geometrical awareness that might be necessary to the creative use of the experiential landscape concept in place making. The discussion that follows covers three categories: mosaics of spatial experience; experiemic scale; and enfolded space. As well as addressing some of the geometrical implications of experiential landscape this also considers the assertion, increasingly implicit in the literature, that certain kinds of geometrical configuration applied to the outdoor environment might themselves contribute to psychological health, particularly in urban populations.

Mosaics of spatial experience

The capacity of outdoor settings to benefit human well-being is well established by research. Examples can be found throughout history and are still applied today in health care facilities, such as healing or restorative gardens for the sick, even though their wider significance in the urban public realm remains insufficiently explored. There are some, though, who argue for fundamental properties of order, present in the natural and cultural world, which are associated with human psychological benefit. Such spatial arrangements, it is asserted, may offer potential to resurrect people's connection with intuitively preferred forms and strengthen beneficial relations between human functioning and the spatial environment. In his book, *Land Mosaics*, landscape ecologist Richard Forman (1995) highlights that we now live in a world where more than 90% of the land surface has been altered in some way by human activity. Against this background he asks, if humanity is now mostly in charge of, and responsible for, most of the land surface, what designs of landscape are best for life (ibid., p.xiv)? Through comprehensive analysis of landscapes and regions he concludes that all land appears to us as mosaic patterns and that mosaic-like attributes are discernible at landscape, regional and continental scales. He argues not only that spatial arrangement matters to ecological integrity, but also identifies an optimal spatial arrangement consisting holistically of three fundamental structures called patches, corridors and matrices. Authority is claimed for this hypothesis because, as Forman demonstrates, this spatial structure is not merely an aesthetic device but appears to arise from the way land presents itself to us as a consequence of the forces, natural and cultural, that shape it.

Forman's relevance here lies primarily with his further claim that this spatial structure is not just important to biodiversity and environmental sustainability, but may equally be applied to achieving human needs. This raises interesting issues for contemporary landscape and urban design theory concerned with the development of understanding about the design of urban settings that can benefit human life quality. It challenges us to explore the possibility that spatial arrangement per se might influence human well-being, as well as the form and content of specific spaces making up the arrangement. It also signals particular features of ecologically beneficial spatial arrangement and raises questions about how to interpret this in the urban environment. Taking Forman's lead we can identify evidence for convergence in elements of urban design theory that certain spatial arrangements, associated with linkages of locational, directional and transitional experiences, can benefit human life quality.

The idea of the restorative potential of networks of small open spaces in an urban centre as an alternative to large parks, for example, has been explored before in the context of urban planning, notably in a proposal by American landscape architect Robert Zion in 1963. Since the opening of Olmstead's Central Park, city planners focused their attention on large parks, ceremonial civic plazas, avenues and parkways. Zion did not accept the belief of the time that to be viable an urban park needed a minimum of three acres to accommodate city crowds. Zion argued that New York would be better served by thousands of very small parks and in 1963 Zion proposed that the citizens of New York build a vest-pocket park on every midtown block of the city to create a matrix of parks. Together these parks would provide spaces for people to rest and gather strength before venturing back into the busy city streets of urban activity. In 1968 Zion's Paley Park, located at 53rd Street and Fifth Avenue opened. Zion imagined that vest-pocket parks like Paley Park would become, in Zion's words, "not amenities, but necessities of city life" (Frankel and Johnson, 1991, p.197). Paley Park was intended to be one of a hundred such parks, in an extensive network. Zion's dream was that each park would be "as ordinary as, say the cafés of Paris" (Frankel and Johnson, 1991, p.191). In fact Paley Park was the only vest-pocket park created by Zion in New York and it has become one of Manhattan's treasures. Zion's vision represents a shift of emphasis from the properties and characteristics of individual spaces to that of networks of spaces as a whole. Implicit is that experience of such networks is psychologically beneficial to urban populations. This more holistic attitude to urban spatial arrangement, as interwoven networks of place experience, might also imply a more fluid and rhythmic approach to design, relevant to sensations of continuity as well as location. If so, then a fundamental question relevant to the design of such settings is what are the geometric attributes of urban open spaces that can facilitate and enhance beneficial sensations of continuity and connectedness?

We can begin to explore this by returning briefly to Richard Forman's ideas about land mosaics (Forman, 1995). Forman's position, after analysis of a wide range of landscape types, is that there are fundamental components of spatial organisation observable in landscape and ecological systems and these are related to ecological integrity. If they are ecologically beneficial, he asserts, the same may hold for human systems. If this is accepted, then it appears to hold quite profound implications for urban and landscape design in particular, not least because Forman's spatial system is fundamentally very simple. Six basic principles can be drawn out that are relevant here.

1. At the root of Forman's system is that spatial arrangement itself matters. This is what gives the landscape its structure which determines

movements and flows between different ecosystems. Certain spatial configurations occur because they are the ones that facilitate ecological activity best.

2. This spatial structure has a particular form reflecting that the real world consists of finely fragmented habitats arranged in a mosaic-like formation. Different parts of the mosaic aggregate, forming distinguishable boundaries, but always as part of the wider whole.

3. The detail of the mosaic is described by Forman in terms of the patch-corridor-matrix model where: patches are relatively homogeneous non-linear areas that differ from the surroundings; corridors are strips of particular types that differ from the adjacent land on both sides; matrices are the background ecosystem or land-use type. Land mosaics are patterns of patches, corridors and matrices.

4. The patch-corridor-matrix spatial structure is scale independent and can be detected at all levels of scale from the submicroscopic to the universal. At the human scale relevant to Forman's work, landscape, regional and continental scales are considered as three distinguishable scales of land mosaic.

5. Land mosaics are holistic spatial arrangements. "It is simply inept or poor quality work to consider a patch as isolated from its surroundings in the mosaic. Designs, plans, management proposals, and policies based on drawing an absolute boundary around a piece of the mosaic should be discarded" (ibid., p.xviii).

6. "Form is the diagram of force" (ibid., p.5). Forman identifies that land mosaics arise as a consequence of a combination of natural and cultural processes that change with time. Solar energy maintains and creates the structure in the landscape within which specific pattern is made by either/or combination of substrate heterogeneity, natural disturbance, and human activity. The form generated is the physical manifestation of the underlying and dynamic forces.

Forman thus presents a conceptual approach to the arrangement of space in a supposedly environmentally and socially sustainable form. The fundamental characteristics of which are that it is essentially holistic, consisting of distinguishable yet inseparable parts emphasising the primacy of linear and non-linear attributes arranged against a common background. The structure is mosaic-like and scale independent and expresses visually the forces that have acted upon the whole system. Crucial is that this kind of spatial concept is not confined to the field of landscape ecology. Echoes can also be detected in facets of architecture and environmental design theory that may strengthen Forman's assertion about the importance of his spatial model to human systems. We have already considered, for example, the phenomenological approach to the built environment advocated by Christian Norberg-Schulz in the late 1960s and early 70s in which he conceptualises that human progression through, and engagement with, the material surroundings can be conceptualised in terms of a tripartite spatial structure integrating sensations of proximity, continuity and change into a collective sense of place.

The similarity to Forman's mosaic-like structure is at the very least intriguing. The spatial sensation of proximity seems resonant with Forman's patches, whilst continuity echoes the linear attributes of corridor. Norberg-Schulz's sense of place is also assumed to include a less clearly defined, but nonetheless coherent, general background that seems similar in principle to Forman's matrix. Furthermore Norberg-Schulz also alludes to the scale independence of his spatial schemata and to its holistic nature. According to Norberg-Schulz's concept, our sense of place, and by extension our existential well-being in the world, is intimately bound together with our subliminal connection holistically to these spatial sensations. The connectivity between locational, directional and transitional spatial experiences are perhaps brought to clarity most vividly in Gordon Cullen's (1971) argument for the importance of serial vision to the experience of townscape. By drawing attention to the sequential nature of urban spatial experience, Cullen begins to elaborate the characteristics of urban settings that stimulate and sustain sequential experience. Cullen articulates the sense of place fundamentally in terms of our reaction to the position of our body in the environment, stimulated by sensations of enclosure and our awareness of when we are outside it, when we are entering it, and when we are in the middle of it. "At this level of consciousness we are dealing with a range of experience stemming from the major impacts of exposure and enclosure" (ibid.). For Cullen, sense of place is associated with our ability to subliminally monitor our position in relation to a kind of balanced tension between awareness of here and there. Furthermore, it is important that here and there are experienced in a fluid and dynamic manner, as elements along a continuity characterised by an unfolding sequence of existing and emerging views. He calls this serial vision and what brings this experience alive is the drama of juxtaposition brought about by awareness of contrast and change: the locations at which here becomes there. Cullen believes these transitional experiences to be crucial to our ability to sustain psychological engagement with our surroundings. Without them "the town will slip past us featureless and inert" (ibid.).

Networks of linked enclosures are associated with social interactions in neighbourhoods, streets and communities by Hillier and Hanson (1984). Their research explored the social potential of urban outdoor space and its relation to networks of convex spaces detectable in figure-ground plans. Hillier and Hanson's assertion here is that the quality of human communication in neighbourhoods correlates with the presence and density of "beady-ring structures" (Hillier and Hanson, 1984, p.90). In essence these consist of points within small convex spaces, discernible by analysing the nature of the site's physical containment, connected by paths between them. The denser the resulting mosaic, the better the potential is for the spatial configuration to sustain a positive social life.

Experiemic scale

We have tried to establish how CDTA can be conceptualised as components that aggregate in mosaic-like structures to form the experiential landscape. In terms of developing the geometrical implications we also have to consider that all four components can be experienced at different levels of scale. The sensation of centre, for example, can happen as a response to the physical or spatial characteristics of a large city plaza, or the experience of it as a hub of social activity, whilst simultaneously, small locations within it may also engender centre sensations for a multitude of different reasons. This characteristic of CDTA resonates with theoretical conceptions developed by anthropologist Edward Hall in the 1960s at a time of growing concern with what many perceived as the placeless consequences of modernist planning and design. Hall and others at the time began to develop an understanding of space as an elaboration of culture where space becomes place as a consequence of what people do in it. This was probably the first time that attempts had been made to give rigorous intellectual foundations to the idea of spaces as living entities capable of growing, changing and declining along with the way people who use them give different meanings to them or ignore them. One of the consequences of giving such an explicitly humanistic dimension to the development of place theory was that it had to be understood, not only as a holistic entity comprising of integrations of material, spatial and human attributes, but also that it was subject to continual change and reformation according to the prevailing local circumstances. This seems to be what has prompted Relph (1976) to regard places to be indeterminate wholes, territories of social activity and meaning projected onto entire assemblages of buildings and spaces. Because of this living quality of place they should be viewed, according to Relph, with the clear understanding that it is not possible to design everything about them. Design action under these circumstances has to be reconceptualised as the generation of conditions under which places will flourish rather than the prescription of finite and static form.

Hall's work began to provide conceptual structure to the idea of places as manifestations of culture by highlighting that social interaction in the external environment may vary in its nature and purpose in response to the degree of privacy that is perceived to be available (Hall, 1966). Hall established that certain types of behaviour are sensitive to conditions of privacy and, especially in public places, perceptual influences may be particularly important. For example, intimacy or secrecy between people may take place in very public places if a perception of privacy can be found. This may be encouraged by the physical organisation of space, such as small-scale spaces adjacent to a main public arena or the presence of a focal point at which to meet. Even relatively incidental features, such as the availability of moveable tables and chairs, have been shown to have a profound impact on people's perceptions of privacy in public. This is because they provide the opportunity to take temporary territorial control through rearranging them to suit the needs of the individuals and groups using them at the time. Hall understood space to be dynamic and stretchy because it relates to human actions and has little to do with the static, mathematical geometry developed by Renaissance thinkers. In his view the general failure to grasp the implications of this had to do with a widespread acceptance that the human skin marked the boundary of the person. Anything inside the skin was part of the person and anything outside of it was not. According to Hall's research this seemed far too simplistic because it failed to take into account that human activity and perceptions project into the surrounding space and impact directly on what an individual does and feels. Significant aspects of what it is to be human are not confined within a material skin but manifest as "learned *situational* personalities" (Hall, 1966, p.115) associated with responses to intimate, personal, social and public transactions. Accordingly space had to be reconceptualised as a series of expanding and contracting fields surrounding an individual and through which different kinds of information was received and responded to. Hall developed these ideas into the theory of proxemic space premised on the idea that humans have innate tendencies to band together in mutually supportive, and usually small, social groupings. Space thus becomes an elaboration of culture and becomes distinctive through the activities of individuals and groups within this context.

The further relevance of proxemic space to experiential landscape lies partly with its elaboration in the late 1970s by Greenbie and Esser (1978) who use the theory to describe how culturally distinguishable urban villages and city neighbourhoods become apparent in large cities. They extend the concept by introducing the term distemic space, referring to the often large portions of major cities which are shared by a diversity of cultural sub-groups. Proxemic and distemic space function in a complimentary manner, but serve different purposes which have implications for the degree to which they can be personalised. In broad terms, proxemic space describes the homeground, which necessarily involves relatively high levels of personalisation relating to cultural needs and preferences. Distemic space, by comparison, is the place of challenge and enrichment that lies beyond. It offers diversity of experience but opportunities for personalisation may be more limited. Experience of both kinds are considered to be necessary to optimise human psychological health by balancing the need to be able to identify places of retreat, security and familiarity with the wider need to extend beyond this to explore and discover. The concepts of proxemic and distemic space together provide a foundation from which to explore the implications of the CDTA model as scale independent spatial experience. Just as we have described the way in which we conceive these four components working together to define different characteristics of place experience within the wider experiential landscape, we can now see how this holistic character works at different levels of scale. We call this characteristic of the experiential landscape experiemics (Figure 7.2).

Enfolded place

Earlier we alluded to an essential characteristic relevant to the design of experiential landscape. This was that it is not meaningful to talk about designing such a landscape in a finite and prescriptive manner because the definition of an experiential landscape has human dimensions that make it a fundamentally indeterminate entity. We suggested that it might be more meaningful to try to consider how to create the conditions in which experiential places might develop instead of trying to determine their precise nature. The question here then, is what

7.2

(a) Experiemic scale
(continued overleaf)

By developing from the foundations
of proxemic and distemic space we
can illustrate experiemic landscape
as an enfoldment of city, neighbourhood, public, social, private and
intimate levels of scale.

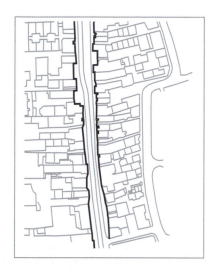

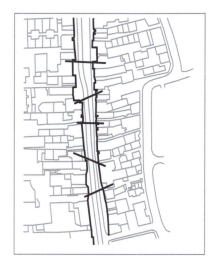

City: At the scale of the whole town or city this part of a street
itself reads as a unified whole against the wider town background. We can say that the street is a constituent part of the
town's spatial infrastructure yet at the same time it has its own
identity with, at this scale, a pronounced experiential quality of
direction.

Neighbourhood: This part of the street has potential as a
distinct neighbourhood within the overall town. The character of
this neighbourhood is given partly by the strong linear spatial
containment generated by the continuous building façades:
threshold transitions marking the boundary between built form
and open space, and partly by the activities it encourages and
supports: trading, living, movement, social activity, watching,
gathering. It is a neighbourhood distinguishable as one of the
town's main arteries. We can also see that the buildings forming the street stand back and forth from a common line creating an irregular, crinkled edge that breaks the continuity of the
street into segments. Each segment holds potential of its own:
a contributor to the overall streetscape and yet a smaller public
realm characterised by its own specific localised activity.

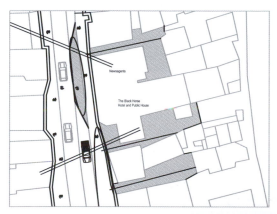

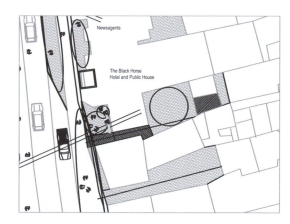

Public: Zooming into one of these segments reveals a picture of developing complexity. The single transition between building and street can now be seen to be
made up of two threshold transitions: one at the building edge and another at the
edge where the road tracking and protruding pavement helps to generate a small
centre offering opportunities for traders to sell goods, places for people to pause or
cross the street, or wait and watch.

Social: Moving in still further reveals that the building edge
threshold is in fact made up from a more complex range of
experiential possibilities. Rather than the general public milling
about, this is the scale of closer social interactions. Recessed
shop doorways create potential centres by encouraging pausing, browsing, shelter and social interaction. Similarly, the public house entrance offers outside seating generating opportunities for watching, waiting, meeting and restorative experiences.
The gap between the public house and the neighbouring property becomes more pronounced at this scale, creating a corridor
or segment transition linking the street with a rear courtyard,
itself another potential centre with a further transition beyond.

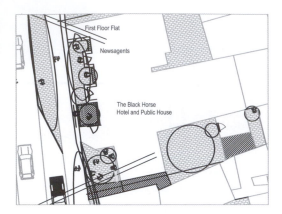

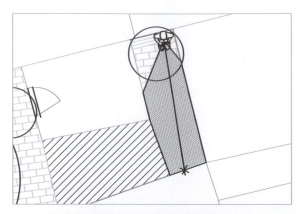

Personal: At this level of scale the recessed active frontage of the newsagent's shop becomes a mini-world of its own. Doorways and windows hold attention at a personal scale as centres and transitions, as do the steps and the landing they define in front of the hotel. A recessed part of the public house seating terrace offers a space for couples and private conversation, itself a small centre and at its edge a transition. In the alley courtyard the doorway where the public house chef meets colleagues on his way to work contributes still further to the build up of centred experience.

Intimate: The chef comes outside at break times to a place where he sits to escape the stress of his job. It is his refuge for a ten-minute break, a place to restore his sense of well-being, escape the demands of a busy kitchen. An apparently insignificant corner it offers the chef an intimate retreat where he can socialise with colleagues, or sit alone in quiet contemplation of the next menu and admire the view.

At the scale of the town this small corner seems almost vanishingly insignificant. Yet its significance to the routine of one of the town's inhabitants seems to amplify its value as a place to be loved rather than neglected. This chef's view is of a dismal brick wall, but disproportionate benefits might arise for him, and possibly the town's gastronomy, from paying attention to relatively small details at this scale, heightening the sense of location with a refreshing and uplifting break in a microcosm of delight rather than a dismal back yard.

7.2

(b) Experiemic scale and movement

(continued overleaf)

The scale of place perception also relates to speed of movement. This picture of a Normandy town, for example, might be taken to represent the clarity of our perception of it as we passed through by car. The nearby environment through which we pass blurs in experiential resolution so that, unless there are specific objects relevant to road safety or navigation, for example, the experiential landscape we form in these circumstances tends to be confined to messages conveyed by overall spatial and built form massing. On foot, and therefore slower, we can detect more detail. The surroundings thus come to sharper resolution enabling more features to influence the overall character of the experiential landscape.

Neighbourhood (left): In terms of experiemic scale we can say, then, that the experiential landscape relating to a journey by car is going to be predominantly characterised by occurrences at the neighbourhood level of scale. Like the street in the previous illustration, at the neighbourhood scale we mainly retain relatively course grain details so, for example, the gap between the buildings defines a threshold transition and the building façades contribute to a sense of segment transition on the main street as we pass through.

Public (right): The slower pace of walking, however, seems to have the effect of changing the experiemic scale. This time the same scene takes on more of the character of the public level of scale as details such as the configuration of the doors and windows adds a level of detail previously unappreciated. Focal points become significant: the coniferous tree above the roof line, the grouping of windows, and the detail of the hanging street lamp above the butchers. These add a finer grain of detail increasing the complexity of the experiential landscape allowing this location to be more easily distinguished from others along the road.

Social (left): Moving closer increases the significance of smaller details adding to the differentiation between the road and the side street entrance. Here it is apparent that there is a further sense of threshold, between the street and building edge, as well as across the street between the buildings. The building's projecting stonework differentiates between its internal floor level and the eaves mark the transition from vertical wall to rainwater gutter and mansard roof. The windows are now segment transitions making the building façade suddenly transparent with views in or out from the rendered elevations. The clustering of road signs, satellite receiver and street light at the street corner make a landmark feature, growing the directional content of the experiential landscape here.

Personal (right): Standing on the street corner the windows increase in significance as visual landmarks and now as individual segments instead of a collective against the walls. The building edge now becomes a vertical threshold to the openness of the street corner that runs downhill and the recessed doorway, now more apparent, offers a potential centre of social interaction, strengthened by the threshold feeling of emerging onto the streetscape.

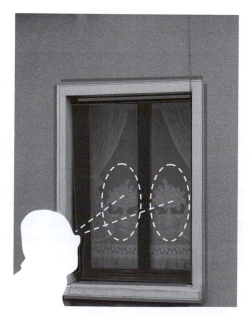

Intimate: Finally, at an intimate level, the windows offer more threshold where the change in material emphasises the recess and progression into the building. The patterns of the net curtains are now visible and, again, glimpses of inside are discerned. The once private has now the potential to be semi-private as details of the interior spill out into and contribute to the experience of the street.

might this mean for geometrical thinking? One way to explore this is by developing the idea of the experiential landscape as a field-like structure characterised by localised variations in the emphasis of CDTA. An important aspect of this conceptualisation of the experiential landscape is that combinations of CDTA are not inside of, or contained by, the experiential landscape. They are instead activities, or forces, of people-space relationships from which the experiential landscape as a distinguishable entity is formed. Experiential landscape places, as compositions of localised CDTA, are enfolded within the experiential landscape and just as cloth is no more or less than the weft and weave of fabric strands, then so the experiential landscape is no more or less than the continuity of experiential landscape place variation from which it is constituted. This amounts to trying to understand ways to create form and space generatively through processes of enfoldment rather than assembly. Conceptually this is quite different from processes commonly associated with the specification and prescription of form and space in a finite and deterministic sense.

A very simple figure that helps to highlight the generative and enfolded characteristics of experiential landscape can be drawn by considering kitchen roll. A recent TV advertising campaign sought to draw potential customers' attention to how much more absorbent a particular brand of kitchen roll was by comparison with its competitors. The secret, apparently, lay with the structural characteristics of the paper, specifically that the decorative pattern on its surface was made by embossing. In a close up view we could see that the surface of the paper was not flat at all but actually had a complex topography, a crinkly terrain of mounds, valleys and crevices all woven together forming an undulating and grainy three-dimensional surface. This, we were informed, not only made the paper more aesthetically appealing, it effectively increased the amount of moisture absorbent surface without increasing the overall dimensions of the sheets of paper. In other words the manufacturers had managed to give a certain sized sheet of paper a much larger effective surface area by crumpling it up. So, although its external dimensions were the same as if it had been entirely flat, its surface area was effectively much greater because of the enfoldment created by the crumpling process. This crumply paper could then hold more moisture than its non-crumply competitors. Another characteristic of crumply kitchen roll is that when liquid is introduced it will spread in an essentially indeterminate way. Until it becomes uniformly saturated, paper and moisture gradually mingle together in response to the conditions and forces prevailing between them. One cannot precisely predetermine, or design, how this will unfold. Moisture occupies and becomes embedded into the structure of the paper and the form of moisture staining develops gradually from the inherent properties of paper and liquid as both change in response to each other.

Moving then from kitchen roll to townscape we can attempt to provide a real world example by considering the urban landscape of a city like Prague. Particularly around the Old Town area in the city centre, Prague has a very complex and permeable character brought about partly by the way in which building façades that define the public realm continuously meander, are regularly penetrated and step forward and back in a wide range of ways to enclose small corners, alcoves, alleys, courtyards and squares, of different shapes and sizes, nearly all of which are occupied in a diversity of use. Prague seems alive with life at every turn. It is as though its irregular, crinkled streetscape has a kind of absorbent thirst for human activity, given birth by the pockets and corners everywhere within its labyrinthine spatial network. People and space in such settings weave together as though in an endless and dynamic dance generating, regenerating and destroying place continuously through action and interaction in and with the spatial structure (Figure 7.3).

The two photographs in Figure 7.4 illustrate this further. The one on the right is of a street in Florence which shows a more or less continuous building façade on both sides maintaining a uniform width of space between. Narrow pavements encourage little other than passage from one end to another. There is a rather smooth, non-crinkly quality to the street which has a bland lifeless appearance. In contrast, the street on the

7.3
Prague's labyrinthine spatial network seems to have an absorbent thirst for human activity of all kinds

left has its smoothness interrupted by a meandering façade that holds space on the pavement, defining a location where something interesting is possible. This sense of partial enclosure, given by the irregular line and permeability in building façade, allows this to become occupied as a place which functions simultaneously as somewhere to stay a while and somewhere through which to pass. Expressed in experiential landscape terminology, we would say that the Florentine street is emphatically directional with few centred or transitional qualities that might slow the directional pace. The Prague street is however much more balanced. It maintains clear directional characteristics, but also has strong centres and transitions that encourage and support sensations of location and engender a sense of anticipation of what might lie beyond (Figure 7.4).

Something of the essence of this can be found in research carried out by Sergio Porta and John Renne to explore the anatomy of streetscape and its relation to social sustainability. Porta and Renne (2005) developed a set of formal indicators of social sustainability and described their application in the analysis of towns in Western

Australia. Eight indicators were presented as ways in which the social sustainability of streets could be quantified. When we look at Porta and Renne's indicators we can see they are, in principle, similar to aspects of the CDTA model. For example, the indicators social width, visual complexity, number of buildings, and sedibility, all relate to measures of the locational attributes that give a roughness, or fine-grain quality, to streets, intensifying their social potential and making them more than mere conduits of movement. The indicators façade, continuity and sky exposure help weave this complexity together, maintaining the sensation of direction, whilst simultaneously providing a further dimension of enclosure. Another indicator is softness and this highlights the need for there to be transparency and transitional sensations. For example, to be able to see from where one is into other realms, by means of windows, for example, or other spatial features that encourage viewing in and out, and also to the need to be able to make, and experience, the sensation of transition from here to there (Table 7.1).

We might conclude from this that the social sustainability of a streetscape increases in

7.4

Crinkly and grainy, rather than smooth, edges seem to enhance the social sustainability of streetscape

Table 7.1   **Formal indicators of social sustainability in streetscape (after Porta and Renne)**

Indicator	Measurement	Significance
Sky exposure	The amount of visible sky in each photo.	Indicates the street's ability to encapsulate the pedestrian.
Façade continuity	The continuousness of the building façade.	Contributes to a sense of enclosure and definition.
Softness (transparency and transitional space)	The amount of window area (transparency) and visually accessible space (transitional space) that fronts onto the street.	Elements that can make a street environment feel safe and welcoming.
Social width	The breadth of the street as it effects human interaction across the traffic area.	Indicates the severance effect that traffic lanes and other features place on human interaction from one curb to another.
Visual complexity	The amount of visual variety in the street, specifically in terms of colour, façade detail, street furniture, pavement.	Describes the degree to which the street has a rich visual tapestry.
Number of buildings	The apparent quantity of buildings visible in the photographs.	Indicates the scale of the street in relation to the potential for human activity.
Sedibility (after Whyte, 1988)	The measure of the number of seating opportunities visible.	Indicates the potential of the street in terms of opportunities for social contact and interaction.
Detractors	Negative features on street social life (blank walls, aggressive automobile facilities, rejecting objects eg. poor graffiti, large dumpsters, low quality light poles etc.).	Indicates the negative effect of a street to provide a good scene for flourishing urban social life.

response to the degree of roughness it has been given by properties that balance the intrinsic directionality of a street with opportunities to pause, feel a sense of local enclosure, and make choices about when and how to deviate from the principal route. It is as though this roughness introduces to the street a kind of friction which acts to slow down the pace of movement by offering a range of ways to become psychologically engaged with the experience of the journey along it instead of it being simply a goal oriented corridor from A to B. Possibly then, the structural conditions we seek to achieve in the experiential landscape are those of a crinkly, irregular quality that is capable of enfolding a wide diversity of distinguishable spatial volumes but without ever making them feel entirely dislocated from one another. Such spatial structures we can regard to be experientially absorbent in that they have an overall sense of orderliness but yet remain in their detailed resolution sufficiently ambiguous to generate and support a diversity of human activity and expression.

Alexander's field of centres

We can develop a more detailed understanding of the nature of geometrical systems that seek to emphasise enfoldment and generative characteristics within the field of environmental design generally by considering aspects of the world view held by architectural theorist and practitioner Christopher Alexander. Alexander is perhaps most widely known for promoting an extremely humanistic stance toward architectural design and building which represents his passionate belief that architecture has become excessively professionalised and dominated by modernist rational ideology, detaching it from authentic human life with detrimental consequences for people and their habitat. The expression of these beliefs in his books *The Timeless Way of Building* and *A Pattern Language* has attracted world-wide attention since their publication in the 1970s and remains the work that Alexander is probably most readily associated with. Implicit in these books and developed in much greater detail in more recent publications however are fundamental aspects of Alexander's thinking that have received far less attention than they deserve.

Of much greater importance to Alexander than the pragmatic content of *A Pattern Language* is the geometry that forms the foundations of his pattern theory. Christopher Alexander's principal preoccupation has been to understand the fundamental nature of order and form and how this relates to the design and building of environmental structure, a formative motivation which has sustained his entire body of work for more than 40 years. His doctoral dissertation at Harvard University marks the first of a series of intellectual landmarks which trace the evolution of his ideas about the nature of environmental form. It was eventually published as *Notes on the Synthesis of Form* (Alexander, 1964). In *Notes* Alexander is concerned with the problem of design which he perceives in terms of a relationship of form and context. The objective, as far as Alexander is concerned, is to achieve a "frictionless coexistence" between the two (Grabow, 1983, p.36). The result of his investigation is, in places, a curious blend of holism and organic metaphor with the logic of arithmetical conventions and it is where several ideas that culminate in his most recent work have their origins. These include:

- the establishment of the primacy of relationships over parts;
- the fundamental role played by the lives and habits of people in the development and adaptation of good places;
- the realisation of the significance of wholes and the importance of relatively independently acting parts within them (Alexander, 1964).

Alexander moved to California after the completion of his PhD and was hired in 1964 to apply the ideas he had developed to an analysis of the San Francisco Bay Area Rapid Transit System

(BART). This provided Alexander with an opportunity to test his ideas empirically and the experience gave rise to several new lines of thought.

- First, the realisation that every system has its own requirements: design solutions are context dependent because the requirements which need to be addressed through design are particular to the specific system in question and arise from its unique circumstances.
- Second, these requirements have a complex, interacting structure like overlapping sets. The whole system is visualised in terms of an interconnected network of relationships between requirements and sets of requirements.
- Third, and most radical in the context of conventional approaches to architectural design, the mappings of these sets of requirements are thought to have a generative capacity (Grabow, 1983).

Alexander proposed that architecture specifically, rather than being seen merely as the product of an architect's imagination in response to problems, should itself be regarded as a generative system capable of bringing to manifestation its own structure from inside the system (Grabow, 1983). Through such a generative system Alexander thought people could re-establish the connection, or fit, between their life habits and their environmental structure directly. Two conceptual structures central to his system are relevant here. These are:

- patterns: which in very simple terms are conceived as the parts of a whole;
- differentiating space: essentially the way in which patterns are combined to make wholes.

PATTERN

"Each pattern describes a problem which occurs over and over again in our environment, and then describes the core of the solution to that problem, in such a way that you can use this solution a million times over, without ever doing it the same way twice" (Alexander *et al.*, 1977, p.x).

The kind of problem a pattern is concerned with can be considered as an event, conceptualised as an *event-spatial ensemble* which represents a particular aspect of the lives of people. A particular feature of the pattern language format, highlighted by Ingrid Fiksdhal-King, a colleague of Alexander's at the time and one of *A Pattern Language*'s contributors (1993), is that the reader is intended to be activated to participate in the inquiry relating to the pattern and its solution, thereby achieving a sense of ownership over the process and encouragement to personalise it. A crucial feature of the published pattern language presented by Alexander is its organisation in terms of scale. This partly reflects that *event-spatial ensembles* exist at different scales, but it is also critical to the process by which they are combined and foreshadows later work in which Alexander develops an explicitly geometric formulation (Alexander, 1993, 2002). Of much greater significance to the discussion here though is with the geometrical nature of what it is that enables different patterns to combine.

DIFFERENTIATING SPACE

"The overall character of these interactions is a very highly differentiated, high density spatial unity – a sort of maximum saturation of ordered interconnectedness, analogous to a poem which achieves, with the bare minimum of elements, the highest possible degree of meaning" (Grabow, 1983, p.201).

The concept of differentiating space represents Alexander's response to the idea that the systems he is concerned with have self-generating capabilities. That is, the final form arises, not from the interventions of external forces, architects' imaginations, for example, but from the activity of the parts within the system: parts which he now conceptualises as patterns. As far as Alexander is concerned the development of order in the built environment is entirely analogous to the development of an organism. Just as genetic codes are rules which influence the development of a complex living entity from within its fundamental material parts, so too does Alexander's language influence the development of environmental structure from within patterns. Differentiating space differs from more conventional ordering systems used in architecture and environmental design through its emphasis on processes of overlapping and integration, instead of assembling (Alexander et al., 1977). Each pattern is intended as an autonomous entity and is also intended to perform an integrative function by combining with other patterns, as a morphologically coherent language, to create larger wholes. The central significance of differentiating space is that it presents a different approach to spatial organisation than the conventional approaches based on Euclidean geometric principles. "It views design as a sequence of acts of complexification; structure is injected into the whole by operating on the whole and crinkling it, not by adding little parts to one another. In the process of differentiation, the whole gives birth to the parts: the parts appear as folds in a cloth of three-dimensional space which is gradually crinkled. The form of the whole, and the parts, come into being simultaneously" (Alexander, 1979, p.370). It is a system which enables environmental structure to arise out of potentially millions of small-scale adaptations. Although Alexander uses a biological metaphor to explain this process of enfoldment, graphic comparison can be made with a mathematical conception called Koch's triadic curve in which the three surfaces of a triangle are successively transformed with additional triangles (Kaye, 1989, p.33). The effect is a continuous crinkling of the straight edges so that, in theory, they progress towards a state of infinite length without enclosing significantly greater area. Three-dimensional equivalents of this also exist in mathematics: the Menger sponge for example (Gleick, 1988, p.101).

Some commentators have also remarked on the apparently unmistakeable correspondence between the underlying principles of differentiating space and fractal geometry, which was being developed by Benoit Mandelbrot around the same time. Mandelbrot was an IBM researcher during the 1960s and 70s and he coined the term fractal to describe a new geometry reflecting the grainy roughness observable throughout the natural world at all levels of scale. By famously pointing out in 1967 that the length of the English coastline was actually relative depending on the length of the measuring apparatus used he demonstrated that conventional Euclidian geometry was inadequate to describe the way that most natural systems appear to fold and unfold to create broken, wrinkled and uneven shapes and forms. One of the more arresting properties of fractal geometry is that it deals with the way objects fill space between the conventional Euclidian dimensions of 1, 2 and 3 revealing that Euclidian geometry, no matter how successful and established, is a very crude approximation when it comes to describing the reality of natural systems. Because of the enfolded and interwoven nature of many objects mathematicians now talk of fractal dimensions between the Euclidian dimensions. A sheet of paper for example in a Euclidian sense is a two-dimensional plane. But if it is screwed up into a rough sphere, the resulting object is neither a plane nor a sphere, but something folded in between the second and third dimensions. In fractal geometry such an object is said to have a dimension of about 2.5.

The Koch triadic curve is one of a number of mathematical abstractions brought into chaos theory by Mandelbrot to illustrate the ambiguity that can occur when objects beginning with one Euclidian dimension gradually, by means of repeated iterations, evolve towards another. There appears to be no clear point at which an abrupt jump is made from one dimension to the next. Instead there seems to be a smooth generative

tendency towards increasing complexity and a gradual transformation from one dimension to the next. The significance of this to the discussion in this section is that it shows how processes of folding and crinkling can act on a system of a given initial extent, increasing its capacity through the gradual packing and condensing of its component parts, without significantly increasing its original extent. This general principle is known to have implications for the bio-diversity potential of eco-systems. Most students of ecology are made aware that eco-tones, the edges where two different eco-systems meet, are potentially richer in ecological potential because the interference between them creates a fusion that merges both systems with a third arising from the conditions caused by their overlap. Instead of arranging the eco-tone in a straight line across the available distance it is best, to maximise bio-diversity potential, to have eco-tones that meander to increase the length over the same distance. This is the same as starting with an eco-tone of significantly longer length and folding it so that its total length can be packed into the shorter distance available, consequently increasing the ecological capacity across that distance. This is essentially the way things are arranged in the natural world (Figure 7.5).

In essence fractal geometry has made it possible to visualise the nature of so called chaotic systems. Fractal patterns are the visible evidence left behind by the dynamic, chaotic forces at work on natural systems and, for Mandelbrot and others since, represent a more accurate way to understand how nature presents to us. This resonates with the view held by Richard Forman, outlined in the previous section, that there appear to be certain kinds of spatial arrangement that manifest because they are the visible traces left by the dynamic forces that shape the world around us. Forman believes that what he observes in landscape ecology could equally be applied to the human habitat. If this is the case then it may be reasonable to extend this to include the possibility that aspects of urban morphology may also exhibit fractal-like attributes and there are those that have investigated this possibility, although for the time being this seems to have been confined to large-scale phenomena like the

7.5

Meandering eco-tones increase biodiversity

a straight eco-tone

a meandering eco-tone

cross section through eco-tone

growth of whole towns and cities (Batty and Longley, 1994).

However, although perhaps rather speculative, a sense of the enfoldment that characterises some fractal systems can be observed in the Cumbrian town of Kendal. The structure of Kendal high street has a rather crinkly nature given by the way in which the building façade subtly steps forward and back from its principal alignment, expanding and contracting the width of the street along its length and creating a series of small pavement enclosures that allow a varied approach to the way shop doorways, and public house and café entrances are used and configured, for example. This line, represented by the black line on the plan below (left), shows the length of the active façade of Kendal high street for the distance contained on the map. The length of the active façade is, in a sense, a measure of the experiential and social potential of the street because, as we have established earlier, the more active a façade the more opportunity exists for locational and transitional experience along its length. These experiences have a tendency to slow the directional emphasis of the street as a corridor of movement, creating a richer and more varied range of experience. But, one of the unique characteristics of Kendal is the way in which the high street façade is punched through frequently allowing access into a wide range of alleys. These alleys are occupied by a diversity of recreational, commercial and residential use, the majority of them accessible to the public using the high street. The effect of this is to dramatically increase the length of the active façade of Kendal high street, represented by the black line on the second plan (right), because it continuously wriggles back and forth as it covers the distance along the street (Figures 7.6, 7.7).

The characteristic enfoldment of fractal systems, for some a fundamental property of the natural and cultural world, is implicit in the way Alexander conceptualises differentiating space. In this he is trying to articulate a kind of alternative geometrical structure by means of which systems progress towards more complex states as a consequence of the cumulative impact of many small actions and adaptations made to the system as a whole. It describes an approach to planning and design that does not begin with a fully formed conceptual solution, predetermined in all its aspects, but an approach which first looks at the existing system and then asks by what sequence of small adaptations the system can be made better, or in Alexander's terms, more whole. In this respect Alexander accepts that the final form of a structure has to be understood as indeterminate because what eventually emerges is the consequence of a generative system rather than the fabrication of a previously fully formed idea. In recent work Alexander has increasingly turned his attention to trying to identify more precisely the geometrical components of his overall concept of differentiating space because he sees this as being instrumental to the way in which a sense of wholeness can be brought to the environment.

Fundamental to this is what Alexander now refers to as centering, the means by which different aspects of a system are connected together to make more complex spatial wholes. Alexander uses the word centre here in a primarily visual sense referring to the perception of centrality and locus in a visual field. In this respect he acknowledges a convergence of view with Rudolph Arnheim's discussion about the importance of centricity to composition in the visual arts as "the self-centred attitude that characterises the human outlook and motivation at the beginning of life and remains a powerful impulse throughout" (Arnheim, 1988, p.2). It is interesting to note that, as well as aligning with Arnheim's theory of visual arts, Alexander also appears to resonate with other theoretical developments in environmental design which, in various ways, highlight an apparently innate human tendency to externalise locational sensations in the environment as part of our orientation processes (Cullen, 1971; Lynch, 1960; Norberg-Schulz, 1971). Alexander's principal interest, though, is with how the visual perception of centre relates to a sense of balance in geometrical systems. This appears to have been stimulated to a large extent by an interest in analysing the visual complexity of patterns in early Turkish carpets (Alexander, 1993). The ones he thought had greater quality seemed to possess certain visual properties that could be seen in the shapes, lines and colours making up the pattern.

7.6

The varied active frontages of Kendal's yards

One of these properties seemed to have more significance than others because it seemed to control the overall sense of coherence and organisation in the carpet pattern. Alexander named this property centre and this was later to become the building block of wholeness, not only in carpet patterns, but in all visual phenomena.

One of the defining characteristics of Alexander's centres is that they are not actually made of anything in particular, but are defined only in terms of order and organisation. "Centers are made up of other centers. A center is an organisation (or field) of other centers. It achieves its significance to the degree that each of these centers which it is made of, is itself significant" (Alexander, 1993, p.49). By conceptualising centres in terms of a kind of holistic visual field, instead of a more conventional, contained shape

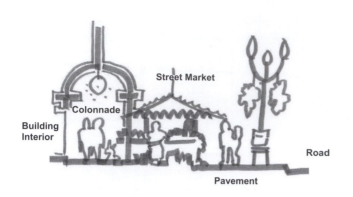

7.7

The experiential equivalent of an eco-tone. Where building meets street there is potential for rich experiential diversity and this can be increased by folding to compress greater length into a given limited distance

as might be understood in a Euclidian sense, Alexander begins to reveal a picture of a geometrical process that seems very much like the characteristic enfoldment apparent in fractal systems. In his most recent work, *The Nature of Order*, Alexander continues to develop the geometrical characteristics that apply to generating a field of centres. He argues, as a consequence of his observations of natural and cultural systems and objects, that structure with wholeness, or life, emerges through a succession of structure-preserving transformations that act on the whole (2002). He sees this transformation as an act of differentiation, an increment in the development of a structure, each stage of which should create a barely detectable change to the existing structure.

The cumulative effect of a long succession of such transformations would however generate a structure very different and more complex than the original: the gradual transformation of an acorn into an oak tree, for example.

So, rather than conceptualise the development of order as something that can be prescribed at the outset and then fabricated, it should instead be allowed to unfold in response to a series of small transformations, each of which must respect the integrity of the structure as it exists at that time so that the unfolding takes place smoothly and in seamless continuity. The mechanism by which these transformations happen is by creating new centres and each time a new centre is created in the system it must do three things simultaneously: it must achieve its own distinguishable identity; it must help to resolve and strengthen centres that already exist next to it; and it must contribute to the development of larger scale centres. The holistic interplay of these three properties of centre is essentially what Alexander means by a field of centres. The wholeness that an organisation of centres produces is not to be understood simply as an assemblage of parts but in terms of the complex organisation evident in the relationship of distinguishable parts which are inseparable from their surroundings.

Alexander uses an explicitly biological analogy to explore the way in which complex wholes are generated and then claims that certain geometrical features can be abstracted for use in human-made cultural contexts. He gives us a vision of environmental order that exhibits wholeness, argues that it is the property of wholeness we should aspire to achieve above all else, and sets out the way that this gradually develops through the integrating effect of many small-scale localised acts distinguishable in their own right but which simultaneously form part of the evolution of larger scale order. In a sense this describes a continuous dialogue that must be established between the parts of a system and the larger whole they gradually generate. Alexander conceptualises this dialogue as a process of differentiation, of splitting and division, rather than fabrication and assembly. The components that allow the differentiation process to successfully propagate are called centres. Alexander insists that, although his inquiry lies with trying to reveal the underlying geometrical structure of environmental order, the centres he describes as the fundamental building blocks are not simply abstract principles but are intended to be a fundamental part of a deeper and more complex attempt to unify geometry, human experience, and spatial form and function. Alexander fervently believes that this kind of holistic spatial structure is intrinsic to all fulfilled human life because he believes it to be an expression of an innate sense of order that primarily Western techno-scientific culture has become detached from. Achieving and sustaining human well-being means, for Alexander, acknowledging that there are geometric and spatial dimensions to human fulfillment and that this should be reflected in the arrangement of our towns and cities.

Conclusions

What we have tried to do in this chapter is relate the characteristics of the experiential landscape concept to geometrical considerations. We have done this because geometrical awareness is fundamental to the activity of design as the principal means by which we conceptualise our surroundings and visualise future possibilities. In relation to experiential landscape, however, we have shown that the prevailing Euclidian geometry is significantly limited because it is predicated on a view of the human-environment relationship that is inconsistent with that at the heart of experiential landscape. Because the experiential landscape is conceptualised as the visible manifestation of relationships of human functioning and where they take place, geometrical systems based on the premise that our spatial surroundings can be detached from human functioning have to be abandoned. Instead we need a fundamental shift of thinking away from this dualism towards a much more holistic attitude capable of embracing that what we do to our material surroundings we do to ourselves. The condition of our nearby world in particular affects how we feel and what we do just as the condition of our material body does. Alexander's conception of differentiating space, its fractal-like character and its emphasis on the geometry of enfoldment presents an alternative geometry in stark contrast to that of Euclid. By conceiving visual entities called centres as a means by which order can propagate smoothly towards more complex, whole and supposedly fulfilling forms he presents possibly the most comprehensive attempt to describe how a holistic philosophy of the human-environment relationship can be translated as creative activity. But, although Alexander's vision of the nature of order is intellectually exciting it seems, especially in recent work, emphatically to be derived from exhaustive analysis of the form, shape, pattern and decorative quality of natural and cultural objects as they appear in the visual field. Although the underlying principles make an undoubtedly important contribution to understanding the geometry of holistic systems, it is often hard to grasp exactly how to translate this form of geometrical order in relation to the spatial sensations of the outdoor environment.

Informed by Alexander's geometrical structure, though, we can look again, for example, at Cullen's vision of townscape as a means to try to summarise geometrical characteristics relevant to designing with experiential landscape. Two things in particular stand out from this. One has implications for the way that space is conceptualised, and the second helps us to develop further Alexander's idea of environmental structure as a field of centres. Gordon Cullen is perhaps most widely known for developing the idea of serial vision. In doing this Cullen aimed to change awareness of the urban realm away from assemblages of discrete locations, objects and buildings to a more dynamic and fluid experience driven by the way focal points, landmarks, views, openings, etc., act collectively to draw people through space. We get the impression from Cullen of a town as an unbroken spatial continuity that we navigate around in response to the arrangement of a diversity of visual devices. Implicit in the way that Cullen talks about this, though, is the suggestion that he sees something more than vision at work here. He is clearly aware, for

example, that people react in different ways according to the rhythm of compression and release felt as they move about. "There is a reaction to being hemmed in as in a tunnel and another to the wideness of the square" (Cullen, 1971, p.10). It is important for Cullen that towns and cities be configured in such a way as to optimise exposure to this rhythmical structure of fluctuating volumes. In so doing he begins to see "how the whole city becomes a plastic experience, a journey through pressures and vacuums, a sequence of exposures and enclosures, of constraints and relief" (Cullen, 1971, p.10).

This appears to imply a concept of space that is not simply a series of empty volumes through which people pass, but instead is something capable of conveying to us fluctuations in the level of containment felt, almost as though containment exerted a detectable pressure-like experience on people. In this respect space is not an external entity at all but more like an extension of the self that projects beyond the body to fill and probe the material surroundings and convey information about its qualities. This presents a spatial dimension to human existence very much like that advocated by Edward Hall in the implication that space can be understood to be a kind of stretchy sensory-like projection that allows us to understand and respond to certain qualities of our surroundings. Indeed, in this respect, we are not actually "in" our surroundings as such, but in some sense our surroundings are more like a part of us. What Cullen appears to be suggesting in essence is that the best arrangements for our built environment are those that can stimulate this aspect of our existence with forms that cause us to stretch and flex the spatial dimensions of our self as we move about. As the diagram below illustrates, this may be more easily achieved in situations that have a crinkly, uneven and grainy quality because this forces our spatial dimension to become compressed and stretched into a greater diversity of configurations as it progresses (Figure 7.8).

If space, as an entity independent of human functioning, is seen to be an abstract artefact of Euclidian geometry then it may follow that there is no separate medium as such through which people move. People, in a sense carry their spatial

7.8

"...the whole city becomes a plastic experience, a journey through pressures and vacuums, a sequence of exposures and enclosures, of constraints and relief" (Cullen, 1971, p.10)

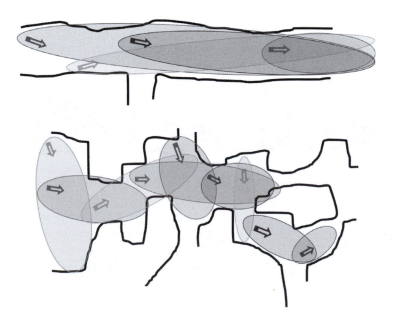

dimension with them and it is through the medium of space that experiential landscape places are created out of a fusion of the human, spatial and material as they act on and integrate with each other. So, by means of this reconceptualisation of space as an extension of human functioning, we can begin now to see how the flexing and stretching of our spatial selves becomes the means by which we create distinguishable experiential landscape places. In Alexander's terms, the diagrams above form fields of centres where at each location of the arrow a subtly different kind of spatial experience occurs. We can therefore see Cullen's conception of townscape as a complex field of centres woven together as a whole. Perhaps because Cullen is concerned with the bodily sensations people encounter throughout urban settings, rather than primarily the abstract geometry of the visual field, the interpretation of the term centre here can be assigned a broader experiential definition according to the sensations that predominate as one progresses. Some centres, for example, may emphasise locational sensations, like squares and courtyards, some may have predominantly directional qualities, like streets, colonnades and passages, others still may engender transitional sensations, like gateways, arches, doorways and windows. Viewed this way it seems as though the crinkly configuration in the second diagram has a greater capacity, or potential, to generate these kinds of

spatial experiences because its arrangement offers a diversity of ways that the spatial dimensions of the human self can be accommodated. This type of arrangement is, in a sense, more absorbent of experiential potential than the other one where the more uniform smoothness tends to limit the diversity of spatial experiences available.

There is also some evidence in Cullen's work that he may have empathised with Alexander's view that complex environmental order must be understood to arise incrementally as a consequence of a series of small transformations. As part of an analysis of the town of Tenterden in Kent, carried out for Kent County Council and the Borough of Tenterden in 1967, Cullen provides a fascinating insight into the way that the final form of a small corner can be understood through an incremental process which breathes life into it by acting in stages to gradually strengthen its sense of location and connection to neighbouring spaces. Although this is in fact an analysis of an existing street corner it is perfectly possible to imagine this illustrating part of a design process involving the kind of smooth structure-preserving transformations that Alexander envisages, beginning with a simple form and acting on that form in relatively small ways to gradually generate the final form of the street corner. Each iteration preserves the initial structure but intensifies it little by little, each detail increasing its complexity and its sense of being a living whole (Figure 7.9).

7.9

Turning a Corner in Tenterden (after Cullen)

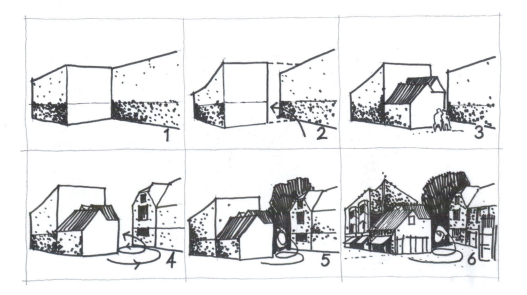

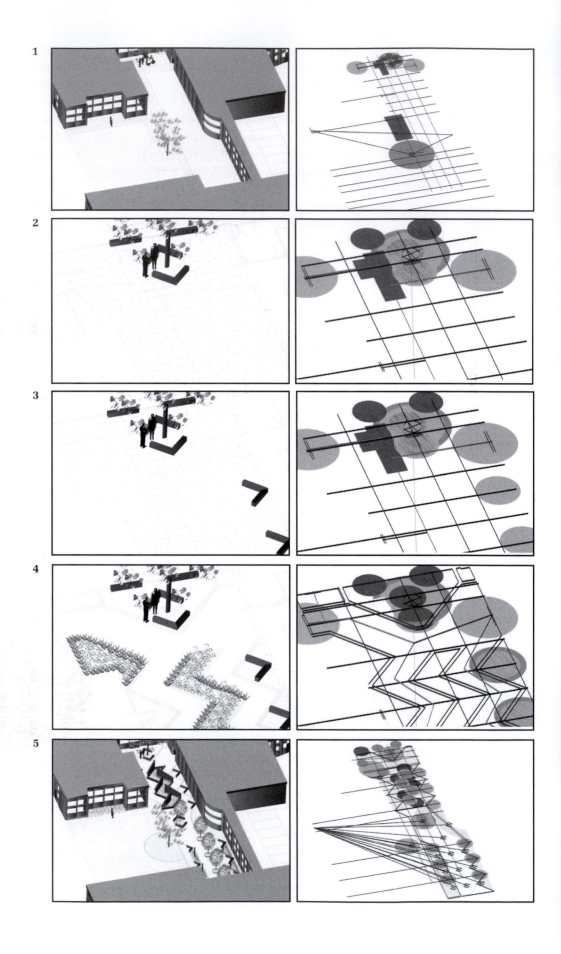

7.10
The incremental growth of an experiential landscape

A corner is a significant event in a street. Here a corner, at the Woolpack, is investigated for its qualities.

1. The T-square solution. A diagram without life but all too common.
2. The space enclosed in the angle is given life by the gap. We can pass through it. It is not a dead corner with little eddies of old newspapers.
3. The impersonal blocks are given scale by the small building projecting from the front line of buildings.
4. The corner is now given its own internal life by the public house which commands it and which corresponds with the shop opposite.
5. The blackness of the tree-shade beyond gives depth and recession in contrast to the sparkling façades.
6. Lastly the façades are given direction or the quality of facing. The street faces out to the busy road, the shop turns the corner and gives in to the space. The Woolpack shares this but gives life to the alley and the Town Hall porch extends the space (Cullen, 1967, p.82).

We have said that experiential landscape is that which is generated from the coalescent effect of experiential landscape places, defined as fluctuations in the extent to which we are aware locally of spatial sensations called centre, direction, transition and area. Experiential landscape and the experiential landscape places from which it is composed are in essence visible manifestations of situated human action, living and indeterminate entities that cannot be fully prescribed in fixed and final form and then fabricated. These characteristics render their design, in a conventional sense, problematic. In an attempt to begin to respond we have explored the structural and geometric implications of experiential landscape. If we accept experiential landscape as a fusion of human experiential and spatial dimensions which appear as a dynamic, fluid field-like structure in continuous change, we have to accept also that its form is, to some extent, a residual outcome of situated human action, rather than an aesthetic, technical or even social aspiration capable of being predetermined. It is the visible

trace of the forces at work in the relationship between human functioning and where it happens. This means that the role of design in experiential landscape is less about prescribing and fabricating form and more about creating the conditions in which to optimise experiential opportunity, accepting that to some extent final form will appear as it will and change and evolve. We have seen through our investigation in this section that attention to small-scale detail is what seems to matter more in this respect than large-scale formal interventions. It is important that a sense of the whole is consistently maintained and that each act of design or change is undertaken in such a way that it achieves and sustains a sense of its own identity whilst at the same time being embedded in its context so that it supports and intensifies its surroundings and does not stand abruptly isolated from it. It appears that this fine balance of self-assertion with integrative tendency seems more likely to be achieved in environments where there is a kind of roughness arising from an irregular, grainy and crinkled structure, than in environments that do not have these properties (Figure 7.10).

The application of experiential landscape

Introduction

In this final section we present four examples to show the potential of the concept of experiential landscape in a variety of contexts. The first of these looks specifically at residential environments and we have chosen three from a wider range of field studies carried out to refine details of the way experiential landscape might be used in site analysis alongside other methods and tools. This shows how aspects of the experiential potential of a residential setting can be read by relating observations of its spatial organisation to experiential concepts. The method used replicates how people actually experience the outdoor environment as a sequential journey to see how variations in spatial configuration along the way might be related to place experience. Experiential landscape maps are used in conjunction with bar charts to provide a visually accessible way to record the fluid, rhythmical changes in experiential character throughout the routes selected. These are used to summarise the main experiential qualities evident and help to identify potential strengths and weaknesses that will help inform change or bring focus to subsequent resident participation work.

In the cases we present in chapter eight, they are the outcome of outside professional observations and do not take into account the place perceptions of the resident population. Our purpose in doing this is to show that experiential landscape methods can be used efficiently and effectively as part of conventional site and user investigations to highlight experiential issues that may warrant further exploration. As we have explained previously they consequently present a partial, but nonetheless valuable, picture of the experiential landscape of the journeys explored. In chapter nine we move on from this to show how experiential landscape methods were used in a comprehensive public participation project. In this case professional observations, similar to the ones undertaken in chapter eight, were used as a scoping exercise to inform the content of a programme of semi-structured interviews. These were carried out as a means of revealing the place perceptions of residents in a North Yorkshire village to help inform a wider study about the village's identity and sense of place. This example shows how findings from the interviews are coded to form experiential landscape maps for each participant and then how these are layered to produce a composite picture of the experiential landscape for the village. Interpretation of this allows us to demonstrate the way in which certain locations and features in the village and beyond come to prominence and how these help to bring an understanding to a range of issues concerned with the village's sense of community, perceptions of its boundaries and its relationship to the surrounding landscape and neighbouring settlements.

Experiential landscape principles, as a cornerstone of participative practice, continue in chapter ten. Here we look at three projects where experiential landscape methods have been used to understand and then inform changes in school grounds. In particular this shows how participative methods, like those outlined in chapter nine, are extended and refined for use with young children. The work with schools shows how experiential landscape techniques help to bring into focus the nature of a school's collective personality, the essence of its physical and psychological character, which emanates from the school's community and how this informs subsequent change. Often the outcomes are relatively low-key, reflecting the budgetary and practical constraints that often characterise school grounds and other kinds of community based environmental improvement schemes. Importantly, in this context, they demonstrate how, by focusing attention on the experiential landscape of the school, designed solutions can be made to be as experientially rich as possible within these limitations.

Our final example explores the experiential landscape characteristics of high profile urban regeneration along the Calls waterfront area in Leeds. The purpose here was to use the concept of experiential landscape to help investigate the development of this part of Leeds city as an evolving urban neighbourhood. A significant increase in residential population here has been the consequence of a major regeneration programme over many years, a programme that has also produced, in many ways, a sensitive blend of contemporary development and traditional character including a fine spatial configuration of streets, yards and public spaces. In experiential terms, we would expect such spatial complexity to be associated with strong sensations of centre, but initial scoping investigations tended to suggest that this may not in fact be the case and we wondered about what implications this might hold for the evolution of the area as a residential neighbourhood and whether spatial issues could be associated with its potential to support a sustaining community. Our work in Leeds has been primarily conceptual and we are indebted to the many students and research colleagues that have contributed to the work over a five-year period. We believe however, that by revealing something of the experiential landscape of the Calls we can identify issues relating to the relationship between spatial and experiential dimensions of urban settings like these that would warrant further investigation as the nationwide programme of urban regeneration continues to unfold.

Chapter 8

Reading the experiential landscape in residential settings

Introduction

In this chapter we turn our attention to residential settings to show how experiential landscape mapping techniques can be used to read aspects of their experiential potential. Where people live and what they experience there probably matters most to them in terms of sustaining a general sense of well-being and we have argued that whatever else might be involved, good health, family and social relations, economic stability, for example, this is partially, yet crucially, related to being able to orientate, become aware of one's own neighbourhood, and be able to attach meaning and significance to particular locations. Routine exposure to these experiences provides foundations from which neighbourhoods form and where communities may establish and be sustained, or indeed fail to be. Our contention is that the experiential potential of a residential setting in this respect, to a limited degree, lies implicit in its spatial configuration and this can be read by recording and mapping the distribution of CDTA for particular settings.

The examples we illustrate here will demonstrate this by exploring the experiential characteristics of a journey through each of the settings. The reason we present this material in the form of a series of journeys is because this is

the reality of how place is experienced. Design professionals, from the very start of their training, become used to looking at the entirety of a setting all at once usually through the medium of a plan. Whilst there are all sorts of good reasons why this should be, it is not how real places are experienced by people: in normal daily life no one ever perceives their surroundings as if they can somehow occupy everywhere at once. Instead our experience of the outdoor environment is more closely related to the expansion and contraction of spatial volume as we move about. Place experience is sequential and continuous and so the most realistic way to explore this is to try to see how experiential character changes fluidly as we make our way around, and to use this to see what aspects of the physical world might be generating these changes.

The residential settings we have chosen to look at here are ones that have been reported in the academic and professional literature because of their association, for various reasons, with aspects of good practice in the application of a range of urban design principles. We were curious to explore what could be learnt by using some of the principles of experiential landscape to understand the experiential characteristics of their spatial attributes. It is important to note that the experiential landscape maps generated for each setting arise from field observations carried out by professionally trained research teams. They do not include other layers of information gathering that would give insight into the place perceptions of the resident population or other setting users. Here, this is intentional because we want to show how experiential landscape techniques can be used relatively quickly as a means of augmenting conventional site survey and analysis work. Applying experiential landscape in this way will add an experiential dimension to conventional processes of site analysis. It will do this to a limited extent of course, but in practical situations where resources or circumstances will not allow more detailed user consultation it will at least highlight where and why, in relation to spatial configuration, a setting may be expected to deliver weak or strong experiential characteristics and also what the nature of that experiential character is and how it evolves and develops with movement through the setting. Even without user group information this gives a valuable extra dimension to help inform subsequent decisions about change. It will also provide an important scoping study for later resident interviews and we will explain this later when we talk about the Kirby Hill village identity project. The approach we outline here will tell of the experiential potential of a setting in relation to its spatial characteristics: mapping the experiences of the resident population as well, however, will give a fuller picture of how it actually is.

Each of the examples we will describe here follows the same format. First, the journey is identified indicating points along the way where photographs give a sense of the spatial sequence. At each of these points a record of the experiential characteristics apparent to the research teams, in terms of CDTA, has been recorded. It is important to note that what is recorded is what is evident at that location and not just what can be seen in the picture: the photograph in this context is merely a device for recording position and sequence. These findings are expressed in tables which first record what aspects of CDTA are evident there and why. This identifies what aspects of the prevailing physical and spatial circumstances the team has associated with stimulating particular experiential sensations. An indication of whether the intensity of awareness of the sensation is deemed to be weak, moderate or strong is also made. Admittedly, this aspect is both crude and highly subjective and it owes more to practical efficiency than scientific rigor. Nonetheless, it is useful because it takes into account that different types of experience, expressed as CDTA, are not either there or not there, like a binary switch, but are more like the volume of music. Sometimes and in different places certain aspects speak more loudly than others. This information is then used to generate an experiential landscape map and the bar chart information from the tables is brought together in a more condensed visual form. This, then, represents the unique experiential "fingerprint" of that particular journey through the residential setting.

The examples we describe here include: The Piggeries in Frome, Somerset, a small infill development in a historic part of town; Friary's Court in Beverley, Humberside, a sequential courtyard development joining the railway station to the Minster and Poundbury in Dorchester, Dorset, the first phase of a town extension. Only the Piggeries is presented in full, showing the completed sequence of tables. The others are summarised with the photographic sequence, experiential landscape map and the condensed bar chart table.

The Piggeries, Frome, Somerset

The Piggeries is an example of new housing that has been well integrated into the existing town. The development consists of 71 social housing units, including a mix of family housing, flats and warden assisted sheltered housing. The site is located within the Frome Conservation area on the edge of the historic Trinity area of the town. It is bounded by Castle Street to its northern boundary and Catherine Street to the south. Both have historical value and contribute to the distinct identity of the town. The site slopes sharply down from Castle Street and a distinctive feature of the Piggeries development is the way in which change in level has been creatively incorporated into the pedestrian access across the site. Within the site there is a strong sense of containment, partly because of the way the new buildings have been arranged along the sloping side. The development along Castle Street helps to define and maintain the integrity of the residential streetscape quality. The use of traditional stone walls extensively within the site gives a distinct character to the development and helps with its integration into the wider town. The built form is varied which adds to its visual appeal, but it is interesting to note that this appears to have been achieved through the repetition of a deceptively simple design language which combines a built form proportioned and rendered sensitively in response to the surrounding area with contemporary detailing, especially in strategically located window details. It was an objective of the development not to produce a pastiche of Frome design but to incorporate characteristics that contribute to its visual identity and produce a modern scheme that would blend with its context. The whole ensemble produces a development that successfully enhances the character of the wider setting whilst at the same time projects a sense of its own identity (Figure 8.1).

The journey we are concerned with on the Piggeries development begins in Castle Street. Strictly speaking this is actually outside of the main body of the development but one of the characteristic aspects of The Piggeries is the way in which it establishes and maintains the integrity of the streetscape along Castle Street with building

form, proportion and finishing responsive to the existing cottages on the north side of the street. Another characteristic feature evident along Castle Street is that the building line is interrupted periodically with gaps that allow pedestrian access into the main body of the site. Sometimes this is quite understated and almost incidental whilst in other places more of a prominent feature has been created with stone walls that signal the points of entry along with other items of street furniture, lamps for example. One of these entrances, about half way along Castle Street, is particularly characterful in the way that the stone wall projects into the street causing a narrowing in the tracking of the road, making a landmark feature and emphasising a sense of pedestrian priority. These entrances lead into passages and gaps between the buildings that take pedestrians down steps into the interior of the development, sometimes giving access to private gardens. These usually afford good views across the site taking full advantage of the elevated position and frequently change direction in a way that seems to intensify the experience of moving through into a different realm. With greater maturity in the adjacent private gardens as shrubs and other plants develop there is potential for their landscape value to develop still further. These features make The Piggeries especially permeable across the site and as well as contributing characterful elements of townscape, have helped to maintain footfall on the peripheral streets and nearby retail area (Figure 8.2 and Plate 7).

Summary

The summary table (Plate 7) reveals clearly that view direction and area are experiential characteristics that are most consistent in the experiential landscape of The Piggeries. This appears to be due mainly to a series of low-key, but nonetheless prominent, visual features (protruding walls, lamppost and corner window detail, for example) along Castle Street itself coupled with the way in which periodic gaps in the continuity of the street façade reveal views into and across the site to the south. These are dramatised by the surprise revelations generated by periodic openings in what appears from the street as an unbroken façade, the elevated position above the main body of the site

8.1
The Piggeries journey with the picture locations marked

Ref	Type	Subtype	What	Why	Intensity
A1	Area		Castle Street	Architectural coherence: colour, roof lines, render, window detail.	Strong
C1	Centre	Social Interaction	Recess in building line	Front door to street. Occasional people meeting	Weak
D1	Direction	Movement	Footpath along south side Castle Street	Wider pavement width; more varied streetscape; fewer cars parked	Moderate

Intensity chart (Strong / Moderate / Weak) across columns:

	Centre			Direction		Transition				Area
	Social Imageability	Social Interaction	Restorative Benefit	View	Movement	Threshold	Segment	Corridor	Ephemeral	Thematic Continuity

Ref	Type	Subtype	What	Why	Intensity
A1	Area		Castle Street	Architectural coherence: colour, roof lines, render, window detail.	Strong
C2	Centre	Social Interaction	Entrance to site interior	Occasional people meeting	Weak
C3	Centre	Social Imageability	Stone pillars and lamp post	Change of material makes visually prominent feature. Recess widens pavement and lamp post anchors	Moderate
D1	Direction	Movement	Footpath along south side Castle Street	Wider pavement width; more varied streetscape; fewer cars parked	Moderate
D2	Direction	View	Stone wall, lamp post, bin, gable	Focal point from combination of features	Moderate

Intensity chart (Strong / Moderate / Weak) across columns:

	Centre			Direction		Transition				Area
	Social Imageability	Social Interaction	Restorative Benefit	View	Movement	Threshold	Segment	Corridor	Ephemeral	Thematic Continuity

Ref	Type	Subtype	What	Why	Intensity
A1	Area		Castle Street	Architectural coherence: colour, roof lines, render, window detail.	Strong
C2	Centre	Social Interaction	Entrance to site interior	Occasional people meeting	Weak
C3	Centre	Social Imageability	Stone pillars and lamp post	Change of material makes visually prominent feature. Recess widens pavement and lamp post anchors	Moderate
C4	Centre	Social Interaction	Space at top of steps	Platform off road at confluence of route across site and private garden gates	Moderate
C5	Centre	Social Imageability	Space at top of steps	Pillars and walls hold square enclosure. Strong entrances and exits	Moderate
T1	Transition	Threshold	Stone pillars and change of surface material	Gateway and framing element	Moderate
T2	Transition	Threshold	Stone pillars and top of steps	Gateway, change in level and direction	Strong
D3	Direction	View	Stone pillars and building facade	Focal point from framing and perspective of stone walls and facade detail esp. column of small windows and stairwell column	Strong

Intensity chart (Strong / Moderate / Weak) across columns:

	Centre			Direction		Transition				Area
	Social Imageability	Social Interaction	Restorative Benefit	View	Movement	Threshold	Segment	Corridor	Ephemeral	Thematic Continuity

8.2

The complete record of experiential observations for the eleven locations along the journey (continues overleaf)

Ref	Type	Subtype	What	Why	Intensity
A1	Area		Castle Street	Architectural coherence: colour, roof lines, render, window detail.	Strong
C6	Centre	Social Interaction	Bin location and front door space	Occasional people meeting	Weak
C7	Centre	Social Imageability	Protruding wall	Enclosure by front door and wider pavement	Moderate
T3	Transition	Threshold	Protruding wall	Narrowing of path and road	Moderate
D3	Direction	View	Stone wall, lamp post, bin, gable	Focal point from combination of features, but more spread out	Weak
D2	Direction	Movement	Footpath along south side Castle Street	Wider pavement width; more varied streetscape; fewer cars parked	Moderate

Bar chart (Strong / Moderate / Weak) with categories:
Centre — Social Imageability, Social Interaction, Restorative Benefit; Direction — View, Movement; Transition — Threshold, Segment, Corridor, Ephemeral; Area — Thematic Continuity

Ref	Type	Subtype	What	Why	Intensity
A2	Area		Stone walls and architectural style	Combination of features, eg building façade, roofscape and widow details, building heights all compressed into complex visual plane	Strong
C8	Centre	Social Interaction	Alcove in footpath	Enclosure and confluence of Castle Street and main route through site likely to be significant local meeting place	Strong
C9	Centre	Social Imageability	Alcove in footpath	Visually prominent recess enclosed by stne walls and strong entrance feature.	Strong
T4	Transition	Segment	Descending steps	Complex changes in level, direction, path width induce gradual passage from here to there. Location of private garden entrances	Strong
D4	Direction	View	Building façade, lamp post, distant tree	Very complex elevated view into and across site, framed by wall pillars, multi-faceted façade to right, focal points in pink building and tree	Strong

Bar chart (Strong / Moderate / Weak) with categories:
Centre — Social Imageability, Social Interaction, Restorative Benefit; Direction — View, Movement; Transition — Threshold, Segment, Corridor, Ephemeral; Area — Thematic Continuity

Ref	Type	Subtype	What	Why	Intensity
A1	Area		Castle Street	Architectural coherence: colour, roof lines, render, window detail. Sense of Castle Street slightly diminished by presence of A3	Moderate
A3	Area		Stone walls and architectural style, esp ornamental window detail	Combination of features, eg window details, stone, roof lines consistent with more contemporary styling of site interior emerging to street and compressed in visual plane.	Strong
C10	Centre	Social Imageability	Corner bay window	Low corner window detail prominent visual feature anchoring the corner location before descending the steps	Moderate
T5	Transition	Threshold	Gap between buildings	Strong sense of change. Area characteristics of site interior protrude onto Castle Street. Window details and stone walls enhance sense of framed gap.	Strong
D5	Direction	View	Window detail	Prominent visual device in corner ornamental window detail	Moderate

Bar chart (Strong / Moderate / Weak) with categories:
Centre — Social Imageability, Social Interaction, Restorative Benefit; Direction — View, Movement; Transition — Threshold, Segment, Corridor, Ephemeral; Area — Thematic Continuity

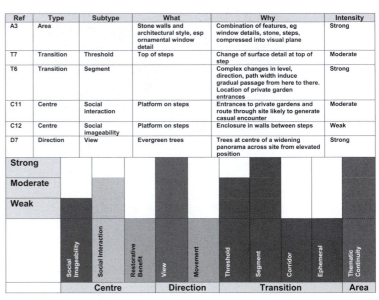

Ref	Type	Subtype	What	Why	Intensity
A3	Area		Stone walls and architectural style, esp ornamental window detail	Combination of features, eg window details, stone	Moderate
T5	Transition	Threshold	Gap between buildings	Change framed by stone walls	Moderate
T6	Transition	Segment		Complex changes in level, direction, path width induce gradual passage from here to there. Location of private garden entrances	Strong
D6	Direction	View	Old buildings beyond site	Strong focal point arising from elevated position, framing containment of stone walls and emphasized gap between buildings and trees	Strong

Strong / Moderate / Weak

	Centre			Direction		Transition				Area
	Social Imageability	Social Interaction	Restorative Benefit	View	Movement	Threshold	Segment	Corridor	Ephemeral	Thematic Continuity

Ref	Type	Subtype	What	Why	Intensity
A3	Area		Stone walls and architectural style, esp ornamental window detail	Combination of features, eg window details, stone, steps, compressed into visual plane	Strong
T7	Transition	Threshold	Top of steps	Change of surface detail at top of step	Moderate
T6	Transition	Segment		Complex changes in level, direction, path width induce gradual passage from here to there. Location of private garden entrances	Strong
C11	Centre	Social interaction	Platform on steps	Entrances to private gardens and route through site likely to generate casual encounter	Moderate
C12	Centre	Social imageability	Platform on steps	Enclosure in walls between steps	Weak
D7	Direction	View	Evergreen trees	Trees at centre of a widening panorama across site from elevated position	Strong

Strong / Moderate / Weak

	Centre			Direction		Transition				Area
	Social Imageability	Social Interaction	Restorative Benefit	View	Movement	Threshold	Segment	Corridor	Ephemeral	Thematic Continuity

Ref	Type	Subtype	What	Why	Intensity
A3	Area		Architectural style	Combination of features, eg window details, rendered walls	Weak
T8	Transition	Corridor	Recess in building	Entrance to alcove from public realm to internal space for doors to private dwellings	Weak
D8	Direction	View	Recess in building	Corner architectural feature including curved stone wall	Weak

Strong / Moderate / Weak

	Centre			Direction		Transition				Area
	Social Imageability	Social Interaction	Restorative Benefit	View	Movement	Threshold	Segment	Corridor	Ephemeral	Thematic Continuity

Ref	Type	Subtype	What	Why	Intensity
A3	Area		Architectural style	Combination of features, eg window details, rendered walls	Weak
T9	Transition	Corridor	Gap between walls	Sense of corridor between open spaces	Weak
T10	Transition	Corridor	Gap between buildings	Framing between tall buildings in mid-distance	Moderate
D9	Direction	View	Pink building window column	Prominent at end of site, framed and drawing the eye to architectural details on facade	Strong

Intensity	Social Imageability	Social Interaction	Restorative Benefit	View	Movement	Threshold	Segment	Corridor	Ephemeral	Thematic Continuity
Strong				■						
Moderate								■		
Weak										■
	Centre			Direction		Transition				Area

Ref	Type	Subtype	What	Why	Intensity
A2	Area		Architectural style inc. stone walls	Combination of features, eg building façade, roofscape and widow details, building heights compressed into complex visual plane	Strong
D9	Direction	View	Pink building window column	Prominent at end of site, framed and drawing the eye to architectural details on facade	Moderate

Intensity	Social Imageability	Social Interaction	Restorative Benefit	View	Movement	Threshold	Segment	Corridor	Ephemeral	Thematic Continuity
Strong										
Moderate										
Weak										
	Centre			Direction		Transition				Area

and the fact that the gaze is held by a range of architectural focal points. The visual harmonisation of existing and new architecture on Castle Street engenders a strong feeling of continuity and neighbourhood identity and this feeling of visual coordination is maintained throughout the remainder of the route by distinctive architectural styling, although with apparently weaker intensity once in the main body of the site. We believe this may be related to an increasing presence of cars and the dominance of car oriented open space that diminishes the strength of the architectural presence.

The route also delivers strong transitional sensations, particularly along Castle Street. This is due entirely to the complex network of thresholds and segments created by the way gaps in the street façade are detailed. It was a stated objective of The Piggeries project to encourage pedestrian movement across the site by using the prevailing topography in imaginative ways to enhance the sense of entrance and exit. What has been made is much more than mere flights of steps and in many ways this has been one of the most significant experiential achievements of the development. A variety of spatial and architectural devices, such as walls that protrude into Castle Street signalling points of arrival and departure and rapid changes in level and direction, intensify the sensation of descent into the site. These details work together generating a sequence of small pause points capitalising on views and offering the possibility for chance encounters at garden gates. Indeed it is revealing that recordings of centre are almost entirely associated with these transitional loca-

Table 8.1   **A summary chart of The Piggeries experiential landscape**

Strengths and weaknesses in experiential potential	
Strengths	**Weaknesses**
Area definition generally strong and consistent with component parts creating potential for distinguishable neighbourhood places (Castle Street, east and west interior courtyards).	Lack of explicit centres in site interior may hinder routine social use (beyond the functionality of access) and the development of a sustainable sense of community. This is an aspect that would warrant focused exploration through resident consultation and mapping.
Transitional and directional experiences very strong, generated by attention to detail and exploitation of elevation and view.	

tions also and are generated by recognition of this social potential and by the presence of prominent features, often the visual impact of the gap itself. Elsewhere the sense of centre as a predominant experiential quality is far less apparent and this in particular contributes to the comparative experiential paucity of the site interior (photo locations 9–11). This was an unexpected finding as the spatial organisation of the site here defines a series of courtyard-like enclosures that would normally be associated with stronger sensations of centre. However, there is haphazardness evident in the way that cars dominate these spaces, often left by kerbs not intended for this instead of in parking bays. The tarmacadam surfacing also tends to reinforce the message that this environment is a part of the wider road network rather than the core of a distinguishable neighbourhood. Although there are exceptions, garden gates do not generally open to this area either and all of this generates an impression of spaces conceived in a rather utilitarian manner for vehicle storage and accessibility rather than to encourage social use, play and a sense of community, for example (Table 8.1).

Friary's Court, Beverley, Yorkshire

Completed in 1990, Friary's Court is a residential setting that mixes together local authority sheltered housing, housing association flats and private housing together with the existing Friary youth hostel, a historic building to the south side of the site. The site occupies a strategic location between the railway station and Beverley Minster,

the latter providing a dramatic backdrop for the development. The architects, LNS Partnership, have created a layout that is sympathetic to the historic townscape of Beverley by using the development to strengthen the streetscape along Eastgate, one of the principal routes into the town, and by arranging buildings to enclose a series of open public spaces connected by what the architects refer to as narrow compression links. These are small openings between the building blocks that give the site a permeable feel whilst at the same time retaining the closely defined nature of the courtyard spaces so that each has its own distinguishable character. An interesting feature of Friary's Court is the way in which the layout deals with the integration of public and private realms. The site is open to the public and indeed its layout appears to deliberately encourage public movement between the Minster and railway station via the main central Paradise Square. But this does not seem to compromise the overriding feeling of the development as a secure, semi-private neighbourhood. This seems to echo the way in which the urban grain of Beverley developed organically over many years as trading and dwelling patterns evolved to eventually generate the spaces and enclosures that defined the boundaries of public and private space. Friary's Court is a distinctly contemporary development but with a layout reminiscent of a historical spatial network (Figure 8.3).

The route through Friary's Court covers the main pedestrian thoroughfare across the development from Eastgate to the railway station. It is formed from three distinctive spaces which together form a kind of spine running between

8.3

The Friary's Court journey with the picture locations marked

residential blocks that form distinct neighbourhood areas within the development. Narrow paths link each neighbourhood to this central public space. The route begins in Eastgate moving in the direction of the town centre from the Minster. Here Friary's Court presents a continuous built frontage of residential development that follows the back-of-pavement line, sometimes with a low railing defining a small private strip. The development makes a significant contribution to the integrity and character of the Eastgate streetscape with its architecture harmonising with existing buildings whilst at the same time maintaining a distinctive identity. Vehicle access into two residential courtyards can be made from Eastgate via two arched entrances that echo those in the older commercial premises on the opposite side of the street. Between them the footpath widens significantly to signal the main pedestrian entrance into and through the development. The presence of traditional railings, stone pillars and gates gives a strong impression of departing from the public street into a residential lane flanked by town houses. Distinctive tree and shrub planting and garden boundary treatments give this lane enclosure and a strong visual identity. Its meandering

edges bring an informal domestic scale which contrasts with the more open and formal Eastgate streetscape. The lane opens out quite dramatically into Paradise Square, the central open space of the development overlooked by sheltered housing. Town houses front onto the square on the west side and flats overlook from the north. Paradise Square joins the top of Outer Trinities, a residential street with a more traditional character and this leads out to Station Square immediately beyond the site boundary (Figure 8.4 and Plate 8).

Summary

Immediately apparent from the Friary's Court summary chart is the higher density of coverage at the top half by comparison to the bottom half. There is also a reasonably even distribution across all experiential components here whereas at the bottom it shows a gradual diminishment leaving an emphatic directional and, to a slightly lesser extent, transitional character. This is borne out by the experiential landscape map which shows the dense clustering of symbols loosening into a more fragmented and less varied range on entry to Paradise Square, the main open space in the middle of the development. This appears to be generated predominantly by the relatively more complex and interwoven spatial configuration apparent in the main pedestrian lane into the development from Eastgate and its crinkly edges. First of all the development maintains a strong sense of integrity and identity along Eastgate by virtue of an unbroken and deflective façade, giving the streetscape a strong sense of area. The entrance to the development is marked by a generously set back space which is detailed in such a way that it creates a multi-centred place along Eastgate as well as a strong transitional experience into the site. The pedestrian lane entered provides a classic example of the transition type, segment. It is evident from the clearly apparent entrance and exit points that on one level this lane is a corridor linking Eastgate with Paradise Square. Yet at the same time it is a place with an identity of its own, given partly by the characteristic planting that strengthens a sense of location and also direction through its perspective effect focused on the distant rotunda, but more so by the complex meandering edge that borders adjacent houses.

8.4
Friary's Court photographic sequence
(facing page)

Particularly on the left side a combination of planting, steps and gates form a sequence of recessed spaces that provide centred and transitional sensations achieving a subtle relationship between the public thoroughfare and adjacent private gardens. This is especially successful in generating a feeling of potential contact and social interaction between occupants and passers-by, whilst also retaining a sense of privacy. The overall effect of this lane is to create, by means of a complex sequence of varied spatial compressions, sensations of entry, arrival, location and exit across a very short distance. The final compression before emerging into Paradise Square is further dramatised by a small change in level before emerging into the wider openness of the Square.

Once Paradise Square is reached however, the experience abruptly changes from being a closely woven network of transitions and centres of varying types held together by a strong sense of coordination, to one in which the sense of direction seems to take over. What this means is that as one passes into Paradise Square the over-riding sensation is of getting across to the other side rather than that of encouragement to pause. Little within the Square seems to hold the attention whilst strong architectural detailing and a street entrance at the far end encourage onward movement. Whilst this is not intended to imply criticism, indeed this may be an entirely appropriate sensation to induce in someone passing through the site, there did seem to be a troublesome ambiguity about the purpose of the relatively large amount of space given over to Paradise Square as well as an uncertainty about how surrounding dwellings related to the

Square. It felt like its edges needed to be more active than they seemed to be, and to this extent shared some common ground with the observations made of The Piggeries. This may not, of course, be the experience of the surrounding occupants and again this outcome of the professional experiential landscape analysis signals a topic for further exploration with the resident population (Table 8.2).

Poundbury, Dorchester, Dorset

Poundbury, an urban extension to the western edge of Dorchester, Dorset, has become one of the most widely cited examples of new settlement development. It attracts criticism and praise seemingly in equal measure. The former usually directed at its eclectic mix of housing styles which, in places, does tend to convey the impression of an exhibition of historical pastiche, an unfortunate picture postcard connotation that is not helped by the media's insistence on referring to it as Prince Charles' model village every time it appears in the news. More positive attitudes generally highlight its layout and spatial organisation which has generated an organic mix of pedestrian streets, quiet neighbourly courtyards and public squares. The familiar "D" shaped plan of the phase one development has become an almost iconic symbol of the application of New Urbanist principles in UK residential design. The complex spatial configuration achieved in Poundbury is indeed one of its defining characteristics and provides an example of how an organic appearance in townscape can be generated from a few relatively simple principles. Poundbury is

Table 8.2 **A summary chart of the Friary's Court experiential landscape**

Strengths and weaknesses in experiential potential	
Strengths	**Weaknesses**
Strong sense of identity and coordination along Eastgate.	Possibly too great a diminishment of experiential diversity within Paradise Square. A large space with little explicit sense of place.
Emphatic sequence of complex transitional experiences interwoven with a balanced range of centres. This contributes to a successful relationship between passers-by and occupants, helping to maintain privacy whilst retaining the potential for social interaction.	

primarily organised around a network of spaces which focus on a main public square with a landmark community building, The Brownsword. It is also quite route oriented in the sense that it is woven from a hierarchy of roads, lanes, passages and mews which meander in apparent informality, generating a rich diversity of courtyards and squares where they meet. The enfolded hierarchy of routeways makes Poundbury a thoroughly permeable setting and this ensures good levels of visual surveillance. Vehicles have full access but pedestrian priority is evident in that road tracking is largely determined in response to the expansion and contraction of the street spaces defined by continuous street façades. Cars are accommodated within internal courtyards, on-street, or in residents' gardens. The way that routes open to create courtyards and squares generates a very close relationship between private, semi-public and public spaces reinforcing clear neighbourhood distinctions. Whilst this is impressive and results in an overall setting that invites exploration and is simply pleasant to stroll around, some of the internal courts do have a rather sterile appearance and have attracted the criticism that they will simply become dominated by car parking. Occasionally there is some justification for this, but developing

maturity in street trees and shrub planting along with the contribution that private garden treatments can make to the public realm may ameliorate this with time.

The route explored in Poundbury begins at the top of Ashington Street at the south side of the phase one development, traverses Pummery Square and begins the shallow upward gradient into Brookhouse Street. Both streets are typical of Poundbury's approach to a pedestrian priority public environment and this is reflected in the surfacing material, the houses that front directly onto the street and the centrally located street trees. Although these streets are fully accessible to the public they have a quiet neighbourhood quality suggesting they are very much under the territorial influence of the street residents and that passers-by are welcome but temporary visitors. The route shows the way in which these streets are integrated into the more public face of Poundbury, particularly in the way that space expands and contracts effortlessly along the way and in the use of landmark features. Two of Poundbury's principal buildings: the octagonal café and the Brownsword community building that dominates Pummery Square are encountered on route. The strategic positioning of these buildings, along with the use of smaller, but equally significant, architectural features (colonnade structures on corners, for example) are important components in the townscape vocabulary of Poundbury. They are prominent visual devices that aid orientation whilst at the same time working to define and hold the organic spatial layout, helping weave its eclectic blend of styles together (Figures 8.5 and 8.6, and Plate 9).

Summary

The most obvious distinguishing characteristic of the Poundbury experiential landscape analysis by comparison with The Piggeries and Friary's Court is the generally consistent distribution and range of experiential sensations throughout the route. Running through this is however a detectable emphasis on directional experience driven mainly by the sequence of strong visual features, mostly in the form of various architectural statements, but also as a consequence of a spatial rhythm generated by the meandering arrangement of

8.5

The Poundbury journey with the picture locations marked

8.6
The Poundbury photographic sequence

Table 8.3   **A summary chart of the Poundbury experiential landscape**

Strengths and weaknesses in experiential potential	
Strengths	**Weaknesses**
Generally consistent distribution and range of experiential opportunities.	Some centres, although evident, can appear rather sterile. This is evident in that no centres of restorative benefit were recorded. This is likely to improve as vegetation matures.
Experiential richness is localised at intervals contributing to the potential for strong associations to develop in particular places. This is likely to aid the development of neighbourhood identity.	
Strong directional and transitional sensations enhance the incentive to explore.	

pedestrian lanes and linked squares. The ever changing scene that unfolds gradually as one moves around Poundbury provides a strong incentive to explore and, because it contributes distinctive characteristics to different regions with the overall development, is an aid to orientation and neighbourhood identity. Along with the directional emphasis, there is also a consistent transitional nature to the journey taken. Mainly this is provided in the form of a series of often subtle thresholds created along the pedestrian streets by minor variations in the building line, and by the positioning of street trees and items of street furniture. Overall these have the effect of breaking down the linearity of streets into smaller segments contributing to the sense of rhythm and in places helping to hold small clusters of perhaps four or five dwellings together as little groupings which, over time, may help stimulate localised social and community cohesion.

As might be expected in a route passing through Poundbury's main Pummery Square, the sense of location as indicated by the occurrence of centre intensifies here. The square itself generates a strong locational sensation produced by a combination of factors including its spatial enclosure, the anchoring visual impact of the Brownsword building, its function both as a main point of arrival for visitors and as a centre for Poundbury's shops and other community services. There are also centres within and around it, creating a nesting effect of locations of different scales, stimulated mainly by the way that the Brownsword columns and the nearby corner colonnade capture spatial enclosure and provide

visual interest, but also by the strategic positioning of the post box. This itself is visually prominent in that nothing else red exists nearby and it is also likely to become a place routinely visited by inhabitants and where casual social interactions might take place. Less predictable, possibly, is the richness of experiential potential apparent in the much smaller square in front of the octagon café. Much like the pedestrian lane in Friary's Court, although harder and smaller, this location is experientially complex. Overall it provides a segment type transitional experience between the end of Ashington Street and Pummery Square. The sense of transition is intensified further by a rapid sequence of thresholds formed from the funneling impact of its enclosing building façades that gradually pinch the space sharply before releasing into the open Pummery Square. The sense of direction here is also tightly controlled and heightened by half hidden views whilst centres are encouraged by the social opportunities offered at the café entrance and by the visual impact of the prominent café building and the space that it protrudes into (Table 8.3).

Chapter 9

In search of the identity of Kirby Hill

Introduction

The village of Kirby Hill lies about a mile north of the North Yorkshire market town of Borough-bridge. It sits on a shallow eminence surrounded by agricultural land and enjoys long-range views across attractive rural landscape, particularly north to the Hambleton Hills. Historically the location occupied by the village is quite signifi-cant. There has apparently been an established community there from before Saxon times and parts of the village's All Saints church can be traced back to this period. The main road through the village, now Leeming Lane, was once the route of the Great North Road from London to Scotland but now the bulk of traffic flow is carried past the village on the A1(M) about half a mile to the west. Once a mainly agricultural village characterised by a clustering of several farms, only one now remains and the past 30 years has seen a succes-sion of residential developments that have transformed Kirby Hill's appearance and expanded its population to about 390. Apart from a pub, church, farm and primary school Kirby Hill is entirely residential, although there is a popula-tion of homeworkers, and since there are no shops in the village, people are dependent, locally, on provision available in Boroughbridge or larger towns such as Ripon and Harrogate. The relation-ship between Kirby Hill and Boroughbridge in particular, but also the closer settlements of Langthorpe and Milby, is in fact a complex local issue and part of the reason for carrying out the work that will be described in this chapter. There is a powerful territorial streak at the heart of Kirby Hill's community and they value greatly their sense of physical independence from neighbour-ing settlements. The agricultural buffer that surrounds the village's built core appears to contribute significantly to the feeling that Kirby Hill is a village in its own right. There is a strong desire to maintain this physical independence against probably well founded fears that Boroughbridge might eventually expand further north, threatening to bridge the rural divide. This is considered thoroughly undesirable because villagers worry that it will compromise the iden-tity and individuality of Kirby Hill and lead to its subjugation as a mere satellite to the larger Boroughbridge.

Walking around the village, looking at the objects and features that contribute to its visual character, relatively little seems evident to distin-guish Kirby Hill's identity as an independent village, apart from being surrounded by fields. At first sight Kirby Hill would prima facie appear to be a rather unremarkable place, much of it having a fairly suburban appearance. A number of resi-dents interviewed during the project highlighted that although they thought of Kirby Hill as a village, it actually had very few physical features that they associated with typical North Yorkshire villages. It has no clearly defined village core, for example, no explicit village green, no village shops, nowhere for the kids to play, and has perhaps suffered a loss of any significant sense of vernacular. Modern day Kirby Hill has evolved to become a collection of residential developments, most of them cul-de-sacs with their backs to the village, contributing little to its visual quality or sense of cohesion. In 30 years the original agricultural village character has been overwhelmed to such an extent that what remains of Kirby Hill's proud historical character and its vernacular is now dispersed and manifest in a few older cottages, houses, the church and farm buildings within a background of suburban-like residential development engendering little obvious sense of place.

So, exactly what identity does Kirby Hill have that its residents feel the need to protect so voraciously? The need to explore this question has gradually evolved in the collective consciousness of the village in recent years as a consequence of threatened development, not in Boroughbridge, but in fact to the north of Kirby Hill alongside the A1(M) motorway. In 1996, a planning application was presented to Harrogate Borough Council for a motorway service station just north of the Ripon Road junction. The anticipated impact of this proposal galvanised local opinion to such an extent that at one protest event numbers turned out that exceeded the entire village population. This brought into sharp focus the need for the Parish Council to consider very carefully the options available that would help it respond effectively to any future development plans it deemed to be undesirable.

In consultation with Harrogate Borough Council Planning Department, members of the Parish Council decided to produce a Village Design Statement (VDS). This is a document that gives voice to local opinion about what is valuable and important about the village so that this can be taken into account when assessing the suitability of planning applications that would affect the village. Developing a VDS requires the collecting and collating of information about the special and unique qualities of the village. It

usually involves drawing out details of the settlement pattern, the character of its landscape setting, building styles, open spaces and wildlife, for example. The general idea is to present information as seen through the eyes of the village community so that it gives a picture of what is important about the village from their perspective. A lot of emphasis was given to the village's historical significance and to the objects and buildings still in existence that evidence this. Kirby Hill's landscape setting, its agricultural context and the distant views across the countryside, along with the contribution of some green spaces, street trees and fields to wildlife diversity all make very positive contributions to the village.

There were more challenging issues however. Among these included a significant lack of clarity about exactly where Kirby Hill started and finished. Looking at a map of the village Kirby Hill appears as a clearly defined, loosely "L" shaped settlement surrounded by fields. However, historical meandering of the political boundaries between Kirby Hill and Langthorpe in particular, seems to have generated a diversity of local views about which buildings to the west of Leeming Lane are perceived in Kirby Hill and which are not. This, coupled with variations in opinion about whether the surrounding fields are "in" the village or "out", makes understanding where the village boundaries are far from straightforward. It appeared that the content of the village was more a matter of individual perception than physical evidence. Another potentially problematic aspect was what to make of the predominant and eclectic mix of relatively recent residential development. It was apparent to the VDS Steering Committee that Kirby Hill's identity and character would be difficult to define. Furthermore, without being able to do this, identifying the way to sensitively protect the village would be potentially problematic as for 30 years it had been ravaged by development that contributed little to the visual appeal of the village and at the same time weakened what visual coherence Kirby Hill might have once had.

But if Kirby Hill's identity and character is hard to express positively in terms of clear boundaries and distinguished architecture, it is much easier to do through the strong sense of community and social cohesion evident in much of the resident population. Most experience village life positively and although, with some notable exceptions, this is not generally manifest in tangible physical "village-ness", Kirby Hill is nonetheless much loved and treasured by its inhabitants. This form of village identity resides in the individual and collective lives and habits of its people. It is a hidden dimension of village order that cannot necessarily be visualised in physical form, but is nevertheless valuable and highly sensitive to change. Another challenge is then to find ways to articulate this in a form that might help development control mechanisms avoid damaging the community and possibly, more positively, take decisions that might actually nurture and enhance it.

The role of experiential landscape

The mapping techniques developed in experiential landscape seemed ideally suited to help make explicit some of the less tangible, but crucially important, aspects of routine village life that seemed to be contributing so much to the sense of Kirby Hill's hidden identity and uniqueness. In particular, by being able to give a spatial expression to the villagers' subliminal experiences of the streets and other outdoor places of Kirby Hill, we expected to be able to shed some light on the confusion apparent in establishing where people felt the village boundaries actually were and, in relation to this, what triggered the sense of arrival at and departure from Kirby Hill. We were also interested to see if we could uncover something about the spatial structure of perceived different neighbourhoods within the village and whether there might be any consensus about significant or meaningful places. In this latter respect it was already clear that some locations of historical significance may justifiably be highlighted. But it seemed probable that other outdoor locations might be equally important in the lives of inhabitants and without the prominence and visibility of, say, the church or war memorial, these might remain overlooked. A brief was conceived that would involve an investigation of local place

perceptions, organised around themes that would focus on, for example: what was special and important about the village and what its distinctive identity was; where there were neighbourhoods in the village and what were its significant places; and, where the village started and finished (Figure 9.1).

The overarching purpose of revealing Kirby Hill's experiential landscape was essentially twofold. First was to explore patterns of routine experience implicit in the way village inhabitants used and felt about the outdoor environment and, crucially, reveal their spatial configuration and characteristics. The second was to give voice to aspects of village life that contributed to the apparently strong sense of community and social cohesion, and to do this in such a way as to be able to identify components of the village's physical and spatial fabric that sustained it. Achieving this would require extensive public consultation to build up layers of individual place perception into a collective view. Practicality inevitably played a role in the number and demographic of villagers that eventually participated in the process and clearly the conclusions drawn from the analysis must be approached with due caution as a consequence. For example, few children and no teenagers were involved and so the place perceptions that made up the collective view produced reflect that of mainly the adult population. Possibly equally significant is that, for reasons of convenience and time, invitations for participants were made via existing community groups and structures, such as at Parish Council meetings, church and school events and by word of mouth from the members of the Village Design Statement Steering Group. In the end 40 people participated, about 10% of the resident population, nearly all of them, though, either involved in or at least accessible through one of a number of community related groups. In other words the analysis may well bias in favour of the active and interested and may be insufficiently representative of inhabitants not involved with or reachable through these groups. This potential skew of participants was identified at an early stage and attempts were made for an inclusive approach through attention to the demographic and locational distribution of participants and a

VIEW TOWARDS
THE HAMBLETON HILLS
AND THE WHITE HORSE

THE POND

MANOR DRIVE

LEEMING LANE

ALL SAINTS'
CHURCH

THE GRANGE

GLEBE CLOSE

BLUE BELL INN

CHURCH LANE

Kirby

Hill

ST JOHN'S WALK

CHURCH BANKS FIELD

WILLOW GARTH

EAST VIEW

N

elp:rdu pEople, pLace, sPace

Experiential Landscape Place
Research and Development Unit

Dr. Kevin Thwaites BA, Dip LA(Dist), PhD
Ian Simkins BSc, Dip LA, PCHE, MI Hort, MLI
e: info@elprdu.com
w: www.elprdu.com

PROJECT: Kirby Hill Village Design Statement
DRAWING TITLE: Village Settlement - Base Plan
DATE: 28/1/2005
RESEARCHER:
DRAWN: IMS
c SCALE: 1:2500
e SCALE: Public/Social

9.1
Kirby Hill

consideration of socio-economic variables and length of residence, for example. But, inevitably, as a consequence of the voluntary nature of participation, only those who positively consented became involved, despite others being sought. Although the circumstances of the project meant that this was more or less unavoidable, it is a potentially significant limitation and indeed the findings do imply the possibility of an over-privileging of certain places in the village that may reflect particular interest groups.

The research team phase

The project was carried out in two phases, the first of which involved the production of an experiential landscape map of the village recording the place perceptions of the research team. This involved a tour of the village during which a voice-recorded commentary was made. This was subsequently transcribed and evaluated to identify the distribution of CDTA around the village according to the observations made by the team. The resulting map helped provisionally identify the range and distribution of distinguishable areas in the village: those places that had some kind of localised thematic continuity that stood out against the general village background. This would provide the opportunity to explore the concept of neighbourhood within the village in relation to the team's observations about the spatial sensation of area. Findings from the research team map were also used to inform the way in which the semi-structured interview themes would be defined and configured. A very provisional picture of some of the experiential characteristics of Kirby Hill, according to the research team's reading of its spatial structure, gradually began to come into view (Plate 10).

This emergent picture of the experiential characteristics of Kirby Hill revealed a linear sequence of six Dobson Clusters. The first of these shows a mainly directional and transitional sequence that seems to mark the southern boundary of the village signalling the beginning of a general sense of entry into the village without yet arriving at its core. South of this location feels outside of the village. The second cluster shows the potential to be strongly centred and marks the first significant location within the village bound-

ary. Also it is from here that visual contact is made with the location occupied by the Blue Bell Inn which feels like the point of arrival, the potential core of the village, although at present this sensation is very weak. Just before this to the south another cluster contributes a further set of transitional and directional experiences that intensifies the sense of either arrival (from the south) or begins the sensation of departure (from the north). Further clusters appear evident along Church Lane and the first of these suggests the possibility of a secondary and more semi-public village core. The final cluster seems problematic in that, although it provides potential as an element of discovery in the village, it seems too detached from the rest of the sequence and feels like an isolated part of the village. In terms of the overall themes the project focused on, this initial phase did not reveal any significant or special qualities of the village taken as a whole from the research team's reading of its spatial structure. Kirby Hill's identity seemed to rest on little more than its existence as a collection of generally unrelated and largely suburban style residential developments contributing little in terms of visual coordination. A number of potentially significant places were clearly apparent although most spoke of unfulfilled potential, and linkage between them seemed to be weak, diminishing their impact on the character of the overall village. It also seemed clear that the sense of where Kirby Hill's boundaries are is complex and, to the south in particular, related in part to the incremental nature of the sense of arrival. This evaluation of the research team's view formed the foundation upon which the next phase of the project was built.

The resident participant phase

The next stage of the project involved interviewing residents so that similar experiential landscape maps could be made for each of them. The interviews followed after participants completed informed consent forms and were carried out in two teams of two: one of whom would lead the dialogue in a conversational style leaving the other to make written and graphical notes that would help with subsequent interpretation. The procedure adopted first involved the development of semi-structured interview themes so that the dialogue with participants would cover all the relevant topics and to ensure as much consistency as possible across the three teams. A timetable for the interviews was established and participants attended at the allocated time to one of three venues. Each interview lasted about twenty minutes to half an hour depending partly on the personality of the participant and partly on the amount of information imparted in response to each of the interview themes. As well as the tape recording equipment, other tools used in the interviews were maps of the village at various scales and model houses. Starting the session by locating their house provided a useful way to orientate participants in relation to the village plan.

The initial impression from evaluating the partial transcriptions of the interviews and playing them all back, was that the responses were unusually rich and detailed, sometimes quite emotionally charged, and full of personal anecdote. It was clear that this material brought a colourful and sometimes highly personal dimension, reminiscent of a more anthropological survey, which required careful consideration during the interpretation. It seemed as though much of the identity and character of Kirby Hill was implicit in the psyche of its residents and, although this had clear spatial implications that the interview structure was able to reveal, this was often so elusive and refined that it challenged the experiential landscape conceptual framework to make it sufficiently explicit. Combining the graphical symbols on the experiential landscape maps with text from the interviews made much of this refined and personal detail more clearly visible. When all the maps were layered together to form a composite this helped to interpret more clearly the significance of certain clusters of symbols. Some places became more pronounced in the collective perception of villagers because of the accumulating effect of individual associations and meanings projected onto that place. What follows is an account of the principal findings from the resident participation phase summarising findings from the composite experiential landscape map. This gives a picture of the experiential characteristics of Kirby Hill as a whole and identifies key locations in the village. Finally we will draw out the main implications for the village in terms of the original brief.

Area

The picture of the village presented by the area map resembles in some ways an abstract cubist painting with its many facets representing clear blocks that are distinguishable from one another. Some areas are well defined, particularly those to the west and north of the village and also the rough "L" shape that corresponds with St John's Walk, suggesting a strong level of consensus that much of the village appears as a mosaic of discrete blocks set side-by-side, each with characteristics that set it apart from its neighbouring block and from the wider village as a whole. It is interesting, and potentially significant however, that there appears to be less clarity evident in the boundaries of areas identified within the main body of the village, broadly extending from the Blue Bell down and to the south side of Church Lane as far as the church grounds. This indicates a lower level of consensus among participants about the configuration of distinguishable places in this region of the village, suggesting perhaps that there may be fuzzier boundaries between places here in comparison to elsewhere in the village (Plate 11).

Centre

Two main conclusions were drawn from reading the distribution of recorded centres. First is that there are places beyond the main body of the village that are important to resolving a picture of what is significant about the village as a whole. It is as though some of the routine experiences of its inhabitants project meaning and association on these places to such an extent that a kind of psychological gravity holds them as components in a full definition of what the village means. Examples of this include, at the extreme, the Hambleton Hills visible in the distance to the north, and closer in, but actually physically in the neighbouring village of Milby, the Coronation Hall. It is also notable that there are places beyond the main body of the village that are embraced as part of Kirby Hill's capacity to deliver restorative experiences. The plan shows these as arms extending out from the village indicating that these are primarily related to short walks that people might take locally. The second is the strong emergence of the vicinity of Church Lane and to a lesser extent, St John's Walk, as the psychological core of the village. This is particularly powerful because it holds associations of different kinds, represented by the three types of centre, and at different levels of scale that are nested together. At the first level, because of the continuity and linkage evident in the distribution of symbols, this region can be regarded as a whole: a kind of super-centre, although there are weaknesses in continuity between the war memorial and church entrance. Within this there are component parts that have a more localised significance, but still at a relatively large scale, such as the Blue Bell, the space at the mouth of the driveway to the old Vicarage, the school, the church and the triangle. Centres are evident at yet smaller scales within these, demonstrating that the larger centres are in fact nested and made up of smaller component parts, each of which hold their own significance in various ways (Plate 12).

Direction

Findings from the spatial sensation of direction tend to add further weight to conclusions high-lighted above. Both categories (movement and view) reveal the significance of experiences that are well beyond the built structure of the village, and sensory tends to support that Church Lane has a special significance in the experiential potential of the village. In terms of kinetic, Kirby Hill appears to be experienced largely in terms of two adjoining triangles. The smaller one corresponds with the "triangle" walk around the Church. The larger is formed by connecting Leeming Lane, Church Lane and Dishforth Road. To some extent this is fairly predictable in that these are the main traffic-carrying roads into and around Kirby Hill, but their routine use links together Kirby Hill with the neighbouring settlements of Milby and Langthorpe in the experience of movement associ-ated with village life. Also revealed is the significance of a roughly defined diagonal route that joins a point on Church Lane close to the church grounds with Leeming Lane south of the entrance to St John's Walk. That this appears quite prominently highlights the significance of the open space across fields to the immediate south-

east of the village to the directional experiences of village life. The experience of view again reveals that places and objects well beyond the village area play a crucial role in the experiential character of Kirby Hill. This is especially notable to the north and north-east indicating again how important are the distant views across open fields towards the Hambleton Hills. That these distant views are possible is partly due to the topography which has Kirby Hill situated slightly proud of its surround-ings suggesting that this modestly elevated position could be an important component to village identity, as well as its historical relevance as a settlement. The sensory map also appears to reveal a focus in the region of Church Lane. Partly this is from where many of the notable view sensa-tions are located but also where most of the view focal points within the village are as well, with a particularly interesting clustering around where the war memorial is located. This suggests that there is a predominance of visually notable features in the vicinity of Church Lane as compared to the rest of the village. Another very interesting observation is the intensity of sensory experience that seems to focus from a relatively short stretch of Church Lane, beginning more or less at the mouth of Glebe Close and intensifying at Keepers Cottage. This appears to be a feature that may be associated with the gradient of the road, the way it changes direction and the sudden break in the built form which dramatises the distant view (Plate 13).

Transition

The configuration of transitional experiences highlights that these spatial sensations seem quite characteristic of Kirby Hill, suggesting a village character that is quite linear in nature composed of a sequence of corridor-like spaces, often with quite well defined "gateways" between them. All the transitional experiences recorded are associ-ated with Leeming Lane and Church Lane only. To the north, the roundabout to the east side of the A1 appears strongly as a transitional experience and, although there are other points along the road approaching the village, the next strongest sensa-tion is where the built form begins. Following that, the location defined by the mouth of Church Lane and the Blue Bell is a very significant threshold experience. Leeming Lane to the north of the village can be defined more or less in terms of three segments. One between the mouth of Church Lane and the end of the village's built structure; the second and longest up to the A1; the last beyond the A1 to the west. Leeming Lane to the south is more complex although again three main segments can be identified, broadly defined by the location of strong thresholds. The configuration of threshold experiences to the south side of the village contributes further evidence for the incremental nature of the sense of village boundary here. The structure of this sequence, and its impact on the incremental nature of the approach into Kirby Hill, appears to be the result of a combination of subtle changes in road gradient, direction, spatial containment, and the gradual visual resolution of the Blue Bell as a focus. The main body of Church Lane appears broadly defined as two segments identified by strong threshold experiences, first at the mouth of the Lane, second at the location of the war memorial and finally at a point between Church Close and the entrance to the primary school. The second of these thresholds appears particularly strong and appears to be so because of a range of physical triggers, including: changes in the direction and gradient of the road; two large trees that arch the road at this point; the presence of the war memorial; and an expansion of space here immediately before a pinch point between buildings on either side of the road. Especially along Leeming Lane, the sequencing and character of these corridors and the threshold experiences that link them influences the way the village boundaries are understood, and the experience of arrival and departure. It also demonstrates, particularly when considered in the light of other findings, that the mouth of Church Lane is of pivotal significance to the spatial structure of the village for many reasons. Not least of which is that it defines the western pole of what appears to be the main experiential core of the village (Plate 14).

The experiential landscape of Kirby Hill

With some notable exceptions in certain places, Kirby Hill does not represent a typical picture-postcard view of a pretty North Yorkshire village. It could justifiably be considered unremarkable, however in revealing Kirby Hill's experiential landscape nothing could be further from the truth. Kirby Hill has, hidden within it, a character and identity of tremendous complexity. This resides in the relationship between its inhabitants' routine experience of village life and the ordinary places that sustain these experiences. Kirby Hill's experiential landscape is multi-layered and rich in character beyond what its visual appearance might suggest. Furthermore, it appears to emanate from a clearly identifiable village core into the surrounding area like a magnetic field reaching out to embrace distant locations, including them also in its sense of identity. Kirby Hill's core lies broadly along Church Lane and within this "magnetic field" has two poles: the Blue Bell forming the western pole and All Saints' Church the eastern. There is much that could be done to realise the full potential of this part of the village as its defining core, but nevertheless, as it is, it is quite clear that currently it is Kirby Hill's richest source of experiential potential. Emanating from this core are waves of village essence. The further away you go the weaker is the sense of Kirby Hill as a discrete independent place. It is as though, beyond certain points, Kirby Hill's essence, or sense of place, gradually begins to blend with the surroundings. The closer in, the more intensely is the sense of Kirby Hill felt. From an experiential perspective Kirby Hill cannot be thought of as having boundaries, like a castle, inside of which it is and outside of which it is not. Instead, its sense of place seems to stretch out, embracing the surrounding fields, elements of the neighbouring settlements, and even the distant Hambleton Hills (Plate 15).

The sense of Kirby Hill projects for some participants out as far as the A1 to the west, over the fields and as far as Hambleton Hills to the north, and beyond Dishforth Road to embrace places along the tracks that run to the east. The southernmost point at which a sense of the village remains detectable is at the bridge over the river at Boroughbridge. These locations, even though quite distant from the main body of Kirby Hill, feature as experiences that some inhabitants interviewed associate with aspects of their village life and in this sense mark the experiential boundaries of Kirby Hill, at some points overlapping with neighbouring places. For example, the bridge over the river at Boroughbridge was revealed as a small part of the identity of Kirby Hill, because it represents for at least one participant the point at which Kirby Hill finally finishes and becomes somewhere else. But, physically it much more obviously makes a contribution to the sense of place that is Boroughbridge. A more significant example is Coronation Hall, technically in Milby. Although this is relatively distant from the main body of Kirby Hill, its influence on the village's sense of place appears disproportionately large. This seems to be because of the significance that it holds as a symbol of Kirby Hill's community cohesion, along with the church and the school. It seems apparent from the interviews that, for many participants, these are not regarded as three separate places but are viewed much more as three parts of the same whole, with their physical separation being almost incidental in this respect.

The increasing strength of Kirby Hill's identity can be experienced particularly by travelling north along Leeming Lane. There is a case to be made for Kirby Hill beginning at the Leeming Lane, Skelton Road junction, developing in strength at the southern boundary of East View and continuing to intensify at Broadacres, eventually culminating in a sense of arrival at the mouth of Church Lane. Travelling north, most people experience an abrupt change at this point from arrival to the beginning of a sense of departure. The village sense of place is generally stronger beginning at East View which locates its southern boundary, includes all the built development to the west side of Leeming Lane, and up to the pond just past The Grange to define the northern boundary. The eastern boundary is the Dishforth Road. This probably corresponds with what most people would intuitively think of as constituting the village of Kirby Hill since it includes all its built elements and its landscape setting of immediately adjacent fields. It is clear from the analysis however, that this does not constitute the strongest sense of village identity in its entirety and here are some examples why. To start with, there is a significant perception among the inhabitants interviewed, although by no means a

consensus, that the developments of Hill View and East View, clearly physically attached to Kirby Hill's main body of built form, do not in fact form a part of Kirby Hill. Some even go so far as to jettison nearly everything to the west side of Leeming Lane, apart from the Blue Bell, from their perception of what constitutes Kirby Hill. To some extent this is encouraged by the counterintuitive position of the political boundary between Langthorpe and Kirby Hill and the location of village name signs. But, along with other evidence from the evaluation, this seems indicative of a feeling that the "real" Kirby Hill actually lies to the east of Leeming Lane. Examination of the historical record tends to lend weight to this point of view. As well as the influence of the settlement boundaries, this may also have something to do with the bisecting effect of Leeming Lane and a certain ambiguity in the character of the location formed by the Blue Bell and the mouth of Church Lane. This place emerges as a pivotal location in the village, particularly from the south and is strongly perceived as the location signalling arrival at the village. But once there, partly because of the influence of the road, there is little that sustains the sense of arriving at somewhere. Instead it appears to be a location that marks the outpost of somewhere more interesting and inviting, and that somewhere happens to be to the east.

The essence of Kirby Hill seems to intensify still further at a closer level of scale. This includes The Blue Bell and the neighbouring Grange Farm as a western outpost. The northern boundary appears marked by the buildings and other physical features that enclose Church Lane at the north side, and to the east the triangle of Church Closes. The southern boundary is effectively given by the Church Banks field boundaries and includes the area known as Willow Garth. It is interesting to note that the majority of the village defined in this way is constituted from green open space on the south and east sides of a relatively small residential settlement currently configured in such a way as to almost entirely turn its back on this open space (Plate 16).

The experiential landscape of Kirby Hill shows clearly though that this is not the whole picture. There is another level of detail revealing that the routine experiences of its inhabitants, their feelings about places in the village and the meanings and associations they hold, collectively define a distinct village core. This is where the experiential character of Kirby Hill's village life comes to focus and is where the strongest essence of what Kirby Hill is appears to reside. Its most westerly point is at the mouth of Church Lane and includes the Blue Bell Inn, its surrounding grounds, and the neighbouring Grange Farm buildings. This works as a beacon signalling where the village core appears to be on its approach. It is far less successful though in delivering a sense of arriving at somewhere distinctive and significant once there. This seems related to a range of factors including weak spatial definition on the Church Lane side, the bisecting impact of Leeming Lane and the surfacing treatment of the Blue Bell car park which continues the tarmacadam of the main road compromising the pub's sense of definition as a separate place. Further down Church Lane a distinctive corridor-like quality begins to develop, given partly by the rows of pollarded trees, and culminates with an implicit sense of arrival at an expansion in the open space afforded by the road swinging a little to the north. This is quite a complex place, partly because the spatial containment makes it one of the few open spaces in the village that does not have a distinct linear emphasis and partly because of features that give a very strong sense of transition out from it. That two of the buildings front directly onto this space seems to lend a sense of a traditional village green that has, in other places along Church Lane, been lost as a consequence of insensitive private development. The fact that Church Lane changes both direction and gradient at this point, coupled with the presence, either side of the road, of two large trees creating an archway gives a very strong sense of a gateway out from this space and into the next. Unfortunately, there seems to be a break in continuity of experiential intensity at this point and this does not pick up again until the entrance to the school. This has the effect of breaking the sense of a village core into two distinct parts.

The next component of the village core begins broadly at the school entrance and includes the grass area in front of the church Lych Gate and the church grounds together. Again this is an experientially important and complex location. Partly this appears to do with the social opportunities generated by the presence of the school and the church, and the wide range of associations that the church holds for people in the village. It seems also related to the strong sense of transition which marks the boundary of the main residential body of the village. It is here also that strong and dramatic views are available across the landscape to the north and east, and where the church as a visual and symbolic landmark becomes clearly apparent. In fact the strong sense of location that appears to be apparent here probably has a lot to do with a sensation of discovery, both of view and of church, afforded by the particular way the road bends and by the abrupt break in the building massing. This aspect of the village core includes the triangle routeway around the Church Closes which appears as one of the most treasured aspects of the village in terms of leisure activity and relaxation. It also appears at the junction with the Dishforth Road to be a crucial part of the sense of arrival at the village from the east and for many represents the first signal that home is close at hand. It also includes the relationship that is clearly apparent between the church, school and Coronation Hall. Although all obviously have independent functions, it is clear from some of the resident interviews that, at a very fundamental level, they are thought of as more or less interchangeable with respect to the social and community identity of the village. They are clearly more than mere buildings within which social activities, functions and meetings are held, but seem to represent three parts of the same whole that collectively symbolises Kirby Hill as a close knit and active community. The church and school are spatially proximate and this is one thing that contributes to the experiential strength of that part of the village, but Coronation Hall is in fact in Milby, virtually a mile away and yet it is very clear that this location is just as much a part of the identity of Kirby Hill as the other two (Plate 17).

The identity of Kirby Hill

Next we turn to consider how revealing the experiential landscape of Kirby Hill has helped inform the aspects of the Village Design Statement by drawing out some issues in relation to the requirements of the original brief.

What is special and important about Kirby Hill?

Because of the over-riding impression presented by the village's physical structure as a collection of independently designed residential developments, largely devoid of any reference to village vernacular, it is not immediately apparent what special and important qualities Kirby Hill has. The region around the church as well as a scattering of other older buildings and elements of open space are without doubt special, but their presence in the village as a whole seems overwhelmed by the impact of the newer development. Visually it has overall coordination only in the sense that it is a collective of built form distinguishable against a wider rural setting. Interviews carried out with village residents reveal this to be a misleading impression. There is an emphatic sense from virtually all participants interviewed of a village defined as primarily a social entity and that the sense of, and desire to sustain and further develop, social cohesion in Kirby Hill overrides the physical structure of the village as its most important characteristic. It is nevertheless clearly evident that there is a spatial and physical expression to this sense of social and community identity. This seems best understood in terms of a gradation of intensity emanating from and with its strongest expression at what we have defined as the village core. Strong and valued though this is we detect an undercurrent of regret or frustration that the green spaces here do not entirely deliver what people would wish. This seems partly to do with their erosion in recent decades as a consequence of development pressure, lack of places within it for respite and relaxation, and some conflict of interests over its use. There are opportunities present to improve on this situation through judicious integration of parts of the large square of land to the west of the junction of Church Lane and St John's Walk. It seems however that this may have been missed as infill residential development continues to remove this from the public realm. Other special and important aspects are that Kirby Hill is surrounded by open fields and thereby retains a sense of physical independence from surrounding settlements. This seems in part to be associated with reports of a rarefied quality to the air in Kirby Hill that is somehow different and superior to that of Boroughbridge. This perception is attributed to the relatively elevated location of Kirby Hill and introduces a topographical dimension to the sense of physical independence that for some seems significant. The openness and views to Hambleton Hills and "The White Horse" are very important and in part explain the attraction to walk the "triangle" a particular way round.

Where is the neighbourhood?

The team's initial survey anticipated a multiplicity of neighbourhoods largely because of the prevalence of block-like, inward looking residential developments. Whilst this was confirmed by the interviews to some extent the experiential reality is predictably more subtle. By far the most prominent impression to emerge from the interviews is that, as with the wider village, people seem to think of the concept of neighbourhood in a social and community sense, rather than in terms of physical or visual coherence. There are exceptions, but many seem to feel that the entire village constitutes their neighbourhood and the reasons for this seem predominantly to do with feelings of safety, fellowship and shared community interests, rather than a consequence of spatial or physical factors. Again though the experiential landscape analysis reveals that this conception of neighbourhood does have a spatial expression, although this manifests as a very elastic structure depending on what individuals wish to include as part of their realm. As detailed earlier, for some this can be quite expansive, extending way beyond where the village boundaries might intuitively be considered to exist, while others have a more compressed perception of neighbourhood.

What is the distinct identity of the village?

There is a strong sense of village identity in a social and community sense and this over-rides its physical structure. At one level this appears to have the effect of weaving together the Church, School and Coronation Hall into a unified social institution and, because the latter is not actually in Kirby Hill at all, seems to generate for some, the feeling that Milby features in some sense as part of the identity of Kirby Hill. In a strictly social sense this also appears to extend to Langthorpe as well. This appears to be because of the galvanising effect that the making of the Coronation Hall has had on residents in the three communities. It seems very clear that the Hall is much more than a convenient shared facility, a receptacle for meetings and social events. It also seems to have an important symbolic meaning representing the collective effort put in by those that participated in bringing it about. This seems to have had a curious effect. On the one hand it seems very clear that there is a desire for the built mass of Kirby Hill to remain physically separate, but that in a social and community sense, Milby and Langthorpe are embraced into the definition of Kirby Hill as a village community. This feeling of social cohesion appears to be strengthened by bonds of association relating to the school catchment area and the fact that people from all three places worship at the same Church. This appears to suggest two things that may be significant: first is that the sense of community is slightly at odds with the village's physical configuration; second is that Coronation Hall appears as an example of how community cohesion can be strengthened by new development projects as long as they are seen to be in the collective good, are generated by local initiative, and are amenable to local participation in decision-making processes.

Where does the village start and finish?

Possibly because of factors to do with the relationship between the village's sense of identity as a community and its physical and spatial structure, defining where it begins and ends seems exceptionally complex. Two principle themes emerge though which help to illuminate the situation. First are issues relating to the village boundaries, and second are issues relating to the sense of arrival and departure from the village. Both have an incremental nature in that there appears not to be specific locations that mark where the village begins and ends, or where one feels a conclusive sense of arrival and departure.

Village boundaries: broadly these appear to extend beyond the line of the built settlement to include the surrounding fields. Most people interviewed seem to regard the A1 to mark the western boundary, although Back Lane to the eastern boundary of Cover Beggar Field seems to mark a significant edge for some. It seems clear that all built form to the east of Leeming Lane is certainly Kirby Hill, but there is substantial ambiguity about the extent to which the buildings to the west of Leeming Lane are included within perceptions of Kirby Hill's boundaries. This seems to be due in part by the impact of Leeming Lane as a boundary, and also to the presence of road signs indicating where Kirby Hill and Langthorpe are. These road signs seem to be providing information about the village boundaries that runs counter intuitive to many people's perceptions and this generates a significant lack of clarity about what is in and out along this western edge. Northern boundaries appear to be marked by the roundabout at the road junction at the A1 and the T junction on the Dishforth Road to the north-east of the village. The significance of the roundabout as a village edge seems to have been heightened by it being the location of a recent village protest against the proposed motorway service station, and to this extent, rather like Coronation Hall, provides another example of a physical structure that has acquired a symbolic significance as a consequence of cohesive community action. The village's eastern boundary seems clearly to be the Dishforth Road. The southern boundary is much more difficult to define, but seems to extend down as far as Milby, and for some includes Milby, to the eastern side of Leeming Lane. To the west side of Leeming Lane, the gap in continuity of buildings at the southern edge of East View represents an obvious boundary, although some seem to regard Hill View and East View to fall outside the village boundary. This sensation seems strengthened by the effect of the poultry farm as presenting an undesirable feature that many would prefer to be associated with somewhere that is not Kirby Hill. There is some evidence that, for some, Kirby Hill actually really finishes at the roundabout by the canal before turning into Boroughbridge.

Arrival and departure: there is a build up to the sense of arrival and departure, rather than a single "gateway" type experience at each point of entry. The clearest to define is at the eastern point of entry. Most people identify the cross roads on the Dishforth Road as the point at which they feel a sense of arrival at the village, and this seems driven by the sensation of change in direction towards the village and sight of the church as a landmark. From the north-west, the A1 round-about seems to provide the first gateway point into the wider village environment. The location at the lay-by and pond provides a second significant point of arrival and then at the point where the road enters between The Grange and Manor Drive. The mouth of Church Lane seems to be the point at which most feel they have arrived at the village core, possibly heightened by the presence of the Blue Bell. From the south there seems to be a more complex incremental sense of arrival and depar-ture that has much to do with a sequential combination of corridors, gateways and focal points acting together. Significant elements include the strong "corridor" effect at intervals along Leeming Lane, given by property and road boundary treatments; "horizon effects"' due to the topography of the road including subtle change in direction; the visual impact of a brick building opposite the entrance to St John's Walk, and the visual draw of the Blue Bell gable end which seems to signal the point of arrival.

Significant places

Three themes appear to characterise the attach-ment of significance to places in the village. These are: because they have historical connota-tions and provide links to the past; because they are socially meaningful; and because they are reminiscent of past enjoyments no longer avail-able. Most of these are concentrated within the location we have defined as the village core and seem to contribute in various ways to an implicit sense of a village green. The strongest perception of a village green is the collective of linear grass verges, trees and open spaces either side of Church Lane and seems to extend from the mouth of Church Lane including the Blue Bell as its western boundary, down to the war memorial. There is however, a sense in which for some the totality of the village green extends beyond this to include the verges along the approach road from the A1, and further to the east to include the grass area in front of the church. There is a strong

feeling that the integrity of the village green has been eroded over the years as a consequence of development pressure and there are signs of this continuing. In many ways this idea of a village green has the potential to act as a unifying green spine for the village core, linking together features and places along it that have emerged from the analysis as significant. These include the war memorial and its setting, the post box, and larger open space features like the triangle around Church Closes. This has emerged as a highly significant and complex social and restorative experience shared by many residents and is an extremely important component of the physical and social identity of Kirby Hill.

The church building and its landscape setting, perhaps unsurprisingly, has emerged from the analysis to be at the heart of the village, from which, as one participant put it, "all else radi-ates". The significance of the church does not appear to lie only in its spiritual significance, although this is clearly important, but more in what it represents as a symbol of Kirby Hill's community and social identity. This seems strengthened by its historic, landscape and archi-tectural value as a village focal point and landmark. It is equally apparent that the church is regarded as one, although possibly the most significant, component in a wider social and community entity that includes the school and Coronation Hall as an integrated whole. Many seem to regard these buildings and what they provide and represent socially, as a collective entity beyond what might be expected by their spatial separation. Importantly, there remains the essence of a view that the Blue Bell should also be included as part of this "community whole", but that recent developments have diminished its value and appeal as a local village pub. There is a general sense of loss apparent in this respect. This sensation can also be detected in respect of the Willow Garth and its nearby hedgerows, and the pond to the north-west of Kirby Hill. These are associated with pleasures past, relating to wildlife observation, relaxation and contact with nature that are no longer available probably largely owing to changes in agricultural practice. They remain though an important part of the way people see the totality of village life.

Conclusions

The analysis carried out at Kirby Hill has helped reveal and illuminate in some detail dimensions to village life, crucially relevant to the sense of village identity, that transcend its superficial visual appearance. These dimensions emanate from the way in which inhabitants experience village life, often subconsciously, through the places they come into contact with routinely and the meanings and associations they hold both at the scale of the whole village and in relation to places within and around it that have particular significance. Revealing Kirby Hill's experiential landscape has given this a spatial expression through revealing patterns of open space experience. These help to explain the complex and elastic nature of the village boundaries, where the essence of Kirby Hill is felt most intensely, and that the village core is a composite of several distinguishable components working together to form its heart. It shows how the habits and emotions of individuals become embedded into the village landscape and how these aggregate into a picture of Kirby Hill's collective social identity and how this is expressed through its buildings and open spaces. It provides a benchmark from which to examine Kirby Hill's strengths and weaknesses in terms of how its spatial organisation might sustain the future evolution of its community. In this respect a number of themes can be identified.

Underpinning all of them is the universal consensus that the social cohesion and community identity of Kirby Hill must be sustained. It is widely appreciated that for this to happen it is necessary to realise that the community of Kirby Hill is a living and dynamic entity and that its continuation relies on periodic revitalisation that has two principal and related implications. The first of these is a collective desire to find ways to encourage greater participation in village life. This seems particularly important for people who do not currently share in the elements of social and community life focused on the church, school and Coronation Hall. The second lies in the generally inclusive attitude to welcome and embrace newcomers, particularly young families, to diversify and sustain life in the village but providing they make a positive contribution to community life. What this actually means in practical terms is hard to define, but it reflects a growing concern in the village that something of its identity as a community may be gradually eroded by an increase in the number of inhabitants that reside there but do not otherwise engage with village life. The really interesting question here then is if social sustainability is as central to the identity of Kirby Hill as it appears to be then in what ways might any future development pressure on the village either help of hinder it? The experiential landscape analysis offers food for thought in this respect as follows.

The most obvious thing not to do is allow any further residential development of the sort that has brought Kirby Hill to its present state. Specifically this means the sort of small self-contained housing developments that ignore village vernacular or are arranged to look inwards on themselves and turn their backs to the wider village. This should apply to development proposals both at the extremities of the village and within its existing main body of built form. The reasons for this are primarily to avoid a spread of anonymous suburban style mediocrity that contributes nothing to the visual identity or appeal of the village. It is also to reflect that internally orientated cul-de-sac type spatial layout is extremely unlikely to be conducive to the sort of social interactions necessary to meet the village's aspirations. What is required instead is development that encourages greater permeability in the village because the more people can walk about, the more they will meet each other and the more they will gradually develop a sense of attachment to locations in the village they come across. This is graphically illustrated by the collective experiential landscape map which records such an intensity of experience focused on Church Lane and, albeit to a lesser extent, St John's Walk. It is no coincidence at all that these two streets are literally the only ones in the whole of Kirby Hill where you can go in at one end and come out at another. Every other street in the village is a cul-de-sac of one kind or another and the only reason to use these streets is if you live there or if you are visiting. This might offer certain attractions but at the same time this sort of spatial organisation sterilises diversity of social activity and interaction to such an extent that the build up of experiential intensity so evident along Church Lane, and so central to its role as the core of the village, will never be generated.

It is very clear, for many reasons and in many ways, that the inhabitants of Kirby Hill see themselves as distinct from Boroughbridge in particular. Even though there are peculiarities with respect to their perceived relations to Milby and Langthorpe, Boroughbridge is different: it even has different air! It is a matter important to village identity that a respectable gap be maintained to preserve Kirby Hill's sense of physical independence from Boroughbridge. There are also implications for perceptions of Kirby Hill's boundaries and the sense of arrival and departure to and from the village. The analysis reveals that Kirby Hill's inhabitants hold a diversity of views about where the boundaries are and as a result we concluded, from an experiential perspective, that where the village starts and finishes is fairly fluid. Perhaps more importantly though is the existence of quite a strong feeling that approaching and leaving the village is incremental. This contributes to a sequential experience which begins at or culminates at the Blue Bell, depending which way one is going. It seems possible that the sensation of arrival at Kirby Hill could be further improved by appropriate enhancement of the spatial sensations that contribute to this rather than through attention to boundaries. The location at the Blue Bell is extremely important because it also signals the beginning of what we have identified as the village core, and this dual role could be strengthened considerably to the benefit of village identity.

During the course of the project there began to emerge a strong feeling that Kirby Hill did not really have a core or centre, at least not in the way this is normally understood in relation to North Yorkshire villages. Nevertheless, many residents mentioned a village green, although where this actually was varied just about as much in local perception as did the village boundaries. It appeared important though that the village should have a clear and distinguishable village green but that somehow the possible candidates were insufficient in this respect. The analysis suggested this might be because many of the green spaces in the village had become so compressed and disjointed as a result of development pressure that a clear sense of the village green had diminished in the collective psyche. During the analysis however, it began to clarify that the largely linear green open space either side of Church Lane was most often identified as village green-like, particularly the wider open space where the war memorial stands. There was also an expression about the desirability of the grass area in front of the church as a potential village green and the experiential landscape map clearly shows this area in particular to be pivotal in the village. It is a pity in some ways that there is an unfortunate break in the sense of continuity between these two locations as together they are obviously important elements in the core of the village. Nevertheless it raises the interesting prospect that, rather than having one single central green open space as might be typical of many traditional villages, Kirby Hill might strike out for independence and be distinguishable by having a sequence of small linked green spaces each associated with, and giving specific identity to, a particular part of the village. It is in fact possible to see in the current village layout that potential for this might once have existed as there are open spaces that could have contributed had they been available. All of these are however, already in private ownership, or are in the process of being built on. In addition to being related to issues of village identity, the lack of socially relevant open space, particularly in relation to provision for children and to reduce conflicts in use of current open spaces, appeared as a recurrent theme from the analysis. This is a very problematic matter for the village because the combination of past and continuing development pressure within the village is reducing ever faster the potential to respond effectively. It is clear though that there are valued and used open spaces, particularly within the fields immediately to the south-east of the village that already feature strongly in the village identity.

Chapter 10

Experiential landscape analysis and design in schools

Introduction

> "parties shall assure to the child who is capable of forming his or her own views the right to express those views freely in all matters affecting the child…" *Children's participation as recognised in the UN Convention on the Rights of the Child* (Hart, 1997). (Figure 10.1).

The everyday environment inhabited by children is increasingly highlighted as an important contributor to their social development and general health and well-being (Thomas and Thompson, 2004). In a recent report the Department of Transport, Local Government and the Regions describes such settings as being composed of incidental spaces, the mundane parts of the outdoor environment that are often overlooked or may even attract attention for being derelict and unsightly (DTLR, 2002, p.47). The DLTR consider these to be a national asset, yet evidence suggests that there remains a significant loss of connection between children and such outdoor settings and that this may have long-term implications. Ken Worpole, author and commentator on open space and social issues, has recently raised the profile of this by synthesising current government and community initiatives in this field. He places the importance of providing

for, and giving voice to, children in policy, planning, design and management of public open space firmly within the Urban Renaissance agenda. His report, *no particular place to go?"…*seeks to make clear that planning for play, and the need to create safe street networks and spaces for young people and children, is a precondition of a healthy community life and 'liveability'" (Worpole, 2003, p.4). Three issues appear to emerge from this aspiration especially prominently.

– It is the everyday environment routinely encountered by children that should receive particular attention because collectively it constitutes the realm of the walkable community advocated by the DTLR (2002).
– The walkable community in this context is understood as the continuous network of varying spaces that form the routine, and usually subliminal, backdrop of daily life. Research shows that this is how young people often inhabit public space, as a series of stopping points in a continual process of wandering though neighbourhoods (DLTR, 2002, p.31).
– The voices of children must play a pivotal role in the arrangement and content of these spatial realms and should focus on developing ways to understand their own notions of

10.1

"parties shall assure to the child who is capable of forming his or her own views the right to express those views freely in all matters affecting the child..."

place as an essential component of individual and social development (Titman, 1994; Worpole, 2003).

These issues help give us some insight into what we might understand as the experiential landscape of the child, as a network of locations strung out along routes routinely taken. Worpole describes this world "as being the continuous network of pavements, streets, amenity land, parks, playing fields, town squares, forecourts and curtilages (e.g. railway station forecourts, or retail car parks) and other paved open spaces, which children and young people use in the course of their daily lives, and which make up that familiar territory of place and attachment so often beloved in the literature of nostalgia in every generation" (Worpole, 2003, pt 1, p.3). They also tell us that the voice of the child is unique in revealing this

experiential landscape because their own notions of place may not necessarily correspond with that of the adult community.

In this chapter we will explore ways to make children's experiential landscapes visible, drawing attention to the need to use special tools and techniques. We will highlight that children's experiential landscapes tend to be generated by responses to place that particularly emphasise: social networks, places and objects, feelings and emotions, and imagination. This is not to suggest that these responses are unique to children, just that they seem to emerge from interviews and workshops we have carried out as the principal ways in which places of all kinds come to prominence for them. We will also discuss how these characteristics of the experiential landscape can help with enlarging our understanding of place experience in the school environment and how this helps to make experientially richer design solutions (Figure 10.2).

10.2

The voice of the child is unique

Field work in schools

A programme of practice based field work has been undertaken since 1999 to explore the concept of experiential landscape with young people, looking in particular at how to develop better participative techniques for school grounds improvement in both primary and high school environments. By working with schools at various locations in the north of England over 900 children ranging from 4 to 14 years (the majority of which have been in the age range of 5 to 11 year-olds) have been involved in a variety of participative processes aimed at building components of methodology by which to reveal the experiential nature of their outdoor space use. The most extensive element of this ongoing research has involved 68 children between the ages of 7 and 11 participating in a three stage participatory process built primarily around different forms of semi-structured interviews and cognitive mapping workshops. This has extended beyond the school boundary to the public realm by examining the journey from home to school to highlight perceptions of place attachment in the wider neighbourhood, a realm which is equally important in the spatial repertoire of children but often overlooked. This has been recently highlighted by

the DfES of being of some importance in the context of enhancing the school run's potential to promote positive behaviour and choice by giving children a say on improving school journeys (DfES, 2003) (Figure 10.3).

Some of the field work has foundations in Single Regeneration Budget (SRB) school grounds environmental improvement projects and aimed to satisfy the funding requirement to consult with each school's populous including staff, children and parents. There are, of course, many relevant methods of consultation in the existing literature and especially through the work of organisations concerned with the relationship between children and open space: *Learning through Landscapes*, for example (Titman, 1994). It became apparent though, in early scoping studies that, from an experiential landscape perspective, a set of participative tools was needed that could provide a

10.3

The journey from home to school is important in the spatial repertoire of children but often overlooked

richer and more qualitative insight into the factors contributing to children's place perception, to more firmly underpin the creation of new places that would promote a sense of ownership and positive behavioural traits.

Early studies using experimental techniques based on developing word-pictures and wish-poems drew attention to the often significant differences in the place perception of adults and children and in particular professionals involved in the design of places to be used by and inhabited by children. There have been numerous occasions encountered in research and practice when this has become apparent. During a project to improve environmental quality at a primary school, for example, the professional perception of the existing site concluded that it was a two-dimensional characterless space of tamacadam-savanah bounded by a low metal fence with no apparent aesthetic qualities or redeeming features. This was identified as an obvious site for improvement and proposals were made to replace the fence with one that matched the other boundaries and related better with the building. Workshops with the children however revealed this as one of the only significant outdoor places in the otherwise bland playground. It turned out this was due to a previous use that had caused the fence to deviate producing a corral effect open on one side. The resulting enclosure was routinely used as a gathering point, a place to shelter from a stray football, and above all and most significantly, as a point of social interaction with siblings. The fence was now low enough to allow engagement with younger brothers and sisters in the neighbouring infant playground. Replacing the fence would have risked removing these opportunities. Fences, in fact, seem especially important to children. On another occasion one was also described as a favourite place during interviews. A galvanised and unpainted 1.8 m high security fence with spikes on top, it was again regarded by professional inspection as a problem to solve. To the children, however, this was the place where they went to find spiders.

Not only do these examples illustrate that places significant in the routine lives of young children do not always correspond with conventional professional priorities, but also that there is

a risk of loss rather than gain if this fails to emerge during site and user surveys. We are not suggesting that these places should necessarily always be preserved, or that beneficial opportunities for the children might not arise from the proposed improvements. But we can only learn the real significance of place attachment if we adopt methods to engage with children that are capable of revealing the subtlety involved in how they assign meaning to place, through informal and sometimes highly clandestine social activity frequently overlooked by conventional methods. In other words we have to be able to see the child's experiential landscape and understand its significance to the life and well-being of that child.

Practitioners do consult and use participation in school grounds design, but traditional participative techniques can frequently attach too much significance to solutions focused on aesthetics, technical resolution and physical features. Frequently lacking is sufficient consideration of the experiential nature of place and its potential to promote positive behaviour by engendering place attachments that bring a sense of emotional well-being. Often out of necessity participation is driven by budgetary considerations or quantitative project auditing requirements and risks falling into the category of what Henry Sanoff has called pseudo-participation (Sanoff, 2000). This alludes to the tick-box approach to participation, or perhaps more correctly consultation, where "the level of participation is that of people being present to listen to what is being planned for them" (Sanoff, 2000, p.8). In these scenarios little meaningful account can be given to the values of people directly involved and outcomes are often unsustainable with no sense of ownership engendered through the process or manifest within proposals.

Collective personality

One of the questions our research sought to address was how to effectively engage with children to ensure that outcomes provided not only desired physical elements, or educational opportunities, for example, but were also experientially rich in the way this is understood in the concept of experiential landscape. This means first developing ways to understand the experiential dynamics of the existing setting so that existing patterns of meaning, so often invisible to conventional processes, could be made visible. Second it means building from what is found to further enhance and enrich opportunities for children to orientate themselves, find places of value and significance to themselves as individuals and groups, and become aware that they are a part of a collective and identifiable whole within which they belong and are an integral part. Part of our response to this has been to concentrate on trying to reveal what we have called the collective personality of a place and then to reflect this in the design. What this means is that anywhere used as intensively as a school will have, represented by its collective experiential landscape, a personality composed of the habits and activities, personal preferences, meanings and associations, of all its users, adult as well as children, projected into the physical surroundings. These places are then as much the product of mind as they are material fabric and if this can be imbued into the way improvements are conducted then a greater sense of place attachment and ownership should be generated. In other words, the resulting scheme means more because it resonates better with the collective personality already there.

The essence of the collective personality can often be very simple and can be translated into symbolic themes that can influence the development of change in the school environment in ways that are recognisable as meaningful by all. For example, at one school this became related to psychological associations of security that children projected onto the geometric form of a circle. The importance of the circle became apparent in workshops as a shape that held strong associations with the certain time of day they engaged in circle time. During this time they got together as a class, with the teacher sitting on the floor in a circle to openly discuss issues that troubled them, including issues of bullying and other social problems. The circle became a recurring theme associated with social significance, sharing and mutual support to the children. Subsequent design work to improve an area of

the school playground made use of the circle as a motif that intended to engender subliminally this same sense of safety and familiarity but also as a place that could be used for circle time as an alternative to the classroom. We will describe an example in which the collective personality was found to be particularly rooted in the faith culture of a school and how this helped the school to connect with the wider community beyond its boundaries. This presents an example where the collective personality is especially explicit, particularly to members of the community who share the same faith. Often, however, what emerges as the collective personality of a school is far less immediately obvious. Significant colours, for example those connected to the school uniform, appeared to predominate in another school, and at another the school's proximity to a railway line appeared particularly significant in providing a catalyst for the school children to mentally project beyond the school to all points imagined to be linked by the railway line and the trains they saw moving along it. These can be very powerful foundations in the psyche of a school community and often come to light only through the layering influence of a multi-method approach and the extended time over which this takes place.

Part of the process of revealing the collective personality in a school resides with the act of participation itself. It has long been recognised by some scholars involved in place theory research that a sense of place is often more robustly embedded when there has been collective and cooperative effort involved in its creation or re-creation. This has implications for the way information is gathered and it is especially important that participants do not simply feel themselves at the receiving end of an enquiry carried out by external experts on their behalf. Experience during early pilot studies showed that an important response to this appeared to be to use a variety of techniques rather than a single method approach. Although this is clearly more time-consuming there seem to be two important gains. One is that different methods tend to highlight different things and so collectively deliver a much richer and potentially more detailed insight than would be possible with single method approaches. Although collating results from this can be problematic, the experiential landscape mapping techniques allows information drawn from different sources to be coded into a common format. Individual responses are then layered using GIS computer software to build up a picture of the composite experiential landscape, a diagrammatic representation of the collective personality of the school in experiential terms. A second gain is that the repeated visits involved with implementing a multi-method approach, coupled with the variety in the tasks that participants become engaged with, seems to embed a deeper sense of participation. Instead of being recipients, those involved experience a sense of being valued participants in the gradual discovery of what makes their place unique, as individuals and as a group, and then in the creative activity of imagining what else might be possible. Some of the principal techniques that make up this form of participatory activity are outlined here.

- **Non-participant observation** (Figure 10.4). Non-participant observation as described in chapter six involves passively observing practices, interactions, and events which occur locationally and contextually. It is beneficial if observations can be carried out at intervals throughout the school day. A potential problem is the nature of observation in that it is fixed at a point in time: it takes no account of what happens before or after the visit. Additionally star actors tend to gravitate towards cameras and clip boards, and the researcher should look towards the less open participants. (Silverman, 2000).
- **Semi-structured interviews** (Figure 10.5). The early studies developed an approach to building trust between the researcher and study group and to determining useful information using a technique of semi-structured interviewing. Predetermined topics guide conversation allowing new questions or

10.4
Non-participative observation

10.5 (left)
Semi-structured interviews

10.6 (right)
Cognitive mapping

insights to evolve as the result of discussion (Pretty, Guijt *et al.*, 1995). The establishment of themes around which discussion is based evolved from pilot work, similar to an ethnographic interview (Flick, 1998 citing Spradley 1979). Themes were categorised into three areas of interest, and are refined to take into account the context of each project or application. In general they seek to reveal children's perceptions of physical objects and features, their experience of place, and placemaking activities, physical or subliminal.

— **Cognitive mapping** (Figure 10.6).
The use of cognitive mapping is effective in finding out how people view their area (Wates, 2000). The technique has been used in urban design methodology perhaps most notably to demonstrate how a city's imageability can be expressed by individuals (Lynch, 1960). The significance of people being able to understand their environment and being able to mentally map it is a prominent component in the development of place perception (Downs and Stea, 1973). Additionally such maps are effective where there are cultural or communication prob-

lems, which can be the case with employing conventional methodologies due to the age and limitations of understanding of the study group (Wates, 2000). During the course of field work it has become apparent that cognitive mapping techniques are useful in two ways. They can be used conventionally to gain insight into perceptions of the existing situation, but they can also be adapted as a means by which children can express how they would like to see things change. In both cases it has been found best to do this by asking basic questions which centre on the child. For example, "This is me and this is what I like doing best and where", and "This is what I would like the outside of my school to be like".

— **Word-pictures** (Figure 10.7).
The use of word-pictures as a means to focus on the way in which people would experience proposed places has roots in Christopher Alexander's development of proposals for the Mary Rose Museum (Alexander *et al.*, 1995). The idea was to develop a means of describing something of the quality of sensations and experience that

WORD PICTURE

We wanted somewhere were you can go and relax. [with no picnic benches] somewhere were its not dull and boring away from the school work and teachers. Were people can meet their friends and hide from teachers. It's a place were you can be yourself, talk to your mates and not have teachers watching you. All the time.

10.7
Word-pictures

10.8
Wish-poems and pictures

the museum would deliver to its visitors in advance of thinking about the physical structure and spatial arrangement in detail. Using Alexander's concepts as a starting point, word-pictures have been developed and refined in work with university students and with year 8 and 9 children as well as groups of adult learners. This work has demonstrated that the word-picture can be a very potent tool through which participants seem to be able to express their feelings about places they want to see more profoundly and in greater detail than is often the case when using traditional visual methods, such as drawings etc. One year 8 student described her aspirations for her school's grounds: "What we will feel like! Chilled, relaxed, having fun, warm, charm, fresh, like everything is new born, crisp and everything is alive." The word-picture does have limita-

We will need!
Logs, trees, flowers, a path, some benches, a pond with a net over the pond, a bird table and a patio tree bench.

What we feel like!
Chilled, relaxed, having fun, warm, charm, fresh, like everything is new born, crisp and everything is a live.

What everything look likes!
Colourful, alive, cheerful, happy, fresh and relaxed.

tions in its application with younger children due to their less developed written communication skills, but transcriptions of oral word-pictures can go some way to circumventing this problem.

– **Wish-poems and pictures** (Figure 10.8).
An adaptation of semi-structured interview is the wish-poem, a technique described by Henry Sanoff (2000) and developed and refined for use with young children over a number of case studies. The wish-poems are gradually constructed by engaging children to think about particular themes, for example, "I wish my playground had". In both the wish-poem and semi-structured interviews the general theme is used to stimulate conversation, to reveal any significance in comments made by participants. In undertaking these workshops, an often overlooked asset is empathic listening to discover the underlying message and an ability to put aside peripheral distractions or preoccupations. Egan (1990) qualifies empathic listening as being "contextual and integrating" (p.131): the act of listening should consider the context and not just the words. This is often experienced in participative workshops and can be especially significant when working with children, where there is more significance in the meaning and context of the words than the words themselves. The earlier cited instance of the differing professional and children's views in respect of the security fence is an example of when listening to the words was insufficient to reveal the contextual meaning and significance of this object, and only on further encouragement and more importantly listening to the children, it was revealed that this was the place where they went to find spiders. The methods used to engage with the children give insights into the children's meaning of place and informal/social activity that would not have otherwise become apparent or recorded without listening contextually. A further adaptation of the wish-poem gives it a visual emphasis by asking children to illustrate their ideas about how they would like to change their outside environment and what they would like to feel there.

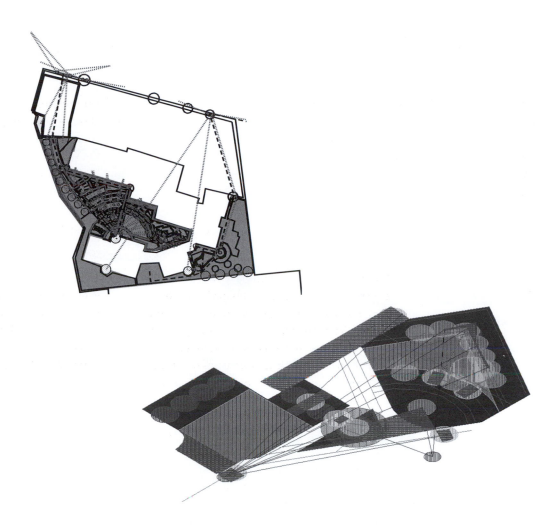

– **Mapping experience** (Figure 10.9).

The mapping techniques of experiential land-scape provide a means by which information from all the above sources can be coded into a consistent format and mapped to reveal spatial implications for the setting being investigated. This coding framework is neces-sary to simplify and make consistent the recording and analysis of the process (Romice and Frey, 2003). This method of mapping spatial experiences produces a composite map made from combining a series of over-lays from the output of each individual participant. This represents the combined existing, or aspirational, experience from information provided by the participatory exercises and observations. Geographical Information Systems (GIS) enables the filter-ing of participant's results to examine a wide range of specific issues. Similar to cognitive mapping, it is a tool with relevance to both the process of revealing information about how an existing setting is perceived and to revealing the spatial distribution of experi-ence for proposed schemes. In the latter case the experiential landscape map does not produce a design for a new site, but it does allow the aspirations that emerge from word-pictures and wish-poems etc. to be translated into an experiential code that often has impli-cations for particular locations on the site.

Findings that have emerged using this multi-method approach highlight the often poetic nature of children's place experiences. They report, for example, the pleasure of watching "long grass swaying" on a windy day, to driving through "a long arch of trees" that on a sunny day

Objects and places

"There's this big thing near where I live, it's got smashed windows, it's a big building next to the sheds. Its been there over a hundred year, and there's a glove in one of the windows. I don't like it because it's scary, there's holes in the roof and pigeons go in it. It's got a thing outside with mud in it and weeds. I'd like to turn it into a swimming baths."

Feelings and emotions

Boat, building alcoves and huddly trees

"I like the feeling you get when you're on rides, it's exciting. I don't feel scared, I feel free, away – from everything…I dream about having the sea outside me front door, and I'm in the speedboat, in the front driving, it's good driving things you feel your in control of it."

"My favourite place to go is the prairie at the bottom of our street, its got loads of trees that are really huddly, which cover you" another child describes how she enjoys walking past a particular hedge "because it feels like its tickling me".

10.10

Children's experiential landscapes tend to be generated by responses to place that emphasise in particular, places and objects, feelings and emotions, imagination, and social networks (continued opposite)

Imagination

"temporal dimensions, place as process, story of flux" (Blizzard, C. (2004) unpublished e-mail correspondence)

"I notice the well and the post box, when I'm on my bike and go over the manholes, it makes me judder and feels like a ride, if I'm walking I still jump over them. There's a road I pass and I used to play with a girl who lived around there, I don't know which house but it still reminds me of her around there. There's like a place where the horses drink from, a trough, by the bush and a gate leading to the grass. Well you can't actually see it from the road but it's all green and rotty and yellowy and I know its there, and I guessed horses drink at the trough, because I've seen it lots of times."

Social networks

"On my way to school, I wave to some of my friends who are walking to the high school, then I see people in the park…Sometimes I see a lady who helps out at my school dropping her daughter off at the high school. I see people delivering things and look in shop windows to see what's new…I see a lady on a motorbike thing walking with her child to school, sometimes I look at the horses in the field, because my friend used to keep hers there, and we sometimes go to look at them. I know when I'm getting close to school because I see my best friend's dad walking to school with his children. If I'm early I see the school bus for the high school, I notice it because I look out for my sister's friend who goes to the high school and gets the bus. I notice a lot of people walking to school and when I get to school I notice lots of children playing and moms and dads."

is fun "like an electric light going on and off" or having a favourite place to go such as the "flower beds, with loads of flowers and lots of colours" and "the feeling of hope you get from them, even when there are no flowers on them, because you know they will come again". Another 7 year-old girl's favourite place was described as; "the prairie, it's got loads of trees that are really huddly, which cover you". Another described how she enjoyed walking past a particular plant "because it feels like it's tickling me". It may be significant that many of these comments appear to allude to pleasurable, comforting feelings, often related to a sense of enclosure and to familiar objects and experiences. Research into the wider spatial implications of these findings and their potential relevance to design processes involving children continues, but it is evident from work undertaken so far that the experiential landscape of children appears to show that certain things are emphasised in the ways children develop associations and attach meaning and significance to their surroundings. Children's experiential landscapes tend to be generated by responses to place that emphasise in particular, places and objects, feelings and emotions, imagination, and social networks (Figure 10.10).

We will move on now to amplify on some of these issues with reference to the way in which

experiential landscape techniques have been used in schools. In the following examples we will discuss in more detail the way in which the collective personality at a Catholic primary school was brought out and incorporated into proposals to improve a courtyard area in the school. The second example shows how experiential landscape mapping assisted with differentiating sense of place in a nursery school playground, and the final examples detail the importance of experiemic scale and the way centres can be nested to form densely packed and multi-purpose social environments for primary school children.

Exploring the personality of place at a primary school

The work at this school took place at intervals over a three-year period and involved both staff and children taking part in workshops, interviews and other activities in the context of three environmental improvement projects. This gradually revealed the unique personality of their school. By adopting this approach we believed that, to be consistent with the concept of experiential landscape, the school's personality would be found as much in the routine habits and emotions of the people using the school, as in its physical characteristics. The purpose of the project was to carry out improvements to the school grounds and in so doing the approach adopted would investigate the pattern of routine use and the values that mattered to those using the school, and then marry this as closely as possible to spaces around the school. This would then inform design decision-making that would ultimately develop a school environment that would not only fulfil the funding objectives and the school's aspirations for functionality and relevance to learning, but also be emotionally and experientially rich with a unique sense of place.

The first site identified by the school for improvement was a courtyard which was to be developed as an outdoor classroom with seating, raised planting beds, and artwork. The main entrance vestibule of the school overlooks the courtyard and on the north eastern elevation is the hall/dining room. On the western elevation are double doors leading onto a pathway giving access to the main playground. The courtyard was bleak, largely featureless and dominated by a floorscape of concrete paving slabs with a central slot drainage channel.

A requirement of the project funding was to involve pupils, parents, teachers and governors and so a significant early issue was to identify ways in which these diverse groups could be meaningfully engaged. Following initial discussions with the head teacher, an evening meeting to discuss the proposed approach was arranged with staff and parent/governors. The design development aims discussed reflected a range of functional, educational and experiential objectives, from the participants and designer, and these included the following.

– To fulfil functional needs by engaging in a range of consultative workshops to establish what physical elements were required.
– To be a resource for learning by maximising the learning opportunities within the design by discussion with the children and staff.
– To promote a sense of ownership by active participation of the school community to enable the project to evolve from the school in meaningful partnership instead of the imposition of an externally generated design solution.
– To promote an emotional response by consideration of the experiential qualities of the design.

Achieving these aims involved recognition of the need to create a unique sense of place, rather than merely an attractive and functional space that would engage the children during their time at school and resonate the experiential essence of the school. Central to this would be to understand what made this school unique in the minds of the staff and pupils.

Finding the personality

The essence of the approach adopted is that it was above all people oriented: attention to the actual site, in terms of surveying its dimensions, physical attributes, analysing its problems and opportunities etc. were to begin with of secondary importance. What mattered most was to get an impression of how the children and adults felt about the school as a place of meaning and as a place of community. Later this would be directed towards the courtyard space to see how it related to its present physical appearance and spatial organisation, and to see how to make improvements to better reflect the values expressed by the school community. This process was informed by a series of workshops, some involving the children and others adults during which a range of activities and discussions, informal and semi-structured, gradually built up a picture of what the school meant. It is important to note that these events, possibly more time-consuming by comparison to conventional processes of client consultation on many school environmental improvement schemes, are not simply a means to gather information. They are also an important means of developing empathy between the school community and the design professionals involved. It is through the generation of such empathy, facilitated by the range of participatory methods employed in the workshops, that it becomes possible to truly begin to understand the culture of the school to the extent that its collective personality becomes apparent. Experience has taught us that this can only be meaningfully established by a multi-method approach and with the investment of time.

The character of the children's workshops reflected the kind of learning experience they were used to. So, for example, time was spent with classes at the outset helping the children to understand what landscape architects do, to help them understand a plan view of a place, and eventually to help them begin to understand the nature of space and scale in relation to activities they would be familiar with. A three-dimensional model of the courtyard was made to help with this and they were invited to think about the fact that you can not fit an elephant into a hamster's cage or play football in a shoebox. They were also taken to the courtyard and with closed eyes asked to say what they could smell, touch and hear, and describe what it felt like to be there. These activities were supplemented by more informal non-participant observation of what happened on arrival and departure from school, at assembly, playtimes, lunch times, as well as in structured lessons. Through the use of wish-poems, mapping, and drawing exercises the children were gradually guided away from thinking about the existing situation and encouraged to use their

imagination to make suggestions, in verbal, text and visual forms, for the courtyard. Although this phase of the work yielded a diverse and creative output, as might be expected, much of it, at a superficial level, reflected the relatively limited environmental experience of the children involved. Findings from this were tabulated to highlight priorities represented by the frequency with which the range of elements appeared in the children's work (Table 10.1).

There was however, a strong undercurrent beneath this wish list that seemed to correspond closely with a more general theme that had gradually risen into prominence during the more informal aspects of the visits. This was the importance of the school's faith culture, reflected in iconic imagery inside the building and in the conduct of the school community in their daily routines and thoughts. Not only was this important to life within school it also linked the school to a wider community. Looking at the findings from the children's workshops in light of this it appeared as though much of it could be related to aspects of the Catholic culture of the school (shaded), suggesting that the fundamental experience of school life rested firmly on these foundations.

Table 10.1 **A table highlighting priorities in the range of elements that appeared in the children's work**

Settings	Plants	Walls	Water	Physical objects	Floor	Themes
Music corner	Flowers	Hang paintings	Pond	Crosses in gravel	Gravels	Nature
Sheltered spot	Grass	Space to write	Rill	Moveable benches for shade	Painted snake	Disney characters
		Patterns and colours	Fountain	Paintings	Crosses	Bright colours
			Fountain with lighting	Benches	Paint ramp	
			Waterfall	Shelter	Maze	
				Bird box	Hopscotch	
				Tables		
				Rocks		
				Drawing table		
				Sand pit		
				Bridge		

Adult users of the school were also observed for patterns of activity and conversations were conducted, some informal and some semi-structured, to enrich the picture that was gradually emerging. Later at a more formal meeting, staff, school governors and the local Parish Priest discussed how the project was unfolding and began the process of identifying particular categories or themes implicit within the range of text, spoken, and visual material generated. This phase of the work tended to emphasise the more pragmatic matter of what elements needed to be included in the proposals to realise the functional aspirations of the school. For example, it emerged that a space was needed that could be multifunctional and able to adapt to the requirements of small groups of children or larger groups to the extent this would be feasible in a relatively small space. Seating ought to offer a choice of location for different times of day and activity, and partitions of some description should be considered to facilitate flexible use and to allow the space to be seen differently from various locations inside the building. Within this, though, the Catholic culture of the school also continued to emerge as a unifying thread with suggestions made to reflect the story of the school's Saint in the design and to respond in some way to the mass held traditionally in celebration of the children leaving to go onto secondary school. This seemed to further the meaning of the school as a part of a wider community and the significance of the children's faith to their place attachment. The totality of this activity works together to develop an evolving understanding, both for the professional designers and the school community, about what is important about the experience of the school: it is much more than simply a matter of data collection.

Designing the personality

Interpreting this in the design of the courtyard involved developing a setting that would reflect the faith culture of the school as a whole and in its parts without becoming so explicitly themed as to become a parody. The over-riding aim was to create a courtyard that fulfilled the school's functional needs in a way that would be an integral part of the collective personality of the school and also optimise experiential opportunity through its use. This meant conceiving a spatial configuration that would let children and adults identify personally significant places within it, explore and discover, and experience the feeling that they were somewhere that belonged to the school and the wider Catholic community, but that also had a sense of its own unique identity.

One of the strongest images in the children's work was that of a snake. This was an interesting image in that it held a theological significance related to the Garden of Eden story that the children were familiar with, and was also associated by them with the game of snakes and ladders, a gentle pursuit of perilous anticipation. This seemed like an appropriate way to begin to think about developing a proposal that could have a playful sense of anticipation based on undertaking a journey, whilst at the same time containing an identifiable theological message. The journey was also the metaphor for life in a theological context. As well as representing the passage through school as a pupil, it also embraces learning in a wider sense through the ups and downs of social, cultural and spiritual development, and the ecumenical chronology of seasons. Once this concept had taken hold, it was made more meaningful by the children exploring similar themes during their Religious Education lessons: a form of feedback loop important to further embedding the collective personality in the consciousness of the school community. This provided a conceptual framework for the courtyard relating to a journey along which travellers would discover a series of places, each with its own distinct identity.

The sense of discovery would be heightened by developing a spatial configuration that offered glimpses of what lay ahead through control of views from within the courtyard and from inside the building. By mapping the proposal conceptually as an experiential landscape map we could explore the sequence and distribution of experiential sensations that would generate diverse opportunities for place attachment and exploration through elements of surprise and discovery within an overall feeling of containment and coordination. The courtyard would be woven into the wider school culture by virtue of its theological underpinning whilst at the same time it would have its own identity: a part of the school but also a place apart. Achieving this would be important to generating the spatial sensation of area, the feeling of being able to experience being inside of somewhere linked to, but also distinguishable from, the surroundings. Within this overall sense of coordination, smaller special locations spread out in a sequence would lay the foundations for sensations of centre, some with a social emphasis, others with prominent features, others that would engender calm, reflective and therefore restorative sensations. As well as being special places, these locations, made as small gardens, and the features they would be composed of, would become landmarks arranged to heighten the sense of anticipation and discovery, key aspects of the experience of direction. Through the generation of contrast at points of entrance and exit, perhaps in the choice and use of materials, planting, natural light and shadows, transitional experiences would also be built into the scheme.

In practical terms, exploration and containment within the gardens would primarily be achieved by a series of panels. Some could be opened to provide varying spatial configurations, allowing small or larger groups to use the gardens and some would be static and serve to allow glimpses through to other gardens, while others could be removed altogether. The use of colour would relate to the ecumenical calendar to define the character of each garden. The significance of colour was a subject discussed in religious education classes and developed from the sequential use of purple, gold and green in the calendar for the seasons of Advent, Christmas, Ordinary time, Lent and Easter. Each garden would then express one of these colours in their physical forms and the integrity of the ecumenical sequence would be maintained if the gardens were experienced in a particular order. In addition to the significance of the colours, which would establish the main visual expression of the courtyard's personality and present a source of thematic continuity, emphasis was given to the allegorical content by the forms used. The panels, for example, were to form part of the metaphor by using shapes cut out of them. Designs for the panels were therefore developed functionally to give a sense of place and enclosure to each garden and provide glimpses of what lay beyond as well as an opportunity to support climbing plants. Additionally they were to serve as a teaching resource in respect of the geometric shapes of the cut-outs reinforcing the theological metaphors, as well as by their subsequent shadow patterns, which would also bring diurnal transitional qualities stimulating threshold experiences. The plant species and composition of each garden was carefully selected not only to add natural and architectural features but also to be colourful within the theme for each garden. Honeysuckle, for example, has fragrant flowers reinforcing the sense of place at a particular location, others are aromatic when crushed such as Rosemary, and focal points are provided by forms of specimens. This is how planting can be used strategically to enhance particular spatial sensations: in these examples, centre.

The final design

– Mary's Garden provides a setting for the school to display a religious icon. This would be the first garden encountered on entering the courtyard and because it holds a statue of the Virgin Mary on a plinth is pivotal to the school's faith culture. Purple is the dominant colour reflected in planting and the opening panels which also have the shape of the cross cut out in 12 places; a theologically significant number repeated elsewhere to represent the 12 apostles. Grid mesh panels divide this garden and the water garden beyond.

– The Orbit Garden alludes to the universe reflecting both the scientific exploration of space and the theological perspective of Christ at its centre. It has a water sculpture as a focal point surrounded by eight circular seats and four painted circular floor graphics surrounding it. The opening panel in gold has cut-outs continuing to maintain both the geometric and numeric continuity by using 12 circles. Golden leafed species or yellow flowering specimens dominate planting.

– The Music Garden offers a place of quiet reflection and opportunities for teaching and interactive pursuits through the provision of a chalkboard with green benches placed either side of it. A musical stave is fixed to

10.11
The final design conceptualised

the wall of the building with the notation spelling the name of the school. A raised stage area with a tarpaulin backdrop provides a performance arena. Climbing plants are encouraged to grow up the grid mesh panels to contribute to the sense of enclosure.
- The Quiet Garden was to be a place of contemplation. The elements in the Quiet Garden are purple to continue the colour theme and the garden is defined by a painted line on the floor between vertical posts of the Orbit Garden and the Music Garden. Seating is provided and a snake is painted on the floor, a fugitive from the jungle area, the next place on the other side of a removable panel.
- Water has strong religious connotations both in allegory and metaphor and in the religious customs observed at mass with the children. To reflect this a Water Garden was developed in an alcove next to a storeroom. A bench in the shape of a "C" encourages social interaction and vertical posts provide support for an overhead stainless steel wire which supports climbing plants. The water feature here is an iguana, selected to be in keeping with the theme of the adjacent jungle garden.
- The idea of a wilderness also has biblical references and this was interpreted as a jungle in response to the outcome of the workshops with children. The dominant features in the jungle area are two chusan palm trees, raised planters and seating in green and the painted snake floor graphic. A bench is for adults to sit on and a triangular planting bed is enclosed on two sides by grid mesh panels.

It was always intended that the courtyard would be an outdoor classroom, but it was also an aim that it would not merely become a receptacle for learning but should promote learning from its forms, colours and geometry. It was possible to use the setting as a resource for lessons in subjects such as Geography, Science, History, English, Art, Music and Religious Education. The children and staff quickly personalised the courtyard with the addition of bulbs, seasonal plants and bird feeders, and an excellent project on the birds observed in the courtyard gardens was displayed inside the school. A permanent record of the development of the courtyard was made for future generations of pupils not included in the process (Figure 10.11).

Differentiating sense of place in a nursery playground

This example illustrates how the participative techniques used in experiential landscape exploration helped to generate a variety of place experience in a small nursery playground setting. It shows how these techniques were adapted to the needs of younger children, an age range of 3–5 years, and as a result how this led to creating a setting that stretched their place experience in the context of their play but in a way relevant and familiar to everyday life outside of school. The existing nursery playground was an uninspiring tarmacadamed area flanked on the northern side by grass with a tarmacadam pathway leading to the front of the school. A small picket fence defined the boundary to the south and extended to include a prefabricated concrete shed. The school wanted to make this into an environment that would provide greater opportunities for passive and active play and social interaction for children during play and lunch times. School staff were keen to make sure that the project reflected the locality, and thought this could be achieved by having a seaside theme. Early discussions explored a range of features that might help realise this including having a boat, sand and stepping stones, and art work to represent sea creatures.

Whilst this provided a useful basis from which to begin developing design proposals for the new playground it was quickly realised that this may not necessarily reflect the thoughts and feelings of the children attending the nursery. The staff did not want simply to impose a set of features which, although would be interesting and entertaining for a while, might not resonate enough with the routine lives of the children. A strong element of the school ethos was to try to make coming to the nursery a comfortable extension of their familiar lives as a means to help with settling in. To address this, workshop sessions involving wish-poem techniques and a lighter form of semi-structured interview gradually helped children to begin to express their likes and dislikes, producing interesting findings about the importance of day trips and holidays, active games like skipping, hopscotch, digging, and ball games. Games of pretend and dressing up also seemed to emerge as favourite pursuits along with places to support this, such as boats, houses, castles, a Barbie garden and the less exotic roads, parking spaces and the local Asda supermarket. There are limits however to what can be achieved using these techniques with such young children and for this reason the methodological balance was shifted more towards non-participant observation.

Watching the way children played in the essentially featureless playground proved revealing. The majority of activity was based on role-play and centred on the various cars, trucks and trailers at their disposal. Beyond this there was no obvious structure to the way children played and they seemed to congregate randomly without any particular point of focus, playing games in groupings across the playground with different, and sometimes competing, clusters of children trying to occupy the same space. Underlying this apparently free-form activity was however a subtle orderliness that seemed significant. This was that the absence of more obvious features in the playground tended to lead to children gravitating to the only things that were distinguishable. These included the covered area at the doorway to their classroom, a shed and its concrete ramp, and staff who seemed to become mobile beacons. Expressed as an experiential landscape map these appear as centres, the only opportunities available to the children to experience sensations of location in the playground. This was a significant, and detrimental, characteristic of the playground given that the main preoccupation of the children was with role-play games associated with their developing awareness that different things were done in different places: you would not do the same things in the Barbie

10.12

An experiential landscape plan of the existing nursery playground. Staff became mobile beacons of centrality in the absence of other features

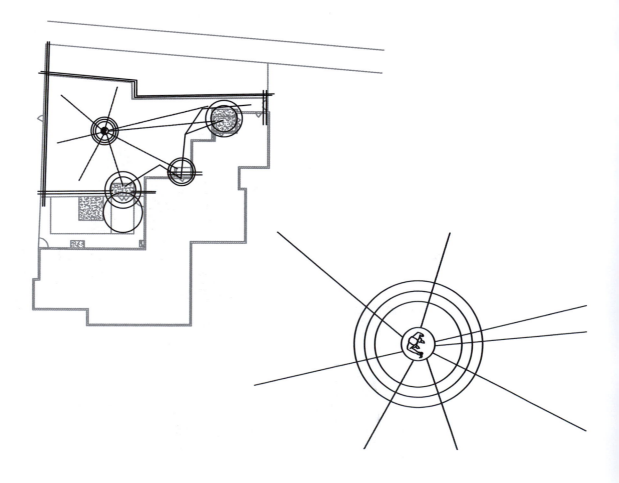

garden that you would in Asda. The association of place with behaviour appeared to play an important part in the social development of the children and in this respect the existing playground was substantially out of phase with the developing complexity of place awareness beginning to be expressed through play. Furthermore, it seemed evident that the lack of a variety of places to occupy and make-believe might be leading to disagreements over possession of toys which, along with the playground staff, were the only features available for the children to gravitate towards (Figure 10.12).

The role-play games often revolved around children exchanging hats provided at playtimes and adopting a persona that went with the particular hat. Discussions about this with staff coupled with the need to expand the diversity of places available in the playground led to the idea of "people who help us". This overall theme gradually grew into a conceptual approach to the development of the playground that would explore how different kinds of people and different activities can be associated with particular places. This would provide a framework of learning through play that simply extended what the children appeared naturally to want to do in the

playground. It would give them different places to go to, and therefore choices to make and it would introduce the idea of journey to and from places, providing opportunities for exploration and discovery. This in particular built from observing that the children played a game with trolleys that involved picking things up from one place and setting them down at another and in giving each other a lift in their go-carts. The new places could be made to be identifiable with what they experienced out of school and so reinforce the connection between school and the real world. Clearly recognisable objects that could be counted and described would help with aspects of the pre-school curriculum. Similarly, shape and colour were ways to differentiate one place from another in the tight space of the playground. Signposts, both physical and metaphorical, using simple graphics could direct the children to these different places. The seaside theme was developed to reflect the town's character and locally identifiable places such as the Fish Quay, shops and the park represented. There would also be a special place with no recognisable features to encourage children to interpret it as they wished. All of this informed conceptual proposals for a town-like setting of different places, centres that could be

10.13

The new experiential landscape conceptualised as a network of centres at distances emanating from a central point of arrival and departure

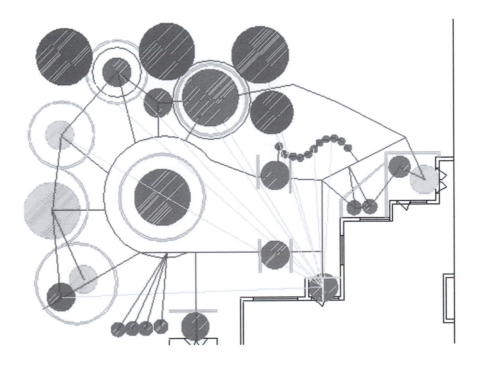

travelled to and from for socialising and activity that would also act as landmarks providing directional qualities to an otherwise featureless space.

One of the children's favourite activities involved re-enacting "going to Asda's", presumably a routine part of the life of a pre-school child that seemed to have raised the town's supermarket to that of a prominent psychological landmark. As the shed was one of the few places to attract children in the playground, its existing prominence in their play resulted in its promotion to the play-town's Asda. Accordingly, it was repainted in appropriate style and the local store manager provided a sign to complete the transformation. Other places in "town" included a bus station, hospital, the local fish quay, home, the park, the beach, a fire station and, to promote a journey outside town, a zoo was proposed.

Figure 10.13 shows how the new experiential landscape was conceptualised as a network of centres at distances emanating from a central point of arrival and departure. This location has the transitional quality of a segment: a location with a significant identity, in this case the main point of access to and from the playground and from which the play-town could be surveyed by the children. This was given the identity of the bus terminus to reinforce its significance as the main point of arrival and departure and helps to dramatise the experience of entry to the playground. Directional experiences are introduced as a consequence of the new centres acting as visual devices from this vantage point, and through the encouragement to move around the site visiting different places via a roadway complete with signs and parking spaces to suit the size of the children's peddle cars. Smaller scale transitional sensations are provided on entry and exit at each of the centres, reinforced by changes in material, colour, direction or level. In this way all the centres are woven together so that they create a coordinated whole, or area, recognisable as the local town that lies beyond the school doorway (Figure 10.14).

- The sea. The town's connection with the sea was represented by including a boat set on a blue safety surface which along with a quayside seat provided opportunities for active and passive play. The prominent visibility of the boat and the strong coloured surface create a playground landmark and give this location a sense of identity clearly distinguishable from others. The mast and funnel of the boat would provide an opportunity for the school to personalise it by making a variety of flags that could be hung at different times of year or special occasions.

- The town centre. The school needed an area of safety surfacing so that portable play equipment could be brought out for the children to use. This was provided in the middle of the playground to be identified as the town centre. As well as providing active play this equipment could be arranged in different ways at different times offering the chance to explore alternative ways to structure the town centre and relate objects variously to the other surrounding areas.

- Home. This was a place that would be less prescriptive than the others, leaving the children to give it whatever interpretation their imaginations wished. Calling it home was intended to reflect that everyone's home is different and so could become whatever they wanted it to be. But it also represents the location of familiar security where safety may be found and it was anticipated that this might be reflected as a point of refuge that characterises many children's games. A simple seat offered either a place to get off the floor or to sit and watch.

- Park. Home has a red seat and, in contrast, the neighbouring park has a green one, differentiating the two places and reinforcing the message of parks being associated with green open space. Planting would further the horticultural theme. The park was to be one of the main places to meet, rest and socialise and so "L" shaped seats were provided that lend themselves to small social huddles. Upright cylindrical screens added to the sense of enclosure and supported plants providing the town with another visual landmark.

- The beach. The beach area comprised of two adjacent centres, the first small centre defined by a yellow painted line containing a yellow bench. The second centre was made from a raised planter in which children could

10.14

A redistribution of active social centres surrounding a central core

dig and plant. A path around the planter gives all-weather access and a sense of exploration. It has mostly grass species to reflect what might be found on a dune.

— The zoo. The zoo resonates with the children's experience of Flamingo Land, a nearby attraction the children are taken to during their time at the nursery. A snake was constructed from vertical poles in the ground and painted in a sequence of different colours and spaced to allow children to wind their way in and out of them. The poles create a further vertical feature adding to the directional qualities of the playground as well as an opportunity for counting and sorting games.

— Fire station. A popular part of the children's role-play had involved firemen's helmets and their activities when wearing them seemed to focus on an area outside the playground store. This seemed to be an attraction because it had a ramped surface in front of it that was different from the rest of the playground. The doors to the storeroom were painted to look like a

fire station and two parking bays provided for "fire station staff only".

Exploring nested centres

The small nursery courtyard outlined above is an example of how experiential landscape analysis was used to create an environment where the experiential potential would not just be increased but would be spread out more evenly across the site. This was to provide children with more opportunity to attribute meaning through their play to a diversity of different locations instead of simply gravitating to doorways. As the conceptual experiential landscape map shows (Figure 10.13), the overall character of the courtyard is a many centred environment linked together by directional features that focus on a main point of access and egress. The emphasis on centres here reflects that the main activities of the children were observed to be primarily locational in nature, driven by their make-believe games, but that the courtyard did not have a spatial structure that

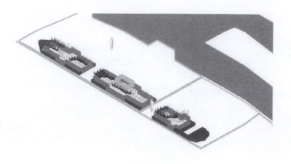

allowed this proper expression. In other words, as it was, the courtyard had an extreme paucity of centres whilst the children's intuitive behaviour was highly centred. Consequently there was a serious lack of harmony in the existing relationship of human and spatial dimensions once the nature of the courtyard, as an experiential landscape, was revealed.

Another project, in a different part of the same school, also sought to explore ways to increase the experience of centre, but this time, instead of spreading them around the site, they would be compressed together, or nested. The reason for adopting this approach was partly a

response to the overwhelming sense of anonymity the site conveyed: the site needed a focal point, a strong beacon that would give personality and interest where none currently existed. It was also a response to the need to create an environment in which a wide range of passive and active pursuits would be possible in more or less the same place, rather than being dispersed to different zones. The need to do this had emerged from participation workshops carried out with staff and children during which the strategic significance of the strip of land marking the edge between the tarmacadam playground and the grass area in front of the school building. From here social interactions occurred while children stood about in small groups watching playground activity and moving back and forth to periodically join in. But, just as with the nursery courtyard, nothing apart from a simple threshold between grass and tarmacadam existed to support or enrich these activities.

The solution explored was to create a strong visual landmark (Figure 10.15) at this location that would mark and indeed celebrate this part of the school grounds. To do this it would need to respond in scale to the façade of the adjacent school building and be something that would bring a distinct sense of character and identity. The school's maritime setting and the relationship of land to sea was a strong feature of the psyche of the children. It emerged frequently in the work they produced in participative workshops relating to its constant visual presence as they moved around town and back and forth to school and also to family ties with people working in a range of maritime occupations. In response the project developed the form of a long cargo ship grounded and with nature taking over. This was an image the school community could readily identify with and it also seemed to symbolise and intensify the nature of the existing site as a threshold. As a prominent visual feature the ship would generate in the playground a strong sense of location: a centre significant because of the social imageability generated by the ship as a landmark feature (Figure 10.16).

But its experiential dimensions would run much deeper than this. It would also be a feature that would intensify the sense of transition from

10.17
Three centres enfolded

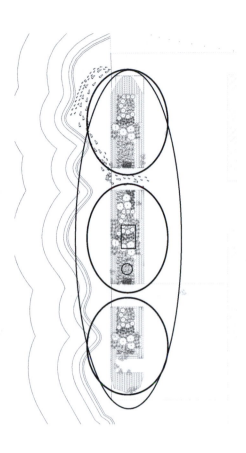

10.18
Many more nested centres

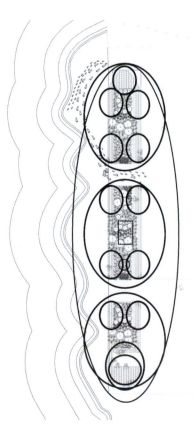

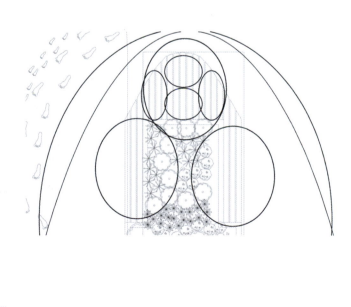

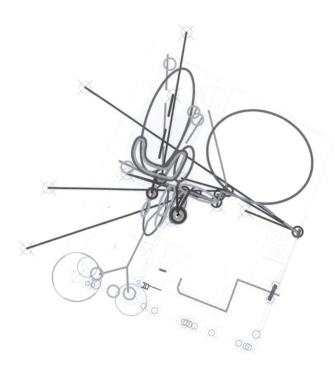

prospect and refuge

The head teacher stands (cup of coffee in hand) outside the school building by the main access/egress door and welcomes the children and their parents. This gives any issues a chance to be aired by the parents before the school day begins, and offers an opportunity for less formal 'social dialogue' with the head teacher. This space, therefore which is bounded by a low wall on one side, and the building on two others becomes a significant locality for engaging with the parents and diffusing any issues that may have manifest themselves overnight. It also gives the head teacher a prominent presence both from the point of view of contact for the parents and supervision of the children that have arrived and are at play.

Some children play football, some sit and chat to each other at benches, while others make noises to babies in pushchairs. The active, play tick but most congregate in the rear playground. The walls dominate and make the spaces 'tight', there is no permeability. Some children – not many – play football in the front playground, these tend to be the older children.

Girls congregate around the railings at the top of the cellar, others wave to their neighbours who are leaving their homes for work or shopping. Benches become focal points for social conversation and observation of more active peers. Some children follow the painted lines on the rear playground floor in what appears to be a horse role-play game.

9.00am The Bell – not a sound.
Second bell, the line up begins.

The year 6 children become team leaders with some from year 5, each 'shepherds' their group of 4 or 5 younger group members to a particular place in a line at right angles to the playground wall.

The young ones fidget and the older ones chastise and coax their team into a straight, still and quiet line. The head teacher awards the 'best' team with the honour of leading the school inside into assembly. Positive behaviour is rewarded with the hierarchy of the assembly parade, the more exuberant, lively, talkative or uneven line remains until last with a few words of carefully chosen admonishment from the head teacher and encouragement that there will be an opportunity to improve.

10.19
Design development using CDTA and experiemic scale
(continues opposite)

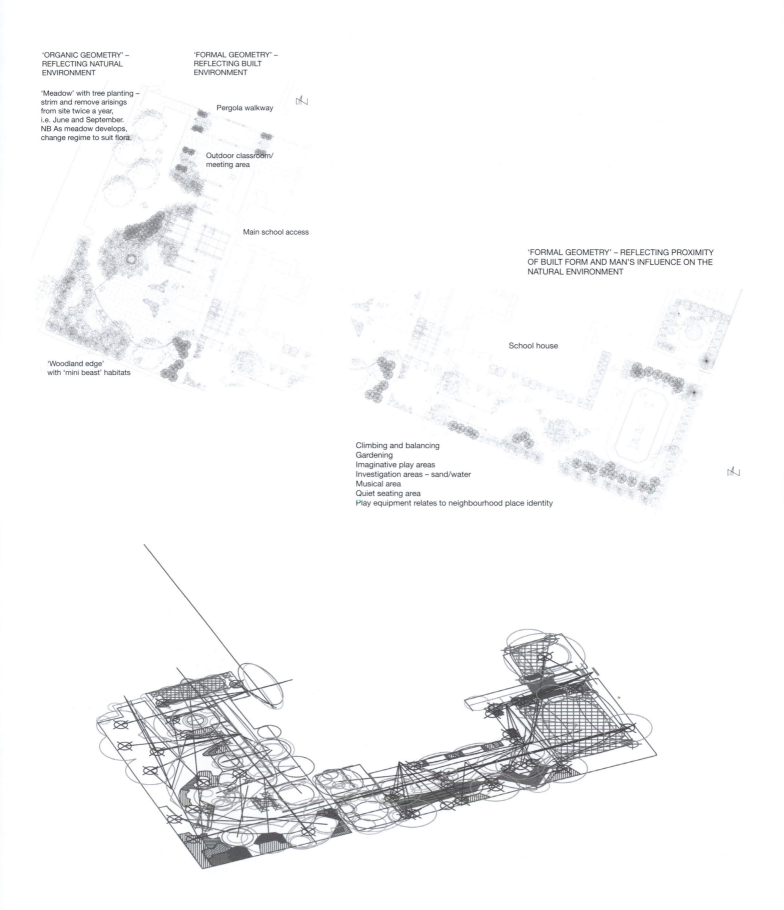

'ORGANIC GEOMETRY' –
REFLECTING NATURAL
ENVIRONMENT

'Meadow' with tree planting –
strim and remove arisings
from site twice a year,
i.e. June and September.
NB As meadow develops,
change regime to suit flora.

'Woodland edge'
with 'mini beast' habitats

'FORMAL GEOMETRY' –
REFLECTING BUILT
ENVIRONMENT

Pergola walkway

Outdoor classroom/
meeting area

Main school access

'FORMAL GEOMETRY' – REFLECTING PROXIMITY
OF BUILT FORM AND MAN'S INFLUENCE ON THE
NATURAL ENVIRONMENT

School house

Climbing and balancing
Gardening
Imaginative play areas
Investigation areas – sand/water
Musical area
Quiet seating area
Play equipment relates to neighbourhood place identity

playground to school by being broken into three sections with gaps corresponding to existing paths. Each of the three sections created smaller centres by offering different reasons for children to pause there: to meet and talk, to watch, to play, or to engage with the plants that were arranged to flow through the whole ship uniting the three parts together in a whole. Partly this was achieved by emphasising that each part corresponded with different component parts of a real ship: a bridge, mid-ships and a stern (Figure 10.17).

A further nesting of centres was created by optimising the potential of the structure for sitting. The edges of the boat were folded in so that small enclosures were formed for children to sit in social groups. Planting was arranged to enhance the sense of enclosure and to intensify the sense of

location at each place with particular smells or tactile qualities. A deeper layer of centres was incorporated by further attention to detail at each location. The bow, for example, would be a location to climb on with seats round the edges, the mid-ships would have a bridge and funnel, and the stern would have a distinct planting theme and seating laid out to form a social niche in the shelter at the back. Yet more centres were made by adding peep-holes to attract and hold attention and by exploiting the sides of the bow to provide shelter and places to hide (Figure 10.18). Figure 10.19 illustrates some of the development sketches and narrative from non-participant observation, along with subsequent translation as experiential landscape maps used to explore experiemic scale in another school.

Chapter 11

Experiential landscape in the Calls and Riverside, Leeds

Over the last two decades or so the city of Leeds has undergone a transformation of its urban character (Figure 11.1). Regions of the city centre, once semi-derelict and neglected backwaters of past industrial and commercial use, have been brought to life with a now vibrant mix of retail, business, leisure and residential development. Much of this has been stimulated by the Leeds Development Corporation, set up by the Government to regenerate over 1300 acres of the inner city by bringing existing land and buildings into effective use to encourage existing and new commercial and industrial activity. A significant objective of the Development Corporation was to achieve this in ways that would also attract people to live and work in the inner city by providing housing and social facilities in an attractive environment.

Core to the Development Corporation's strategic plan was the need to help the city centre expand southwards. This required overcoming a number of major obstacles. In particular the railway viaduct had, for many years, acted as a physical barrier more or less confining the retail and business centre to its northern side. South of the railway viaduct the city was characterised by mainly industrial development, much of it a Victorian legacy with historic value and architectural merit but largely unused and in places derelict. Through this area ran the River Aire corridor, once a vital commercial artery for the

city's growth, but since the development of the railways, a declining feature that the city had long since turned its back on. The Leeds Development Corporation recognised that an area in the south-east corner of the city centre known as the Calls offered potential to begin the process of overcoming these obstacles. They thought that its distinctive character and location could play an important part in the regeneration of Leeds by providing necessary expansion to the south-east of the city centre. Its location meant that a positive relationship could be re-established between the city centre and its river corridor and, by exploiting the historical appeal of its existing Victorian warehouses, buildings and small-scale historic street pattern, a characterful city quarter could be developed that would attract new uses and draw people from the city. The Development Corporation envisaged regeneration of this area as a careful blend of conservation and imaginative new development.

The Calls is actually the name of a street that runs roughly parallel to the river on the city centre side of its north bank. But as the regeneration process moved on, the name has become more generally associated with the wider area either side of the river held at the east and west sides by the Crown Point Bridge and Leeds Bridge respectively. As development work gradually came to fruition on the south bank, the southern

boundary of the Calls, as a distinguishable city quarter, now extends to Waterloo Street and Bowman Lane. An interesting feature of the Calls regeneration is a developing ambiguity about where its northern boundary now lies. Whilst this is still defined in large part by the imposing presence of the railway viaduct, more subtle forces are now at work gradually dovetailing the Calls into central Leeds at sites north. A physical link to the city centre was established early in the regeneration process by punching a route through one of the railway arches. Aided by the construction, in 1992, of a new pedestrian river crossing, this is now a well used route from south of the river into the city and effectively pushes the

visual and social characteristics of the Calls through the railway, embracing the Corn Exchange and Assembly Street area into a lively urban quarter of shops, hotels, flats and town houses, offices, bars and restaurants. Further work to penetrate the railway viaduct by opening more arches is underway at the time of writing. This will send more fingers from the Calls out towards Kirkgate and this, along with significant new residential development at the junction of Cross York Street and New York Street, will create strong connections between the Calls, Leeds' majestic indoor market and the city's bus station. This development, by the developers Urban Edge, is actually two separate schemes

11.2

A Calls resident's experiential landscape

either side of Harper Street, called the Iceworks and New York Apartments. A mixture of private and housing association dwellings arranged around internal courtyards with shop units to the ground floor street, it has powerful strategic value at this location relevant to the integration of the Calls into central Leeds. Its architectural style brings the two developments together to create an impressive gateway feature that will emphasise Cross York Street as a significant corridor into the Calls area.

The Leeds Development Corporation's vision for the Calls, to create a thriving, characterful blend of conservation and innovation to encourage and support a working and residential community in an attractive environment, has largely been achieved. It is often cited in publications as an exemplar of quality urban regeneration fulfilling many of the aspirations of Lord Roger's Urban Task Force to breathe new life into towns and cities through generating a strong sense of

place. That this has happened, and indeed continues to happen, probably owes much to the approach adopted by urban design consultants, Llewellyn-Davies, who set out to produce a masterplan that emphasised spatial rather than merely planning considerations. As a consequence a template for regeneration emerged that paid careful attention to the quality of the streetscape and to enhancing the network of small spaces and squares implicit in the historic layout of the Calls area. It is evident this has contributed to lifting a neglected part of Leeds into prominence, creating an attractive and popular place to live, work and socialise and there is now a substantial residential population.

Places like the Calls in Leeds are in many ways becoming models for the repopulation of cities, presenting to us a potential appearance for the new urban neighbourhoods. The question is though, is this model the right one, or not? The Calls has many impressive features: sensitive architectural regeneration, relationship to the city centre, exploitation of its waterside setting, vibrant social opportunities, impressive visual character, for example, but questions remain about the extent to which developments like these are conducive to creating communities. The Calls has an increasing number of inhabitants, but like many city centre developments that follow similar models this tends to be composed from an often transient population of mainly young professional people who may not establish the kind of long term roots in the area that will nurture and sustain a stable neighbourhood identity. An informal inquiry using experiential landscape mapping techniques helped reveal aspects of this that seemed to hold implications for place identity within the Calls (Figure 11.2).

We began to see that Calls inhabitants, residents and non-resident workers, identified the Calls area, or significant parts of it, as a neighbourhood in the sense that it stood out or had special associations that set it apart from the wider city. Although variously located there were also features that established physical or psychological points of transition suggesting that the Calls had clear boundaries and points of entry and exit. Significant sensations of centre and direction, however, tended to be associated with locations within the wider city with comparatively few within the Calls area itself. As the map shows, the experiential landscape of this particular Calls resident stretches out across the city. Of course, there is no implication here that there is anything wrong with this and indeed it is what might be expected of a city dweller whose routine life reflects the diversity of opportunities that a vibrant city centre offers. What was perhaps unexpected, however, was that the rich visual and spatial qualities so evident within the Calls area did not appear to register more prominently in the experiential routine of its users. In particular, the network of small spaces, courtyards and streets that characterises the Calls, to which Llewellyn-Davies' masterplan sensitively responds, gives a spatial configuration with many attributes of a setting that might have been expected to be more locationally significant than it appeared to be. People did not seem to be forging the kind of meanings and associations there that anchor a sense of belonging to a neighbourhood.

This is no doubt due, in part, to the wealth of experiential opportunity available in the central city which draws people from the Calls area, a situation exacerbated by an absence of neighbourhood supporting facilities: there are plenty of expensive bars and restaurants, for example, but no local grocery shop (there now is one on Dock Street), post office, doctors or dentist, for example, and certainly no school or community centre. Other influencing factors, though, seemed to relate more to a lack of understanding about how space can be encouraged to develop into place in a mixed-use setting. Unimaginative approaches to car parking make some office and residential courtyard spaces unavailable for better social uses, for example, and some open spaces in newer residential blocks are at best ambiguous as to their intended purpose and, in one particularly memorable case, completely inaccessible to surrounding inhabitants. Routing a section of the Leeds city centre loop road down High Court has effectively destroyed the Development Corporation's hope for better pedestrian priority and new development here, a decision that flies in the face of Llewelyn-Davies' masterplan and completely compromises an obvious potential to create quality public squares in this key central location. It began to seem as though, hidden beneath the impressive veneer of the Calls regeneration was a fundamental lack of confidence about how to optimise the place-making potential of its spatial infrastructure (Figure 11.3).

A much more comprehensive study, like that carried out in Kirby Hill, would be required to draw general conclusions about the experiential character of the Calls. Nevertheless, with the help of postgraduate landscape architecture students from the Department of Landscape, University of Sheffield, over a three-year period we began to explore the Calls as an experiential landscape in more detail. This provided an opportunity to examine the potential of the developing experiential landscape approach as a means to visualise some of the experiential characteristics of the Calls as an emergent urban neighbourhood, and explore how and where improvements might be made to encourage better locational balance and neighbourhood identity.

11.3

Traffic management has severely compromised place-making potential in a key central location of the Calls area

The material presented here follows the process adopted by one particular group of students as they set about exploring a particular journey through the wider Calls area, firstly to reveal details of its experiential character and then to explore potential design responses influenced by some of their findings. The main purpose of this work was to generate a situation within which we could explore the Calls area through the concept of experiential landscape. Its focus is therefore very much on the potential of experiential landscape as a means of revealing and then responding to hidden experiential qualities within its spatial structure. We are not suggesting that the material here necessarily presents wholly feasible and viable design solutions: there was neither sufficient time nor resource available to deal with the complexities involved. Consequently, readers should be mindful that the resolution of design ideas is less important here than what is revealed about the potential of experiential landscape as a means of visualising usually hidden dimensions of place experience in urban settings, and highlighting the value of this in design decision making. Throughout the process, however, we are confident that we have developed interesting and valuable insights into the way in which the Calls area, and by implication other similar urban regeneration schemes, could evolve towards a better sense of neighbourhood identity and social sustainability.

The Calls experience

Twenty-six students were involved in the project illustrated here over a six week period which first involved reading the experiential characteristics of the Calls area using the GIS based mapping methodology. The findings from their field work, undertaken in groups of about six, informed subsequent sketch design proposals for a part of the wider site area and by this means they were able to see how the concept of experiential landscape could help them to understand the site and then focus on appropriate design responses. As a consequence of work done in previous years we decided to begin the project by identifying six journeys across the site area. These drew from observations made previously and broadly corresponded with real patterns of movement to draw attention to the way in which the Calls area is actually experienced by real users, including the resident population, people coming to the area for work and leisure, or those simply passing through. The students involved assembled themselves into groups to look at one journey each and were encouraged to decide how best to adapt and apply the principles of experiential landscape within the constraints of available time, resources and project focus. The following illustrates this with the work produced by one of the groups who decided that they would try to develop a detailed profile of a roughly north-south journey through

11.4

Postgraduate landscape architecture students, Fran Curtis, Peter Koch, Neil Northrop, David Wesselingh, Lu Zhong, Veronica Meacham

11.5

Key locations along the journey through the Calls area

the Calls covering both sides of the river using a professional survey and role-play techniques (Figure 11.4).

The journey (Figure 11.5)

The journey examined begins at the Leeds city bus station and market and moves towards the Calls area via the new gateway Iceworks and New York Apartments development and through the central Calls area where there is a clustering of bars, restaurants and a hotel, as well as office and residential accommodation. It crosses to the south side of the river over the Centenary pedestrian

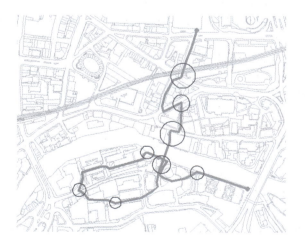

bridge alighting at a contemporary public square surrounded by restaurants, offices and the Hilton hotel. The hotel is a part of a cluster of new and refurbished buildings that have begun to define a sequence of new public spaces linking with Dock Street, the main westerly access into the Calls area south of the river Aire. This is in many ways a pivotal point at which new squares converge with Dock Street and the entrance to mixed residential development around the Aire and Calder Dock. This development of 120 units, completed in 1988, was the first major private housing scheme on the Leeds waterfront and it remains a visually distinctive neighbourhood with a sympathetic synthesis of traditional and contemporary styling. The journey emerges from here, meets the waterfront and returns to the Centenary Bridge continuing east along the water's edge to new apartment blocks by Crown Point Bridge (Table 11.1).

The team made a detailed photographic sequence of the journey and summarised their observations on tables like the one here for locations along the way that they felt were experientially significant. These were then interpreted as a sequence of Dobson Clusters and associated bar charts to give a first diagrammatic expression to the experiential characteristics observable at each location (Figure 11.6).

Plate 18 shows the experiential landscape map generated from the observations of the research team. As expected with professional experiential landscape surveys, this represents a distribution of place perceptions stimulated largely by visual information: the team is making observations based mainly on what they see in the material and spatial setting that stimulates, for them, sensations of centre, direction, transition and area, rather than what places mean to them as a consequence of routine use, for example. In very general terms what this shows is evidence for a part of the city of Leeds that has a rich visual complexity working to define a tightly knit sequence of areas. So, just as we can talk about the Calls as a whole being a thematically consistent region, or area, distinguishable within the wider city, we can also talk of it as an area itself made up from a series of distinguishable areas at smaller levels of scale. Another predominant experiential

Table 11.1   **Observation summary table for each location**

A2	Social Centre	Area	The use of traditional materials and active and façade continuity create the sense of an area along Wharf Street. This is further emphasised by Kirkgate which severs this space from adjacent spaces.	Main roads play a major part in dividing distinctive areas of 'the Calls'.
A2, C3	Wharf Street	Very isolated car-park Social interaction Negative centre	Very much 'private space' entrance to it very unclear. Fencing a visual eye-sore.	This very functional space has a visual gateway beyond, but it is blocked by fences.
A2, T3	Wharf Street	Threshold	Change in materials and colour, move in more enclosed space because of buildings.	
A2, T4	Entrance to Shear's Yard	Threshold	Movement into narrow passage between tall buildings, transition in colour, light and scale.	
A2, D5	Down alley to Shear's Yard	Direction view	Change in spatial rhythm and deflective facades draw your eye down narrow alley.	Fairly insignificant view contributing little to experience of place. May be intimidating to some.
A2, D6	View to ball fountain	Direction view	Metallic ball water feature as unique focal point and landmark feature draws the eye.	Potential to enhance movement to this focal point.
A2, M7	Alleyway to Shear's Yard	Direction (strong)	Sense of perspective and views into yard.	Strong sense of direction with little opportunity for free movement.
A2, T5	Wharf Street-High Court	Threshold	Change in materials and enclosure.	
A2, D7	View to trees	Direction view	View to street trees form significant focal point as lack of trees in area.	Trees have potential to contribute to directional views across other parts of journey.
A2, D8	View to St Peter's Church	Direction view	Strong view of spire of St Peter's Church helps with orientation.	Maintain views of landmark feature.
A2, M6	Wharf Street	Direction (strong)	Deflective facades, sense of perspective, and linearity of floor-scape.	Strong sense of direction and movement.
A2, C8	Fountain at the Entrance to Calls	Social interaction and imageability positive centre	Interactive sculpture, strong focal point, however not an obvious gathering space.	Thought to total use of space not well thought through.

sensation is that of direction, mainly stimulated by views. Frequent linear continuity in spaces, façade features, prominent visual devices such as architectural detailing, framing structures and free standing objects, all contribute to a sense of rhythmical continuity. This can be seen on the summary bar chart where the colours on the bars indicate the CDTA element that has greatest impact on the experience throughout the journey (Plate 18).

To an extent the directional emphasis of the Calls experience is being reinforced by the sequence of transitional features. Sometimes these are observed as prominent and strong, but at other times, although the sense of transition is clear it has seemed less well resolved leaving an impression from time to time that adjacent spaces appear

to leak into one another in a loose and ill-defined manner. This appears to be especially evident in the Simpson's Fold area where the configuration of built form ought to be supporting a clearly defined spatial sequence, but the resolution of this appears unsatisfying. Partly this seems due to weaknesses in transitional clarity and partly due to ambiguity in centre definition. These two aspects of place experience are in fact closely related because to a degree the intensity of a centre is related to the clarity of transitions that signal the sensations of arrival and departure. In very general terms, where there are weak transitions, there may be loosely defined and ambiguous centre definition. This appears, from the research team's findings, to be a characteristic feature throughout the Calls area as a whole. The

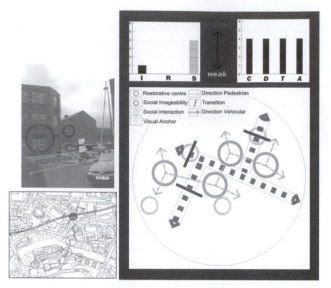

CROSS YORK STREET

Kirkgate Road creates a strong east–west directional sensation and at the same time has a spatial configuration that generates a number of distinct centres of social interaction. These are disjointed however and this appears to contribute to a sense of confusion and poor legibility. The viaduct and its associated archways provide a strong transitional feature to Wharf Street where a bright red brick building façade acts as a focal point, strengthening the transitional sensation and drawing the eye to the neighbouring space.

Strengths: engaging architectural detailing; potential as a key transitional location from bus station into Calls; deflective façades and continuity of floorscape encourage forward movement.

Weaknesses: Kirkgate Road a significant obstacle to fluid pedestrian movement; centres lack clarity and linkage.

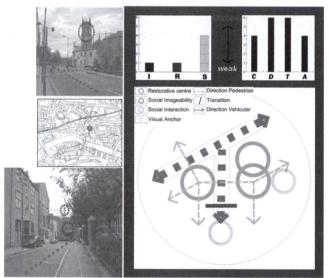

CROSS YORK STREET

Kirkgate Road creates a strong east–west directional sensation and at the same time has a spatial configuration that generates a number of distinct centres of social interaction. These are disjointed however and this appears to contribute to a sense of confusion and poor legibility. The viaduct and its associated archways provide a strong transitional feature to Wharf Street where a bright red brick building façade acts as a focal point, strengthening the transitional sensation and drawing the eye to the neighbouring space.

Strengths: engaging architectural detailing; potential as a key transitional location from bus station into Calls; deflective façades and continuity of floorscape encourage forward movement.

Weaknesses: Kirkgate Road a significant obstacle to fluid pedestrian movement; centres lack clarity and linkage.

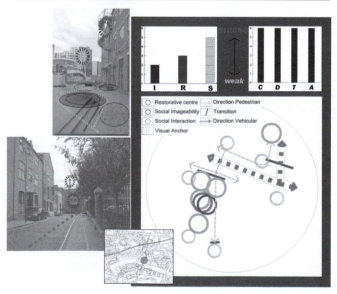

NORTH CENTENARY BRIDGE

Significant change in spatial rhythm and façade detailing encourage exploration towards Pool Court restaurant. Strong transition from enclosed to open aspect. Very strong directional sensation provided by centenary bridge structure and distant hotel block. This emphasizes awareness of Pool Court restaurant courtyard which appears to have multiple centres, but ambiguity of use.

Strengths: local and distant visual cues increase legibility and sense of continuity; strong transitional sensation at footbridge; diversity of materials strengthen courtyard as a social imageability centre.

Weaknesses: some interruption to pedestrian flow across the Calls; ambiguity in courtyard centres.

11.6
Analysis record for the journey (continued overleaf)

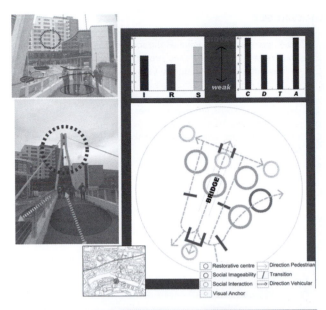

SOUTH CENTENARY BRIDGE

A strong transitional space acting as main entrance to Brewery Wharf, but which has multiple poorly defined centres generating a lack of coherence.

Strengths: strong directional and transitional sensations.

Weaknesses: poorly defined centres.

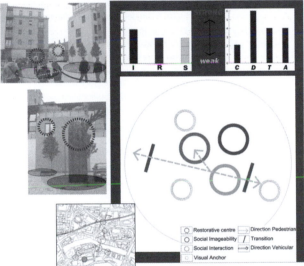

SIMPSON'S FOLD EAST

Strong directional qualities with movement funnelled between buildings. However the sense of spatial rhythm and transitional qualities are weakened by the void created by a car park to the southern side. Sculptural features and engaging façade detailing contribute to the social imageability in places, but there is a sense of unfulfilled potential in centre definition and poor connectivity between interior and exterior spaces that compromise orientation.

Strengths: strong direction to Simpson's Fold West; emergent structure of centres.

Weaknesses: poor spatial enclosure (centre definition) to part of southern side; sequential sense of transition; ambiguous centre definition.

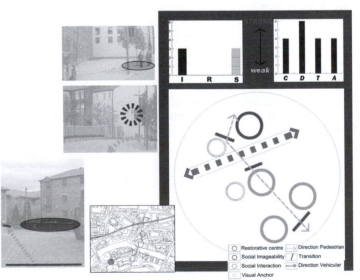

SIMPSON'S FOLD WEST

A larger enclosed courtyard with an adjacent smaller courtyard space which again has multiple potential centres that currently lack definition and clarity of purpose. Directional devices on buildings and in spaces work to a limited extent with orientation.

Strengths: strong sense of transition created by pinch points between buildings; some sense of anticipation generated by spatial sequence and partially obscured forward views.

Weaknesses: directional cues tend to draw attention away from locality and weaken sense of centre; poor connection between and lack of clarity in centres.

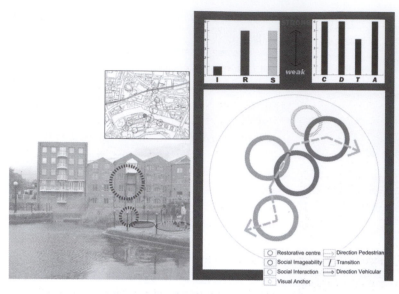

QUAY SIDE

A distinctive and intimate semi-private residential area with multiple centres which appear to offer restorative and social opportunities. Enclosure and prominent architectural detailing strengthen sense of direction and there are clear boundary points heightening transitional qualities.

Strengths: attention to detail enhances social imageability; potential for restorative and social interaction centres.

Weaknesses: some ambiguity in transition between private and semi-private space; unfulfilled potential in centres.

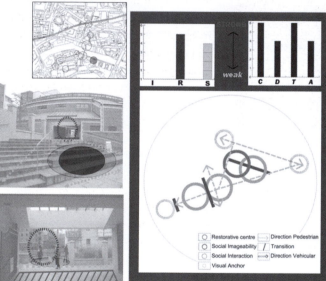

CROWN POINT STEPS

A strong transitional area with changes in level and contrast from open to enclosed. There is again strong potential in centre generation, especially for restorative and social opportunities, whilst strong architectural styling adds to social imageability. Steps offer potential to enhance river view capitalizing on directional sensations.

Strengths: strong and frequent sequence of transitions; potential for centre definition.

Weaknesses: unfulfilled centre potential.

Dobson Cluster analysis clearly identifies many centres and this is exactly what might be expected from an environment with a rich and varied spatial structure like that of the Calls. But it is significant that the sensation of centre does not feature more often as a dominant part of the experiential character. So although structurally there is considerable evidence of enclosure, confluence of route, prominent features etc., all indicators of centre, it does not seem as though, for whatever reason, these features are anchoring locational experiences to the extent that the spatial structure might imply. This indicates an experiential landscape structure emphasising orientation over location. Put in terms of our earlier reflections on the geometric implications of experiential landscape, the Calls appears rather a smooth, fluid experiential landscape which, despite what first impressions of its spatial structure might suggest, does not seem to have sufficient coarseness, or roughness, in its structure by comparison to slow the pace of movement down to successfully cultivate and hold a stronger sense of location. In terms of centre, then, it appears as though the

11.7
Structurally a potential centre, but experientially dead

11.8
The Iceworks and New York Apartments under construction

Calls is a story of experiential potential as yet largely unfulfilled (Figure 11.7).

Looking at this in more detail as we move through the journey sequence from the bus station we can see first that the junction of Cross York Street and Kirkgate Road is an example of new development likely to increase the centre definition, or sense of location, for this part of the city. The completion of the Iceworks and New York Apartments development will introduce a new residential community here, bringing life to Cross York Street as a consequence of the routine to and fro of inhabitants. Dwelling entrances that front directly onto the street may increase opportunities for social interaction as will activating the ground floor façades along Kirkgate Road with shops. The architectural impact of the development will also simultaneously improve the potential for social imageability centres, emphasise the transitional and directional experience of Cross York Street as a key gateway from the City into the Calls area enhancing the connection between north and south sides of the viaduct, and improve the continuity and therefore sense of direction along Kirkgate by tying in with existing buildings (Figure 11.8).

The area beyond the viaduct is already dramatically framed in views through the brick archways and this imageable feature of the city here will be further enhanced with plans to punch through additional archways opening up the future possibility to develop patches of open space at present largely inaccessible and neglected. The detailing of building façades, including the impact of St Peter's Church, act as focal points and contribute to the potential for centres of social imageability, and nearby green spaces offer restorative opportunities. However, the north end of Wharf Street is experientially confusing with an intensity of traffic disrupting pedestrian movement and the sense of a smooth transition between Cross York Street and Wharf Street (Figure 11.9).

Wharf Street itself is revealed to be a distinctive area characterised by traditional cobbled street surfacing and brick building façades. The street also has a strong sense of direction as a link between adjoining areas and a good sense of spatial rhythm. However, the unimaginative

11.9
Beyond the viaduct

11.10
Wharf Street and Centenary Bridge

11.11
South end of Centenary Bridge and Brewery Place

provision for car parking here, in High Court Road, Kirk Ings Yard, and elsewhere, interferes with the inherent sense of continuity and provides an example, repeated often throughout the Calls area, of the potential of space to deliver better locational experience compromised because of a poor approach to car storage. To an extent this observation, along with a lack of clarity about use, holds for a small square between buildings at the north entrance to Centenary Bridge, and identified a strong cluster of potential centres at a very significant location at the heart of the Calls area. Strong deflective façades along the Calls coupled with innovative architectural detailing generates a strong sense of direction here, contrasting quite dramatically with the highly centred space which seems to invite pause before moving onto the bridge. The bridge creates a strong sense of social imageability and its transitional impact combines to create a place which, although small, feels like it should be delivering a strong sense of arrival, a satisfying place to pause, reflect and contemplate at a main gateway to and from the central city. There is no doubt that this remains a wasted opportunity (Figure 11.10).

Much the same can be said for where Centenary Bridge meets the southern bank of the river. The recently completed Brewery Place with its edges activated with bars, restaurants and the routine activity of hotel and office use, compensates to some extent with a strong sense of centre, especially during lively summer evenings. The potential to enhance Brewery Place with a better sense of arrival, capitalising on the interesting level changes to provide attractive and intimate riverside centres, linked to the restaurant terrace,

encouraging sitting, eating, working, taking in fine river views, or just wondering, is largely ignored. In what seems to be a triumph of disjointed thinking a combined step and seat structure is provided a little way to the east at a point where comparatively few people will routinely pass. Instead, at the bridge where this should be, litter, graffiti, harsh concrete and uninspired attention to detail combine to deaden what ought to have a bold and stimulating sense of place (Figure 11.11).

The story of structurally evident, yet experientially dead, centres continues along Brewery Wharf. It is true that, at the time of writing, this area is very new and its current spatial structure, defined largely by new buildings capturing space at the rear of existing buildings that front onto Dock Street, offers considerable potential to develop with use. Nevertheless, there seems to be a curious blurring of the clarity between what is front and what is rear which, coupled with a hotel car park that contributes nothing positive to spatial integrity, generates sufficient ambiguity to weaken again the implicit sense of location here. The dominant experience here is once more the sense of direction and transition. The sense of centre is clearly evident but just not as strong and it seems that in this location the power of the sequence of squares to hold a stronger sense of location ought to be greater than it is. Speculation among the research team about why this should be the case focused on what could be achieved through attention to better interplay between indoor and outdoor space, to give clearer reasons for users of the surrounding buildings to use these spaces. One of the strongest aspects of the Brewery Wharf development lies in the space at

11.12
Brewery Wharf and Victoria Quays

the western end that links with Dock Street. From an experiential perspective this is a pivotal location simultaneously being part of the directional continuity of Dock Street and also acting as the point of transition into Brewery Wharf and, opposite, the Victoria Quays residential development. Possibly a consequence of the greater maturity of Victoria Quays, the transition from Dock Street into the development signals a distinct change in place character. Alterations in spatial rhythm and interruptions in site line are effective in slowing the sensation of continuity with a more enclosed domestic atmosphere. At the same time the linearity of Navigation Walk establishes linkage with the river's edge, with sculpture and a footbridge acting as focal points and establishing a sense of location. An increase in the amount of vegetation here also indicates the potential to increase the restorative potential of some of the open space around the Calls more generally (Figure 11.12).

If the opportunity had been available to carry out a systematic experiential landscape investiga-

tion of people who routinely used the Calls, in all likelihood the prominence of centres in the balance of its experiential character may well have risen. The expectation from other experiential landscape field work suggests that when this is done locations not apparent to outside professional observers rise into significance because their routine habits in relation to the spaces used becomes visible through interview and mapping processes. Whilst the range of informal interviews and conversations carried out with Calls users, coupled with numerous role-play studies carried out with students and researchers, bears this out, it still remains evident that the Calls area appears primarily as a place to pass through rather than linger in. There are some exceptions to this though. The density of retail and recreational opportunity continuing to grow in and around the Corn Exchange and Assembly Street immediately north of the viaduct, coupled with its distinctive streetscape and architecture, and its role as a main public transport stop, has made this area a powerful attractor with an emphatic sense of location for social interaction and imageability. The much more recent Brewery Place has similar potential, although so far this seems confined to the summer months.

Our exploration of the Calls area in this respect appears to be consistent with the adage that life attracts life. The sense of centre appears to be strengthened wherever human activity congregates, whereas even attractive spaces offering enclosure and interest can sometimes convey only feelings of emptiness and discomfort, a disincentive for a true sense of location to develop. It is interesting to note however that these negative connotations appear significantly mitigated by the presence of vegetation which seems to be consistently active in inducing contemplation and relaxation, turning awkward emptiness into tranquil and restorative experience.

With these notable exceptions, though, many of the centre sensations recorded by Calls users, or people role-playing as such, tended to be outside

of the Calls area or at the northern boundaries. They also seem to be primarily associated with the specific work place or residence and with points of arrival and departure. When there were exceptions these tended to be few in number and disparate and usually along main routes to and from the central city. The area at the northern end of the bridge around the Pool Court restaurant, the bridge itself, and the small square with the ball fountain at the junction of High Court and the Calls were routinely registered as having locational sensations for people. It is probably no coincidence that these are along the main pedestrian route from south of the river into the city centre and are spatially and visually prominent in various ways (Figure 11.13).

Interestingly, other prominent locational sensations were associated with the increase in regulations to control smoking in offices. Office doorways with alcoves or recesses offering shelter rose to significance for this reason for some.

11.13

Role-play to simulate user place perceptions

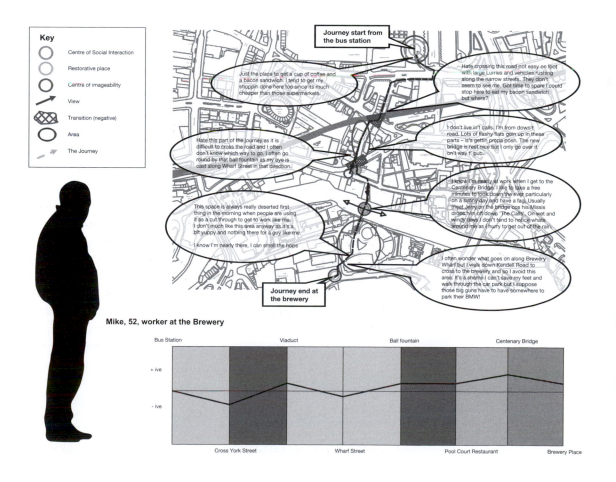

Mike, 52, worker at the Brewery

Smokers venturing beyond the office doorway tended to favour places at a short distance away with shelter, a view, seating or a sculptural object. This sort of activity increases the locational significance of Centenary Bridge, both in the middle and at either end. The southern end of the bridge seemed especially important to older children and teenagers who did not live in the area but came via the bus stop at the Corn Exchange. The steps of the Corn Exchange appear as an extremely significant socialising location for groups of young people, particularly those with a preference for the sort of clothes sold inside. Sometimes, some venture towards the river in search of recreational opportunities both passive and active. The slightly shabby and sheltered enclosure offered beneath the footbridge at its south side seems a popular haunt and this is close to appealing edges such as steps and other forms of change in level attractive to skateboarders. There is evidence in Brewery Place of measures being taken in design detailing to discourage this sort of activity.

Taken together then, this insight into the experiential landscape of the Calls reveals that it has a strong directional emphasis which draws people through the site with a rhythmic continuity of landmarks features and spaces, and coherent streetscape. Structurally there are many opportunities where centres could develop but, with notable exceptions, these are comparatively weaker and this seems to be because architectural aspects that signal a sense of location are not anchored with a clear experiential dimension. The Calls is a rich and diverse spatial resource and many of its spaces have developed into places with strong directional and transitional characteristics. Comparatively, though, it seems that few deliver an equivalent level of locational experience. This may be indicative of an imbalance in experiential opportunity that might have implications for its sustainability as an emergent urban neighbourhood.

Design concept development

We will now follow on by describing some aspects of the process the student research team adopted to respond to these findings. The purpose was to explore how the principles of experiential landscape could be used to develop conceptual ideas relevant to achieving better balance of experiential opportunity by enhancing the potential for locational experience. One of the methods used was to develop a word-picture. A word-picture is a technique used to focus attention on the experiential content of a setting rather than its physical form. In essence this is a way of expressing a sequence of emotional responses relating to places before considering the spatial and physical elements of site design. The concept of a word-picture comes from an approach to design developed by Christopher Alexander in 1991 during the development of ideas for a proposed museum to house the Tudor battle ship, Mary Rose. The idea was to try to create a highly detailed mental image, or map, of the kind of experience they wanted visitors to have. Alexander's principal concern in adopting this approach was to try to convey the feelings that visitors might have as they passed through the museum. Their task was to design a building that would realise this experience in physical form. For example, in Alexander's word-picture, in the first section is this passage. "One sees these windows from outside – the sun glistens on them, and shines on the glass. At night especially, the banners and emblems glow darkly" (ibid.). So, not only do we have the presence of objects like windows banners and emblems, we also have a sense of the quality of light they are supposed to generate. There is a deliberate attempt to reveal the poetic potential of place experience here, particularly evocative in the implications of a phrase like "glow darkly" (Alexander, 1995, p.26). The question is how do you get inanimate things like banners and emblems to live in this way? The word-picture also has a structure. It is broken down into short sections, each of which has its own title, to give the word-picture a sense of sequence and continuity.

This is a word-picture developed by landscape architecture postgraduate student David Wesselingh. It explores the potential of a subtle blend of sensitive design intervention, conserving and enhancing existing qualities and introducing more ambitious features and redevelopment at

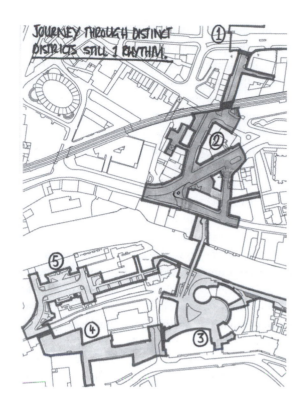

11.14

Exploring variations in different districts

targeted locations. David interpreted the essence of the problem as one of achieving a better balance, rhythm and pattern of directions and centres to help develop an urban landscape which is socially active but also has more passive and restorative opportunities. Providing these in a rhythmic sequence would be a way to balance the experiential landscape of the Calls (Plate 19).

These plans show how the concept can be expressed diagrammatically in relation to the site plan. The plan on the left shows the pattern of directions and centres through the journey with red representing where the sense of centre, in a general sense, would be developed or enhanced, and blue those that would remain with a directional emphasis. The white circles on the plan on the right show in more detail how centres are intended to be distributed along the journey, often by punctuating a directional shopping street. In this configuration the new and enhanced centres help to distinguish distinct districts by either providing a stronger sense of transition or by contributing to the sense of place in each area. The concept is elaborated as a word-picture that distinguishes five areas (Figure 11.14).

– Area 1. Movement into Cross York Street and the Calls is invited by the recently completed New York Apartments and the Iceworks buildings. These stand as landmarks on the convergence of the Calls area and Leeds town centre. The modern façades promote the character and quality of the Calls area. Passage onto Cross York Street offers an immediate appreciation of a quieter more pedestrian-friendly district. Cross York Street itself feels enclosed, not only by the buildings which run the length of the relatively narrow street but by the bustling street behind and the railway line and arches ahead. The same railway arches serve as a visual anchor towards the junction at the north end of Wharf Street.

– Area 2. The sense of transition provided by passing under the railway arches is strengthened by the change from modern to more vernacular materials. A collection of small containing centres contrast the dominating directional elements at this major node. These centres serve as social meeting points, offer restorative opportunities and generally create a more open feel to the junction. They offer opportunities for pausing rather than resting. A choice of routes are offered by directional views towards St Peter's Church, back under the railway bridge along Kirkgate or the deflected views down Wharf Street. Curiosity and a hum of activity persuade continuation into Wharf Street. Progression is rewarded with the arrival into a bustling shopping street. Active frontages and vernacular detailing provide a rich environment on a human scale. A brief but engaging journey along Wharf Street is punctuated by a large open space bisected by a very busy High Court Road. Again this junction provides a choice of routes suggested by their representative visual anchors. Equivocal pedestrian activity is drawn towards the new development and its neighbouring public square on High Court Lane. Associations can be drawn between the detailing of this development and that along Wharf Street. The related open space encourages outdoor seating and copious opportunity for social interaction. Café and bar frontages soften the edges of the space and provide a glow which radiates through the space. Despite the relatively open nature of this square the new development frames the neighbouring space and communicates a feeling of refuge whilst retaining a substantial element of prospect into other ongoing activities. An archway carved out of the new building leads the way through the heart of the building and its activities and into a now familiar style of narrow street with contextually ingrained architecture and detailing. An elegant deflective façade conceals the route ahead and inspires progression towards a rewarding wealth of sensory stimuli and experiences across the River Aire.

— Area 3. A curious semi-private space adjacent to the restaurant marks the transition into a more contemporary design area of the Calls. From here the natural draw of the water coupled with the impressively modern form of the sculptural Centenary Bridge dictate the continuation over the River Aire. Centenary Bridge provides very rich and obvious experiences of freshness, exposure and visually stimulation. A gentle decline on the bridge signifies the passage from the brief but invigorating jaunt across the River Aire into the more reposeful surroundings of Brewery Wharf. Reflections and precise lines in the concave façades of the buildings stand as a landmark and testimony to arrival into a recent and opulent rejuvenation of the area. Leisurely pedestrian exploration through and around the arcades of the shop and bar fronts is contrasted by the more purposeful direc-

11.15
The identification of an area to develop in greater detail

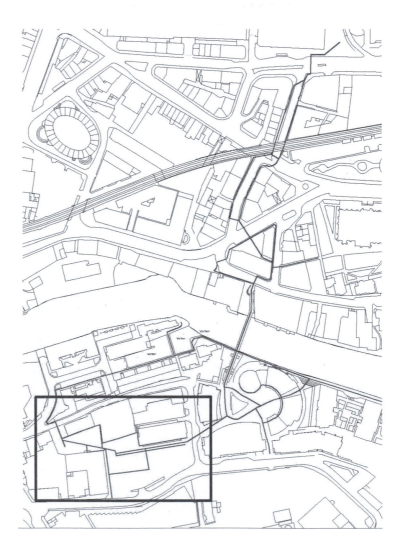

tional movement through the centre. This is generally a quiet open square with occasional opportunities for passive reflection. The exacting landscape elements, broken façades, and curiosity, lead movement around the corner into Brewery Place and a brief but significant experience of enclosure. Containment between two imposing buildings offers a comfortable immersion into the shadowy frame to the impelling sequence of sinuous centres, directions and transitions lying beyond.

– Area 4. The passage through the Brewery Place corridor and across Kendell Street is marked by experiential changes in colour, scale, activity, enclosure, sound and sight. The street beyond is an active street with simmering edges and the spatial rhythm also allows for plenty of opportunities for sitting and being passive. Modern landscape detailing is continued through from Brewery Wharf, adding a sense of continuity. However the spatial experience alters considerably, distinguishing it from the large and impersonal scale of Brewery Wharf. A more varied but generally more intimate scale is noticeable with a real sense of cohesion and community along this street. Building use is reminiscent of that of a small village and social activity is triggered by associations and

recognition. Negotiating the direct route along the street often offers the chance to catch the smell from the bakers or the florist positioned on the corner and allowed to spill out onto the street.

– Area 5. Quieter more intricately detailed spaces and paths prevail in Victoria Quays, assuring its recognition as a more private space. A pleasant waterside environment and locally provided services ensure that there is regular pedestrian activity from the residents and passers through. Private and semi-private spaces and courtyards display personalised planting and evidence of ownership, which coupled with the change in materials, style and colour confirm this as a distinct district (Plate 20).

Plate 20 presents a graphical representation of how some of the ideas from the concept might begin to be realised on site. It includes new built form proposed at Kendell Street, High Court and Wharf Street. The concept of rhythm and movement has been represented here through the activity of people throughout the journey. The blue and yellow colours suggest pace of movement, areas shown in blue are very directional areas, while yellow areas suggest a containing or centred element: the stronger the shade of yellow the slower the movement. The parallel black lines

11.16

Exploring how the overall concept can be interpreted experientially for the detailed site

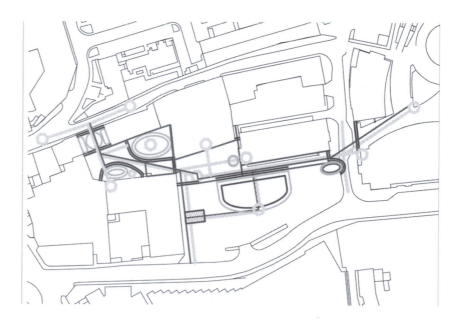

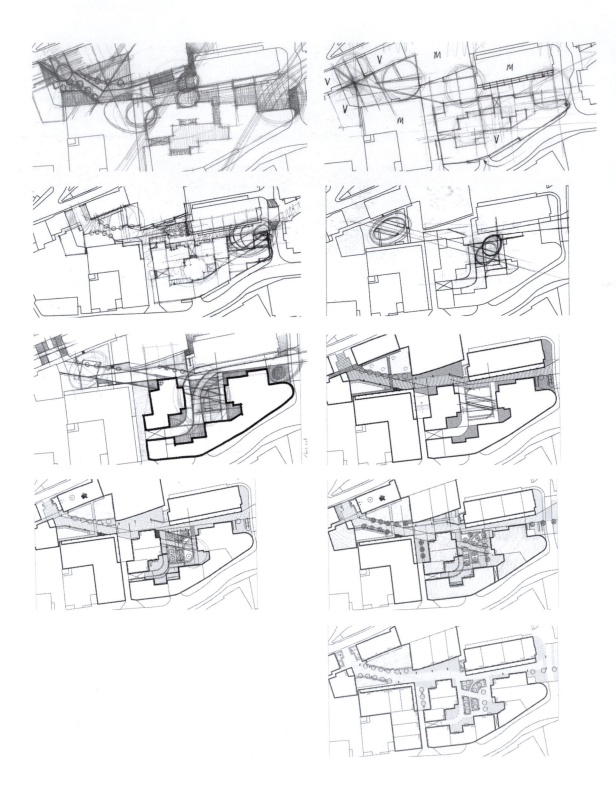

11.17
The gradual evolution of a design solution

11.18

A sequence of here, there and change working seamlessly to bind the whole together

along the journey represent how active the spaces are. The closer together the lines the busier the area will be, for example black lines along a building façade suggest an active edge such as shop fronts. The edges of the buildings along the journey are defined by a black line of varying thickness. This represents the sense of enclosure in the external space surrounding the particular building, heavier lines indicating a greater sense of enclosure. The dots around the plan signify visual anchors and are intended to stimulate movement. This main concept represents a unifying theme running through the journey and its distinct districts. The passage through distinctive districts in the Calls area is anticipated to

increase the experiential value of the journey and add to the sense of place in the wider area (Figure 11.15).

These conceptual ideas are followed on with an exploration of how they might influence the detailed development on one of the areas, from Brewery Wharf to Victoria Quays. The aim is to develop a centre of activity particularly for the residents of the surrounding buildings. It currently serves as a cut-through and feels very much like a back street. Despite not being very well used this area has much potential. There is an unusual spatial configuration making the passage more of a series of centres and pinch points than a street. There are also some interest-

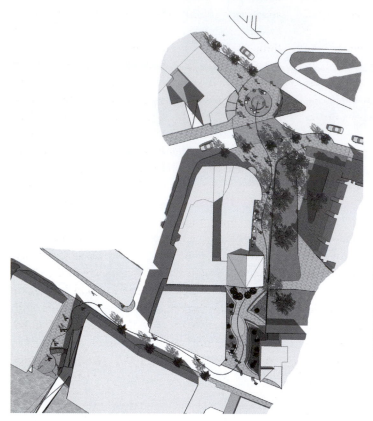

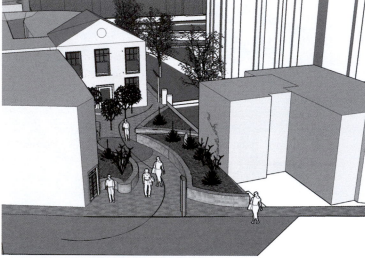

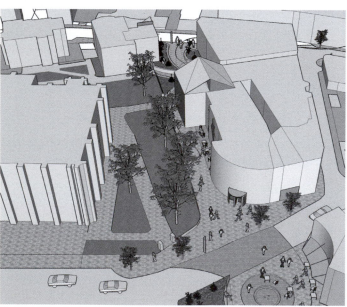

11.19
Steve Watt's proposal to improve experiential potential and spatial rhythm to the west side of St Peter's church

ing buildings with a mix of modern and vernacular styles. The concept of rhythm and movement has been represented here through the activity of people throughout the journey. The blue and yellow colours indicate pace of movement. As with the larger masterplan, areas shown in blue are very directional areas, while yellow areas suggest a containing or centred element: again, the stronger the shade of yellow, the slower the movement. Yellow adjacent to building fronts indicates slower movement and could be interpreted as browsing shops or outdoor space to a café (Plate 21 and Figure 11.16).

The following images show how the experiential aspirations gradually evolve into a final form with interwoven centres and direction working together to create a medley of distinguishable places combining seamlessly as one whole (Figures 11.17, 11.18).

Existing sculpture has been relocated to the gable end of the building to create a small centre of social imageability and restorative benefit whilst allowing continuation of shop frontage and a stronger sense of direction along the street. Bay windows, outdoor stalls, recessed doorways and arcade frontages help to soften the definition between internal and external space. The streetscape accommodates a variety of movement, the smooth straight concrete slab path running through the street offers an efficient cut through the site, while the treatment of the floorscape around the buildings with rougher granite setts slows down movement, allowing internal activity of shops and bars to spill out onto the streets. The crinkled edge of building also encourages a slower, more meandering pace around the buildings. Building uses on ground floor change along the whole street from residential to more public uses, such as shops, cafés, bars, services, doctors, etc. to create a network of neighbourhood facilities within a distinctive extended courtyard. These units are on a small scale, as they are only intended to support the local community. This will also allow a greater variety of uses leading to a more active street scene. The streets are still casually overlooked by the residential units above. New built form add to increase the enclosure and containment of the street, increasing social activity and enhancing the spatial configuration of the street (Figures 11.19).

References

Alexander, C. (1964) *Notes on the Synthesis of Form*. Cambridge: Harvard University Press.

Alexander, C. (1979) *The Timeless Way of Building*. New York: Oxford University Press.

Alexander, C. (1993) *A Foreshadowing of 21st Century Art: The Color and Geometry of Very Early Turkish Carpets*. New York: Oxford University Press.

Alexander, C. (2001) *The Nature of Order: An Essay on the Art of Building and the Nature of the Universe*. Book One, The Phenomenon of Life. New York: Oxford University Press.

Alexander, C. (2002) *The Nature of Order: An Essay on the Art of Building and the Nature of the Universe*. Book Two, The Process of Creating Life. Berkeley: Centre for Environmental Structure.

Alexander, C. (2005) *The Nature of Order: An Essay on the Art of Building and the Nature of the Universe*. Book Three, A Vision of a Living World. Berkeley: Centre for Environmental Structure.

Alexander, C. (2004) *The Nature of Order: An Essay on the Art of Building and the Nature of the Universe*. Book Four, The Luminous Ground. Berkeley: Centre for Environmental Structure.

Alexander, C., Black, G. and Tsutsui, M. (1995) *The Mary Rose Museum*. New York: Oxford University Press.

Alexander, C., Davis, H., Martinez, J. and Corner, D. (1985) *The Production of Houses*. New York: Oxford University Press.

Alexander, C., Ishikawa, S., Silverstein, M., Jacobson, M., Fiksdahl-King, I. and Angel, S. (1977) *A Pattern Language*. New York: Oxford University Press.

Alexander, C., Neis, H., Anninou, A. and King, I. (1987) *A New Theory of Urban Design*. New York: Oxford University Press.

Allsopp, B. (1972) *Ecological Morality*. London: Muller.

Altman, I. (1975) *The Environment and Social Behaviour: Privacy, Personal Space, Territoriality and Crowding*. Monterey,C.A: Brooks/Cole.

Altman, I. and Rogoff, B. (1987) World Views in Psychology: Trait, Interactional, Organismic and Transactional Perspectives, in Stockols, D. and Altman, I. (eds) *Handbook of Environmental Psychology*, Volume 1. New York: Wiley.

Alvarez, L. and El-Mogazi, D. (1998) *The Language of Fractals: An Enhanced Design Vocabulary*. Presentation to the Council of Educators in Landscape Architecture (CELA) conference, October 22–27, 1998, Arlington, Texas.

Arnheim, R. (1998) *The Power of the Center: a study of composition in the visual arts*. Berkeley: University of California Press.

Barker, R.G. (1968) *Ecological Psychology: Concepts and Methods for Studying the Environment of Human Behavior*. Stanford: Stanford University Press.

Batty, M. and Longley, P. (1994) *Fractal Cities: A Geometry of Form and Function*. London: Academic Press.

Baxter, A. (1998) *Places, Streets and Movement: A Companion Guide to Design Bulletin 32, Residential Roads and Footpaths*. London: DETR.

Bell, J.S. (1987) *Speakable and Unspeakable in Quantum Mechanics*. Cambridge: Cambridge University Press.

Bentley, I., Alcock, A., Martin, P., McGlynn, S. and Smith, G. (1985) *Responsive Environments*. London: Architectural Press.

Berleant, A. (1997) *Living in the Landscape: Toward an Aesthetics of Environment*. Kansas: University Press of Kansas.

Berlin, I. (1965) "Herder and the Enlightenment" in Wasserman, E.R. *Aspects of the Eighteenth Century*. Baltimore: The John Hopkins Press.

Berlin, I. (1999) *The Roots of Romanticism*. London: Chatto and Windus. Edited by Hardy, H.

Bernstein, R. (1978) *Beyond Objectivism and Relativism*. Oxford: Basil Blackwell.

Bohm, D. (1980) *Wholeness and the Implicate Order*. London: Routledge.

Bonnes, M. and Secchiaroli, G. (1995) *Environmental Psychology: A Psycho-Social Introduction*. London: Sage.

Briggs, J.P. and Peat, F.D. (1985) *Looking Glass Universe: The Emerging Science of Wholeness*. London: Fontana.

Brook, I. (1998) "Goethean Science as a Way to Read Landscape" in *Landscape Research*, vol. 23, no. 1, 1998, pp.51–69.

Canter, D. (1977) *The Psychology of Place*. London: Architectural Press.

Capra, F. (1975) *The Tao of Physics: An Exploration of the Parallels Between Modern Physics and Eastern Mysticism*. London: Wildwood House.

Capra, F. (1982) *The Turning Point*. London: Wildwood House.

Carr, S., Francis, M., Rivlin, L.G. and Stone, A.M. (1992) *Public Space*. Cambridge: Cambridge University Press.

Chermeyeff, S. and Alexander, C. (1963) *Community and Privacy: Toward a New Architecture of Humanism*. New York: Doubleday.

Chew, G.F. (1968) "Bootstrap: A Scientific Idea?" in *Science* vol. 161, May 23, pp.762–765.

Clamp, P. (1981) "The Landscape Evaluation Controversy" in *Landscape Research*, 6(2), pp.13–15.

Corner, J. (1990) "A Discourse on Theory I: Sounding the Depths – Origins, Theory and Representation" in *Landscape Journal* vol. 9, Fall 1991, pp.61–78.

Corner, J. (1991) "A Discourse on Theory II: Three Tyrannies of Contemporary Theory and the Alternative of Hermeneutics" in *Landscape Journal* vol. 10, Fall 1991, pp.115–133.

Cullen, G. (1967) *Tenterden Explored: An Architectural and Townscape Analysis*. Maidstone, Kent. Kent County Council.

Cullen, G. (1971) *The Concise Townscape*. Oxford: Architectural Press.

Davies, P. (1983) *God and the New Physics*. London: J.M. Dent and Sons.

Davies, P. (1987) *The Cosmic Blueprint*. London: William Heinemann.

DfES. (2003) *Travelling to School: an action plan*. Nottingham: Department for Education and Skills.

DTLR. (2002) *Green Spaces, Better Places*. London: Department of Transport, Local Government and the Regions.

Day, C. (2002) *Places of the Soul: Architecture and Environmental Design as Healing Art* (2nd edn.), Oxford: Architectural Press.

Descola, P. and Palsson, G. (eds.) (1996) *Nature and Society: Anthropological Perspectives*. London: Routledge.

Dovey, K. (1993) "Putting Geometry in its Place: Toward a Phenomenology of the Design Process" in Seamon, D. (1993) *Dwelling, Seeing and Designing: Toward a Phenomenological Ecology*. Albany: State University of New York Press (pp.247–270).

Downs, R. and Stea, D. (eds.) (1973) *Image and Environment, Cognitive Mapping and Spatial Behaviour*. London: Edward Arnold.

Egan, G. (1990). *The Skilled Helper: A Systematic Approach to Effective Helping*. California: Brooks Cole.

Fiksdhal-King, I. (1993) "Christopher Alexander and Contemporary Architecture" in *Architecture and Urbanism*, August 1993, Special Issue.

Flick, U. (1998) *An Introduction to Qualitative Research*. London: Sage.

Forman, R.T.T. (1995) *Land Mosaics: The Ecology of Landscapes and Regions*. Cambridge: Cambridge University Press.

Frankel, F. and Johnson, J. (1991) *Modern Landscape Architecture: Redefining The Garden*. New York: Abbyville Press.

Gadamar, H.G. (1975) *Truth and Method*. London: Sheed and Ward.

Gadamar, H.G. (1981) *Reason in the Age of Science*. Cambridge: MIT Press.

Geddes, P. (1915) *Cities in Evolution*. London: Williams and Norgate.

Gleick, J. (1988) *Chaos*. London: William Heinemann.

Grabow, S. (1983) *Christopher Alexander and the Search for a New Paradigm in Architecture*. Stocksfield: Oriel Press.

Greenbie, B. (1978) "Social Privacy in the Community of Diversity" in Greenbie, B. and Esser, A.H. (1978) *Design for Communality and Privacy*. New York: Plenum Press.

Greenbie, B. (1981) *Spaces: Dimensions of the Human Landscape*. New Haven: Yale University Press.

Gudeman, S. (1992) "Markets, Models and Morality: The Power of Practices" in Dilley, R. (ed.) (1992) *Contesting Markets: Analysis of Ideology, Discourse and Practice*. Edinburgh: Edinburgh University Press.

Hall, E.T. (1959) *The Silent Language*. Garden City, New York: Doubleday.

Hall, E.T. (1963) "A System for the Notation of Proxemic Behaviour" in *American Anthropologist*, 65, pp.1003–1026.

Hall, E.T. (1966) *The Hidden Dimension*. New York: Doubleday.

Hart, R.A. (1997) *Children's Participation*. London: UNICEF

Heisenberg, W. (1963) *Physics and Philosophy*. London: Allen and Unwin.

Hillier, B. and Hanson, J. (1984) *The Social Logic of Space*. Cambridge: Cambridge University Press.

Horton, G. (1956) "Johannes Kepler's Universe: its Physics and Metaphysics" in *American Journal of Physics*, 24, pp.340–351.

Howett, C. (1998) "Ecological Values in Twentieth-Century Landscape Design: History and Hermeneutics" in *Landscape Journal*, Special Issue, 1998, pp.80–98.

Hunt, J.D. (1992) *Gardens and the Picturesque: Studies in the History of Landscape Architecture*. Cambridge: MIT Press.

Ittelson, W.H. (1973) *Environment and Cognition*. New York: Academic Press.

Jacobs, J. (1961) *The Death and Life of Great American Cities*. London: Jonathan Cape.

Jeans, J. (1930) *The Mysterious Universe*. New York: Macmillan.

Jencks, C. (1995) *The Architecture of the Jumping Universe*. London: Academy Editions.

Jones, C. (1980) *Design Methods*. London: John Wiley and Sons.

Jones, C. (1984) *Essays in Design*. London: John Wiley and Sons.

Kaplan, R., and Kaplan, S. (1989) *The Experience of Nature: A Psychological Perspective*. New York: Cambridge University Press.

Kaplan, R., Kaplan, S. and Ryan, R.L. (1998) *With People in Mind: Design and Management of Everyday Nature*. Washington: Island Press.

Kaye, B. (1989) *A Random Walk Through Fractal Dimensions*. Weinheim: VCH.

Kellert, S.R. and Wilson, E.O. (eds.) (1993) *The Biophilia Hypothesis*. Washington: Island Press.

Kelsey, J. (1970) "A Design Method" in *Landscape Architecture*, May 1970, pp. 425–428.

Koestler, A. (1978) *Janus*. London: Hutchinson.

Koh, J. (1982) "Ecological Design: A Post-Modern Paradigm of Holistic Philosophy and Evolutionary Ethic" in *Landscape Journal* vol. 1, Fall 1982, pp.76–84.

Lincoln, Y.S. and Guba, E.G. (1985) *Naturalistic Inquiry.* California: Sage.

Lovejoy, A. (1974) *The Great Chain of Being.* Cambridge: Harvard University Press.

Llewelyn-Davies. (2000) *The Urban Design Compendium.* London: English Partnerships.

Lozano, E.E. (1974) "Visual Needs in Urban Environments and Physical Planning" in *Town Planning Review*, no. 45, pp.351–374.

Lyle, J.T. (1985) "The Alternating Current of Design Process" in *Landscape Journal* vol. 4, Spring 1985, pp.7–13.

Lynch, K. (1960) *The Image of the City.* Cambridge: MIT Press.

Lynch, K. and Rivkin, M. (1959) "A Walk Around the Block" in *Landscape*, 8, pp.24–34.

Martin, M. (1997) "Back-alley as Community Landscape" in *Landscape Journal*, Spring 1997, pp.138–153.

McAvin, M. (1991) "Landscape Architecture and Critical Inquiry" in *Landscape Journal*, 10, pp.155–172.

McCall-Smith, A. (2001) *Morality for Beautiful Girls.* Edinburgh: Polygon.

McHarg, I. (1971) *Design with Nature.* Philadelphia: Falcon Press.

Merchant, C. (1980) *The Death of Nature.* New York: Harper and Row.

Merleau-Ponty, M. (1962) *Phenomenology of Perception.* London: Routledge and Kegan Paul.

Moore, K. (1993) "The Art of Design" in *Landscape Design*, February 1993, pp.28–31.

Motloch, J.L. (1991) *Introduction to Landscape Design.* New York: Van Nostrand Reinhold.

Naess, A. and Rothenberg, D. (1989) *Ecology, Community and Lifestyle: Outline of an Ecosophy.* Cambridge: Cambridge University Press.

Norberg-Schulz, C. (1971) *Existence, Space, and Architecture.* New York: Praeger.

Norberg-Schulz, C. (1980) *Genius Loci: Toward a Phenomenology of Architecture.* London: Academy Editions.

Nothnagel, D. (1996) "The Reproduction of Nature in High Energy Physics" in Descola, P. and Palsson, G. (1996) *Nature and Society: Anthropological Perspectives.* London: Routledge.

Palmer, R. (1969) *Hermeneutics.* Illinois: North West University Press.

Palsson, G. (1996) "Human-environment Relations: Orientalism, Paternalism and Communalism" in Descola, P. and Palsson, G. (1996) *Nature and Society: Anthropological Perspectives.* London: Routledge.

Parnes, S. (ed.) (1992) *The Source Book of Creative Problem Solving.* London: Creative Education Foundation Press.

Penrose, R. (1989) *The Emperor's New Mind: Concerning Computers, Minds, and the Laws of Physics.* Oxford: Oxford University Press.

Pepper, D. (1984) *The Roots of Modern Environmentalism.* Beckenham: Croom Helm.

Pepper, D. (1993) *Eco-Socialism: From Deep Ecology to Social Justice.* London: Routledge.

Pepper, D. (1996) *Modern Environmentalism: An Introduction.* London: Routledge.

Perez-Gomez, A. (1983) *Architecture and the Crisis of Modern Science.* Cambridge: MIT Press.

Porta, S. and Renne, J. (2005) "Linking Urban Design to Sustainability: formal indicators of social sustainability field research in Perth, Western Australia" in *Urban Design International*, vol. 10 pp.51–64.

Poundstone, W. (1985) *The Recursive Universe.* New York: William Morrow and Company.

Pretty, J.N., Guijt, I., Scoones, I. and Thompson, J. (1995) *A Trainer's Guide for Participatory Learning and Action.* International Institute for Environmental Development: London

Prigogine, I. (1980) *From Being to Becoming: Time and Complexity in the Physical Sciences.* San Francisco: W.H.Freeman.

Proshansky, H.M., Fabian, A.K. and Kaminoff, R. (1983) "Place-Identity: Physical World Socialisation of the Self" in *Journal of Environmental Psychology* 3: pp.57–83.

Proshansky, H.M., Ittelson, W.H. and Rivlin, L.G. (1970) *Environmental Psychology: Man and His Physical Setting.* New York: Holt, Rinehart and Winston.

Relph, E. (1976) *Place and Placelessness.* London: Pion.

Rivera, A. (1990) *Conversations in Colombia: The Domestic Economy in Life and Text*. Cambridge: Cambridge University Press.

Rohde, C.L.E. and Kendle, A.D. (1994) *Human Well-being, Natural Landscapes and Wildlife in Urban Areas: A Review*. Reading: English Nature.

Romice, O. and Frey, H. (2003) *Communities in Action*. Glasgow, Dept. of Architecture and Built Science, University of Strathclyde.

Rosenberg, A. (1986) "An Emerging Paradigm for Landscape Architecture" in *Landscape Journal* vol. 7, Fall, pp.75–82.

Rudlin, R. and Falk, N. (1999) *Building the 21st Century Home: The Sustainable Urban Neighbourhood*. Oxford: Architectural Press.

Russell, P. (1991) *The Awakening Earth: The Global Brain*. London: Arkana.

Salaman, G. (1974) *Community and Occupation: An Exploration of Work/Leisure Relationships*. Cambridge: Cambridge University Press.

Sanoff, H. (2000) *Community Participation Methods in Design and Planning*. New York: John Wiley and Sons.

Schumacher, E.F. (1973) *Small is Beautiful: A Study of Economics as if People Mattered*. London: Blond and Briggs.

Several Authors (1992) "Most Important Questions" in *Landscape Journal* vol. 11, pp.160–181 (Scarfo, pp.166–167).

Silverman, D. (2000) *Doing Qualitative Research – A Practical Handbook*. London: Sage.

Sommer, R. (1959) "Studies in Personal Space" in *Sociometry*, 22, pp.247–260.

Sommer, R. (1969) *Personal Space: The Behavioural Basis of Design*. Englewood Cliffs: Prentice Hall.

Spivak, M. (1973) "Archetypal Place" in *Architectural Forum*, October, pp.44–49.

Spradley, J.P. (1979) *The Ethnographical Interview*. New York: Holt, Rineheart and Winston.

Stapp, H.P. (1971) "S-Matrix Interpretation of Quantum Theory" in *Physical Review* D, March 15.

Steinitz, C. (1990) "A Framework of Theory Applicable to the Education of Landscape (and Other Environmental Design Professionals)" in *Landscape Journal* vol. 9, Fall 1990, pp.136–143.

Stiles, R. (1992) "Determinism Versus Creativity" in *Landscape Design*, July/August, pp.30–32.

Stiles, R. (1992) "The Limits of Pattern Analysis" in *Landscape Design*, September, pp.51–53.

Stokols, D. (1981) "Group X Place Transactions: Some Neglected Issues in Psychological Research on Settings" in Magnusson, D. (ed.) *Towards a Psychology of Solutions: an Interactional Perspective*. Nillside, N.J: Lawrence Erlbaum, pp.393–415.

Stokols, D. and Altman, I. (eds.) (1987) *Handbook of Environmental Psychology*. Vol 1. New York: Wiley.

Taylor, C. (1975) *Hegel*. Cambridge: Cambridge University Press.

Taylor, C. (1989) *Sources of the Self: The Making of the Modern Identity*. Cambridge: Cambridge University Press.

Taylor, C. (1991) *The Ethics of Authenticity*. Cambridge: Harvard University Press.

Thomas, G. and Thompson, G. (2004) *A Child's Place: Why environment matters to children*. Green Alliance/DEMOS.

Tibbalds, F. (1992) *Making People Friendly Towns: Improving the Public Environment in Towns and Cities*. London: Longman.

Titman, W. (1994) *Special Places; Special People – The hidden curriculum of school grounds*. Surrey: WWF UK

Tuan, Y.F. (1974) *Topophilia: a Study of Environmental Perception, Attitudes and Values*. Englewood Cliffs: Prentice Hall.

Tuan, Y.F. (1977) *Space and Place: The Perspective of Experience*. Minneapolis, University of Minnesota Press.

Tuan, Y.F. (1979) "Thought and Landscape" in Meinig, J.W. (ed.) *The Interpretation of Ordinary Landscapes*. New York: Oxford University Press.

Tuan, Y.F. (1980) "Rootedness versus Sense of Place" in *Landscape* 24: pp.3–8.

Turner, T. (1991) "Pattern Analysis" in *Landscape Design*, October 1991, pp.39–41.

Turner, T. (1996) *City as Landscape: A Post-Post Modern View of Design and Planning*. London: E. and F.N. Spon.

Uzzell, D.L. (1991) "Environmental Psychology Perspectives on Landscape" in *Landscape Research* 16 (1) pp.3–10.

Uzzell, D.L. and Lewand, K. (1990) "The Psychology of Landscape" in *Landscape Design*, April, pp.34–35.

Walter, E.V. (1988) *Placeways: A Theory of the Human Environment*. North Carolina: University of North Carolina Press.

Warnke, G. (1987) *Gadamar*. Cambridge: Polity Press.

Wates, N. (2000) The Community Planning Handbook, London: Earthscan Publications.

Whitehead, A.N. (1926) *Science and the Modern World*. Cambridge: Cambridge University Press.

Whyte, W.H. (1980) *The Social Life of Small Urban Spaces*. Washington: The Conservation Foundation.

Worpole, K. (1998) "People Before Beauty" in *The Guardian* newspaper, 14 January.

Worpole, K. (2003) *No Particular Place to Go: children, young people and public space*. Groundwork UK.

Zmyslony, J. and Gagnon, D. (1998) "Residential Management of Urban Front Yard Landscape: A Random Process?" in *Landscape and Urban Planning* 40, pp.295–307.

Zukav, G. (1979) *The Dancing Wu Li Masters: An Overview of the New Physics*. London: Rider Hutchinson.

Index

Note: the terms centre, direction, transition and area appear throughout the text. References here are confined to elements of explanatory discussion rather than their use in the interpretation of fieldwork in Section three.